DONKEYS ON MY DOORSTEP

HOOFING IT IN THE MALLORCAN HILLS

ANNA NICHOLAS

summersdale

DONKEYS ON MY DOORSTEP

Summersdale Publishers Ltd
46 West Street
Chichester
West Sussex
PO19 1RP
UK

www.summersdale.com

Printed and bound in Great Britai

ISBN: 978-1-84953-038-5

Substantial discounts on bulk quantities of Summersdale books are available to corporations, professional associations and other organisations. For details contact Summersdale Publishers by telephone: +44 (0) 1243 771107, fax: +44 (0) 1243 786300 or email: nicky@summersdale.com.

For the irrepressible cockney queen, Dooda Joyce

CONTENTS

ACKNOWLEDGEMENTS

This latest tome has taken me on a fascinating historical and literary journey in Mallorca and I am indebted once again to friends and locals who have pointed me in the right direction along the way. In no particular order I would like to thank my friends M. J. Ripoll for his fascinating insights into the Spanish Civil War, Ignacio Recalde for his excellent book, *Los Submarinos de Sóller*, and for loaning me so many historical tomes, William and Elena Graves for sharing their pearls about writer Robert Graves and Mallorcan history and culture, and Sari Andreu (aka Catalina) for her *joie de vivre*. I am hugely grateful for the kind support of Pere and Margarita Serra, Ignacio Vasallo of Turespaña, Roger Katz of Hatchards, Jason Moore, editor of the *Majorca Daily Bulletin*, Lluc Garcia, editor of the *Sóller* newspaper and Biel Aguareles, editor of the *Veu de Sóller*. Once again I would like to give a special mention to Jennifer Barclay, the commissioning editor of Summersdale Publishers, for her continuing support, and to the company's editorial and publicity teams.

My inestimable thanks go to Alan and Ollie for their unwavering patience and enthusiasm, and to my sister, Cecilia, and nephew, Alexander. Finally, I would like to thank the Sóller community for its warm friendship and my readers for having so loyally supported my work.

ABOUT THE AUTHOR

As a freelance journalist, Anna Nicholas has contributed to titles such as *The Telegraph*, *Financial Times*, *The Independent*, *Tatler*, the *Daily Express* and the *Evening Standard*. She contributes a thrice-weekly Majorcan Pearls blog to *Telegraph Expat*, a monthly column to *Spain* magazine and a weekly column to the *Majorca Daily Bulletin*. She is a fellow of the Royal Geographical Society and has been an international adjudicator for *The Guinness Book of Records*. Together with explorer Colonel John Blashford-Snell she has also organised an expedition to carry a grand piano to the remote Wai Wai tribe in South America, which was the subject of a BBC TV documentary. Her author website is at www.anna-nicholas.com.

AUTHOR'S NOTE

Most of the local vernacular used in this book is in the Mallorcan dialect. Although Mallorcan is derived from Catalan and is believed to have been spoken for more than five or six centuries, it varies greatly when written. During the Franco era, Mallorcan was forbidden in Balearic schools and this has made it an oral language, reliant on Catalan when transcribed to print because no dictionary in Mallorcan exists. Today, Catalan is the main language used in Mallorcan schools with the Mallorcan dialect being spoken in the street and in the home. The vocabulary and spelling often varies greatly from village to village in Mallorca. I have taken advice from local language experts and so hope to have accurately transcribed the Mallorcan language to print. However, I apologise unreservedly to any fervent linguists who may care to differ!

Some of the names of those appearing in the book have been changed to protect their privacy but most are authentic – in fact local Mallorcans positively encouraged me to use their real names and that of their businesses. One error of judgement was in giving my friend Sari Andreu the fictional name Catalina, rather than calling her by her real name. She has never quite forgiven me. Well, almost.

ONE

POETIC JUSTICE

At the far end of the orchard a white bird, possibly a dove, appears to be caught in the higher branches of a lemon tree. It's seven in the morning and I am standing at the bedroom window of our *finca* in Mallorca in yawning mode but the sight of those limp wings fluttering helplessly from behind a clump of leaves has me wide awake. I'm puzzled. How on earth has a bird got stuck in one of our trees? It's surely not the sort of thing birds generally do. If that were Orlando up there, our terminally dim though lovable grey cat, I wouldn't turn a hair. Despite my having to rescue him several times from the clutches of a predatory shrub, he continued to try his feline paws at more ambitious and vertically challenging leafy projects. It was on the spikes of the enormous cactus by the front lawn that he finally came a cropper. Now the only thing he tends to navigate is the duvet on our bed. My husband, Alan, commonly nicknamed 'the Scotsman', is running water from a tap in the bathroom and is none too happy to be summoned mid shave. He joins me at the window, a half-robed Santa with a frothy white beard and a razor poised in the air.

'What's up?'

'I think a bird's stuck in a tree.'

He pulls open the window, allowing cool autumnal air to waft into the room. I give a little shiver. Summer is certainly over even though September has not quite past. He surveys the dewy orchard beyond with some impatience until his gaze rests on the tree with the bird. He leans out of the window to take a closer look.

'You're right, although I think I can see several wings fluttering. Maybe it's a group orgy of doves?'

I tut. 'At this time of the morning?'

'It has been known. Why don't you get the binoculars?'

With some impatience I don a pair of old flip-flops and head for the stairs. There's only one way to find out what's going on up in that tree. As I leap over the assault course of cats on the staircase, Minky, brother Orlando and the queen of the house, Inko, I find a loud chorus of felines on the patio beyond the back door. These are the local feral cats that have recently formed a Wailing Wall day and night outside the kitchen. Word seems to have got out in the local cat community that we're a bunch of mugs, willing to feed any feline within a ten-mile radius. Rather like a fugitive under fire one has to prepare oneself for the onslaught when exiting the house, zigzagging through their midst and clapping loudly until out of the danger zone. I've christened them all and, much to the Scotsman's fury, I've been known to slip them the odd morsel. There's Scraggy the tabby, albino Baby Boris, his black brother, Demonic Damian, a stripy bruiser named Tiger the Terrible, and Tortoiseshell, a flirty female with Cleopatra eyes and smoky pelt. Now as I make my way hurriedly across the back terrace, clearing the cats from my path as I go, they start up a terrible din which has the Scotsman huffing and puffing from the open upstairs window.

'Damned cats!' he curses to the breeze.

I descend the stone staircase into the field and scythe a path through the wet grass, my feet slippery with dew and my nightdress damp at the hem. I pass the corral on my left and see that Salvador, our indignant cockerel, is already on the march. He lifts his head and turns it right and left in small jerky moves, his eyes blinking fretfully as he steals a backward glance at his uppity harem behind. Last year our hens, Minny and Della, disappeared one night without trace. There were no feathers in evidence, so I like to think they made a break for freedom and are living happily on some other paradise isle frequented by holidaying fowl. In truth, a tear in the corral netting indicated that they were carried off by a genet but I don't like to dwell on that. Salvador now has some new feathered female companions, a trio of sisters christened Goneril, Regan and Cordelia. There's a good reason why he watches his back. It's only Cordelia who cuts him a little slack while her bossy sisters give him a good pecking and an earful if he oversteps the mark by attempting to snaffle their grain or shadowing them too closely.

I reach the lemon tree and peer up through the branches. The white fluttering wings have taken a new form; that of paper. I potter off and find our wide, old orchard ladder leaning against a wall and drag it over. Carefully, I climb to the top rung and hoist myself onto a thick branch. The papers are almost within my grasp when a party of curious ants tickle first one then the other leg, prompting me inadvertently to shake both flip-flops to the ground. I lose my balance and the ladder goes tumbling after them. I lunge at the tree trunk and curse my stupidity. Now I'm going to have to take my chances at leaping to the ground barefooted. There's a loud rustling in the long grass and heading purposefully towards me across the orchard are the Scotsman, clad in pyjamas, and Ollie, fully dressed in his school uniform. How humiliating is this?

'I always wondered what a tree hugger looked like,' sniggers the Scotsman.

'Why are you always so impetuous?' huffs Ollie.

'That's a big word for a twelve-year-old at this time of the morning.' I say.

He narrows his eyes. 'Give me a break.'

'So it's not a passionate trio of doves?' asks Alan.

'No, just some sheets of paper that have got wedged in the branches.'

'How boring,' sighs Ollie.

He hauls the ladder up and perches it against the trunk. 'Can I come up?'

'There's hardly room, Ollie, and besides you'd better get ready for school.'

He hunches his shoulders. 'It's such a waste of time. I could do more useful things at home.'

'Such as?' I say.

'Sorting my stone collection, getting my football cards in order or trading my coins on the Internet.'

Alan tousles his hair. 'All in good time.'

He shakes himself loose and heads back to the house, muttering as he goes. Alan steadies the ladder until I manage to grab the papers and make my descent. I slip on my flip-flops and straighten out the sheets of crumpled paper. There are four pages in total, all a little damp and streaked with tears of maroon ink. The blurred writing that remains is tiny and compact, elegant and elaborate and written in Catalan.

'Bother, I can't make out a word. I'll have to consult the dictionary.'

Alan looks over my shoulder. 'What is it? A letter of some kind?'

I shrug. 'It's hard to tell. I'll just have to try to decipher what little handwriting remains.'

He removes a pair of secateurs from his pocket and begins snipping fruit off some nearby trees. 'Might as well pick some lemons while we're at it.'

I'm trying to make head or tail of the small writing when he calls to me, pointing at the far wall.

'Come over here! There are more sheets of paper stuck in the brambles.'

I stride through the long grass, a pale sun now glimmering overhead, and see to my delight that the Scotsman has a good clump of sheets in his hand. Better still the writing appears to be intact, probably because they have been sheltered by the wall.

'It's a little voyeuristic to read other people's mail, isn't it?' he asks as I take them brusquely from his grasp.

'Well finders keepers, and besides they are on our property.'

He laughs. 'Oh well, I suppose it'll be good for practising your Catalan. The paper's quite thin and yellowed. These haven't been written recently.'

What sort of historical treasure might we have stumbled upon on our very own patch? I leaf through the pages and with growing excitement see that the first random page I study is dated 26 November 1936 in tiny Roman numerals – the year that the Spanish Civil War began. Since early childhood I have had a passion for antique books and historical letters and at one time was a collector. Alan holds a pile of lemons to his chest.

'You've got a dangerous gleam in your eye, as if you've just found treasure.'

I fold the letters carefully and give him a wink. 'I do believe I have.'

I gaze up at the towering Tramuntana mountain range beyond our land with its bald grey torso, bushy midriff of pine and holly oak trees and dense citrus and olive orchards at its feet. At this time of the morning when the sky turns from ink to a soft pallet of blue, diffusing pale light across the valley, I wonder if I have somehow stepped into a live canvas, rather like the children in the *Mary Poppins* film. I follow Alan slowly across the orchard, past the corral and back up the steps to the terrace. The swimming pool is a hive of activity. Tiny ripples of water scour the surface as if hit by raindrops but the culprits – or victims – are insects that every morning dive unwittingly to their deaths. I suppose if your entire life cycle lasts but a few days, it's not such a bad way to go. Ollie appears, the corners of his mouth betraying evidence of my home-made chocolate mouse.

'You'd better come quickly,' he giggles, 'Orlando's just got stuck up the chimney.'

I'm huffing back up the track which leads to the *finca*, our stone-built country house, when I hear an urgent 'toot toot' behind me. I pull over to the side, wondering why on earth I continue to assault my body with daily runs but there's an inherent worry that if I stop the whole thing might dissolve into blancmange. Besides, running a marathon each year, as I do, has meant that I can raise funds for one of my favourite charities so at least I know that it's all for a good cause. I am currently training for the Athens marathon, which I have been warned is somewhat challenging. Catalina leans out of her car window, the engine running. Her short, glossy dark hair is tousled and her brown eyes full of laughter.

'Hey! Crazy woman. Where you been this morning?'

I catch my breath. 'Believe it or not, I've just been up to Fornalutx.'

She rolls her head back with laughter. 'If you'd knocked on my door, I could have given you a lift!'

She elbows Miquela, the companion sitting in the passenger seat next to her. 'She runs up to my house and runs back again. How mad is that?'

Miquela juts her head forward and gives me a grin.

'Actually, Catalina, that's the whole point of the exercise,' I say.

She shakes her head and drives on ahead of me up to the house. This is Monday when Catalina, like a whirlwind, works her magic transforming our muddle of a home into a shiny, clean palace. Her army consists of bleach, washing powder, copious amounts of hot soapy water and all manner of brushes and floor cloths. In the last few months she has brought reinforcements in the form of Miquela, a cheery young mother of three from a nearby village. She is lean and willowy where Catalina is curvy and of moderate height. Catalina and I have been firm friends ever since the time she au-paired for my sister back in the UK, and it was thanks to her that the Scotsman and I originally decided to holiday in Mallorca. That idyllic summer break inspired us to buy and renovate an old wreck of a *finca* in the Sóller Valley and when it was habitable we upped sticks from London for a new life in Mallorca. So for the last eight years I have happily subscribed to a dose of Catalina's cheeriness on a Monday morning and her news-gathering skills, which keep me abreast of gossip in the valley.

The front gate is wide open and Catalina's car is parked wildly across the gravel as I trudge into the courtyard. The Scotsman hasn't arrived back from dropping Ollie off at his school near the university but is due any time soon. I survey the wild profusion of blood-red bougainvillea that hangs in heavy bundles over our old rock wall, shedding silky sepals on to the gravel below. The dry and delicious tones of rosemary pervade the courtyard, mingling with the sweetness of the lavender. The front doors are thrown back and just as I am getting into my painful stretching routine Catalina appears like a scowling fairy godmother, brush, not wand, in hand. Her eyes are narrowed and hands are placed firmly on hips. This means trouble.

'What have you been doing with the chimney? *Hi ha molta brutícia*!' It's filthy!

'Orlando climbed up it this morning and got stuck.'

She shakes her head. 'There's soot everywhere. That cat is a menace!'

'I can help clear it up,' I say lamely.

'Per favor!' Please! She chortles loudly and plods back to the kitchen.

I slip up the stairs, shower and head for my office. Miquela is doing battle with our sitting room on the top floor. Rugs have been draped over windowsills, cushions plumped and the vacuum cleaner, like a demonic Dalek, is being guided by Miquela about the room, gobbling up dust and spitting out errant marbles and sweet wrappers secreted under sofas and chairs by Ollie. I creep by and close the office door softly behind me. Glimpsing the large calendar above my desk, I note that I am due back in London in November. Despite my desire to cut loose from the frenetic world of public relations, I continue to commute back to the UK every month or so to meet with clients and catch up with my staff in my Mayfair office. My dream is to find a like-minded agency with which to merge so that I can devote my time to setting up a cattery on our land and freelance writing, but it hasn't proven easy so far. Rachel, MD of my PR company, and I continue to keep tabs on potential buyers in the offing, while carrying on with day-to-day business. Much as we have received business offers, none of them so far has fitted the bill.

The computer screen is awake, revealing a huge stack of emails in urgent bold print awaiting a reply. Rachel has sent an email about a new client she's signed up called the Chelsea Mad Hatter, not surprisingly a hat emporium, owned by a couple called Marcus and Pippa Darley. A long report follows about some other potential PR business, including a couple with a country estate called Frithington Manor in West Sussex. Quickly scrolling through the pages, I read that the manor's visitors have tailed off since a new family attraction arrived nearby. She doesn't specify what it is. Frithington Manor's owners, the Claverton-Michaels', appear to think a dynamic PR programme is needed to get them back on track. I decide to visit the estate's website but a shrill ring from the phone stops me in my tracks. It's Rachel, she who must be obeyed, and the world's greatest slave driver.

'Are you tailing my every move? I've only just switched on the computer.'

'I assumed you'd have packed in a few hours work by now,' she tuts.

'Very funny. Actually I've just been reading your PR report about the Claverton-Michaels'. Are they normal?'

She gives a little giggle. 'Of course not. They're completely barking!'

'Great. Well, don't involve me in the account.'

'Too bad, I've fixed up for you to visit the estate with me next month. A weekend in the country.'

I groan. 'Thanks. So what's this rival family attraction that you mentioned?'

'Oh, some grim labyrinth of plastic tubes that visitors crawl through. It's called an interactive assault course and, unfortunately, it's only a five-minute drive from Frithington Manor.'

'Why interactive?'

'God knows, just marketing speak I imagine. Still, the Claverton-Michaels' have got a huge USP.'

Unique selling point – more marketing spiel. 'What's that then?'

'You haven't read my report that thoroughly, have you?'

I've been rumbled. 'Go on, dazzle me.'

'It appears that Frithington Manor is haunted.'

'And you're asking me to stay there for a whole weekend? Are you completely nuts?'

She gives an exasperated tut. 'You don't seriously believe in ghosts? It's all a load of codswallop but we can create a great PR story around it. The media love haunted house stuff.'

'I despair of you, Rachel. Anyway, I hope for your sake that it is a load of old tosh because if I see one medieval white sheet gliding towards me down a musty corridor I'm out of there.'

Her voice ripples with laughter. 'Look, the Claverton-Michaels' say that since they bought the house ten years ago they've never seen or heard anything disturbing. The previous owners probably made it all up to attract interest in the property.'

'What sort of history does the house have?'

'Oh, the normal sort of thing; murder, mayhem and suicide – nothing too sinister.'

I let her rattle on about other business for some minutes and finish the call. It doesn't matter what Rachel says, I've an uncomfortable feeling about my future sojourn in the English countryside. I shall most definitely check out that Frithington Manor website. Forewarned is forearmed.

I get up and wander over to the window just as the Scotsman pulls into the courtyard. I watch him swing open the car door, peering surreptitiously around before lighting up a *puro*, one of his stinky, large cigars. He saunters up the small flight of stone steps to the front lawn, inspecting the peachy roses by the boiler house and his collection of old terracotta pots teeming with seedlings. Crouching down to feel the soil, I notice a scowl suddenly cross his face. He looks around and catches sight of Damian, the black feral cat, creeping behind a bush. With some passion he begins remonstrating with him before stomping towards the house. Oh dear, I feel a gardener's rant in the making. I sit back at my desk and, as if on cue, he bursts into the office.

'Those wretched cats have peed in my seedling pots!'

'Surely not?'

'It's true. There's soil everywhere and several seedlings have been uprooted. Those cats can't stay.'

He plonks himself heavily in an office chair. 'And another thing, they're eyeing up your beloved frogs so be warned.'

This is a clever move. If there's one thing the Scotsman knows will grab my attention, it's the welfare of our frogs. In our small pond by the front lawn, which is forested by lily pads and tall rushes, we have at least forty frogs and one corpulent toad that I've christened Johnny. They are my constant companions during the day, chirruping and croaking up at my open office window.

'What do you mean?'

He taps the arm of his chair. 'That devious little black blighter is stalking them. I've seen him lurking by the side and dabbing a paw in the water whenever a frog is about.'

I throw out my arms. 'Oh come on, the poor creature might just have been having a drink! Besides, this is a cat-friendly zone.'

He gives a little groan. 'Ferals are different. They're just a nuisance. It's like walking the gauntlet for our own poor mogs. They're frightened to step out of the house.'

He has a point. I worry that a sign I bought in Gruyère that reads 'Bienvenue Chats' and which I hung by the front porch might have encouraged the onslaught. Of course, the irony is that for the last year we have been trying to set up a small cattery in our field. After one attempt at a modest wooden structure, which proved too flimsy for the cold weather, we have employed a British cattery manufacturer to come up with a custom-made building that will withstand the bitter winds and rains that hit us in the hills during the winter. It will be some months before the finished design is agreed and ready to construct. Alan, my poor beleaguered Scotsman, has gone along with the idea in good faith but when he retired from the corporate world and stress of London I imagine he thought he'd be in for an easy time of it in rural Mallorca, tending his gardens and relaxing out on the terrace every day. The reality is proving to be a little different, given my compulsion for new business schemes and constant activity.

A fly buzzes noisily by.

'That's another thing,' says the Scotsman, pushing a hand through his grey hair, his tall frame blocking out the meagre sun. 'There are flies everywhere. If I'm not tormented with the damned ferals, it's the flies.'

He bats one away with his bronzed hand.

'What you need is a comforting cup of coffee with Catalina downstairs.'

He nods his head. 'You're right. I might just do that.'

On that note off he trots, leaving me to contemplate my workload.

Out of the corner of my eye, I see the crumpled sheets of paper that I rescued from the lemon tree. I push them in front of the computer and stretch down to pick up my Catalan dictionary, which sits permanently on the floor by my desk. Surely the work can wait for a little while longer?

Ollie is sitting at the desk in his bedroom with a perplexed expression. In front of him is a piece of paper.

'How on earth am I supposed to learn this?'

'Well, what sort of a poem is it?' I ask.

He stands up and in thespian mode holds the paper before him and begins reciting.

'*Mon cor estima un abre! Més vell que l'olivera, més poderós que el roure, més verd que el taronger…*'

He pauses. 'Still with me?'

'Hang on. It's something about loving a tree that's older than an olive tree. Who wrote it?'

'Who cares?'

I give him a dark look. 'Come on, don't be silly. Your Catalan teacher must have given you the poet's name.'

He stares at the paper begrudgingly. 'He's called Miguel Costa i Llobera. The poem is "El Pi de Formentor".'

'The pine tree of Formentor? That sounds rather nice. Well, if your Catalan teacher says you have to learn it you'd better get on with it.'

'It's not fair!'

'Life isn't, I'm afraid.'

He tosses the poem on his desk and stares out of the window at the darkening sky. 'Did you like going to school?'

An interesting question. 'I liked aspects of school life.'

He laughs. 'That's the sort of answer a politician would give.'

'Touché. I liked the Classics and English. I hated maths and made no effort in science, which I now regret.'

'Why?'

'Because it's a fascinating subject.'

He shakes his head. 'The best thing about school is sport and break time.'

I give him a wink. 'You see, there's always some aspect that's likeable.'

He looks at his watch. 'If I finish my homework on time, can I watch some English TV?'

'Maybe.'

'It's been a funny week starting ESO. We're getting far more homework than in Primaria.'

ESO, *Educación Secundaria Obligatoria*, is the Spanish equivalent of secondary school and Ollie has just returned from his summer holidays to take up a place in ESO 1 at his all boys Spanish school. Unlike the British system, there's a graduation ceremony on leaving the primary school. Ollie and his classmates were given a grand send-off and each awarded scrolled certificates to show that they had passed their end of year exams as well as mortar boards which they threw in the air for an end of term school photo. Returning to 'big' school has been a little daunting for him, especially as he's the only British boy in his class.

'You'll get used to it,' I say as cheerily as I can. 'There can't be many English boys who could recite a Mallorcan poem.'

'No, you're right about that,' he mutters. 'There wouldn't be any mad enough!'

A gale is chasing the plant pots about the front porch and rain spills down in torrents from a scowling sky – so much for the prediction of a mild September. The electricity has died and the *entrada,* our large entrance hall, is gloomy and dark. A stray shutter is thumping against a wall somewhere in the house, screeching like a tormented banshee as it swings back and forth against the window. I try to work out which room is hiding the culprit but can't be bothered to hunt it out. It's only ten in the morning and yet it feels as if the night is setting in. Alan has gone off to Palma to buy new supplies of potting compost and Ollie is at school. I am waiting impatiently for the lights and computer to turn back on so that I can get on with some work. This weather is predictable, though. Every year, *la gota fria*, as it is known, arrives with the regularity of snails, the postman and the equinox. As freezing air passes over the warm waters of the sea, the climatic reaction is dramatic with storms, terrific downpours and flash floods. It usually occurs after the first week of September and there's nothing to be done but wait patiently until it passes.

There's the muffled sound of a bell clanging from the front gate. When the rainy weather starts and electricity cuts occur with some frequency, we keep a bell by the gate in case the electric buzzer stops working. I walk over to the front door and peer through the pouring rain. There's no car in evidence but a large black umbrella is battling to stay erect in the gale. Without engaging my brain, I run into the kitchen and push the button that activates the gate mechanism, forgetting that of course there's no electricity. I hear the distant ring of the bell above the rain. Hell! Who can this be? I push on some old espadrilles by the front door and, grabbing a brolly, rush out into the courtyard. In a few moments I am pretty drenched. At the gate it takes me some time to operate the manual lever but finally I get it moving. The rain-coated figure hobbles in, stick grasped firmly in one gnarled hand, his face obscured by a dark beret and the umbrella. I beckon him to follow me across the gravel and up to the porch which he dutifully does, albeit slowly and painstakingly. When he arrives, he shakes out his umbrella, stands it by the stone pillar and with a quivering hand wipes some drops of rain from his pale face.

'Please come in,' I say above the howling wind.

He gives a grateful nod and follows me into the *entrada*.

'It's wild out there,' he says quietly in Spanish.

'Yes, it's terrible. I'm sorry it's so dark but there's no electricity.'

There's a sudden burst of light and the house is illuminated like a giant Christmas tree.

'I am a magician,' he replies.

I laugh. 'So it seems!' I throw off my soaking espadrilles and push back my wet hair.

'I apologise that, thanks to me, you are now drenched.'

'I'll dry off in a minute,' I say with amazing good humour.

'May I remove my hat and coat and sit down?' he asks.

I still don't know who my guest is or what he wants, but he is old and infirm and hospitality seems the name of the game. I wait until he laboriously unbuttons his coat and then usher him to a chair in the kitchen. He places his polished wooden stick on the floor at his side, his beret on the table and blows his nose with a large white handkerchief. I'm not quite sure what to say. After a few moments, he turns his snowy head and surveys the kitchen and the *entrada* beyond. He strokes his chin and then fixes a pair of penetrating brown eyes on me.

'I think you have something that belongs to me.'

I feel my brow crease. 'Really? I'm not sure what that could be.'

'Some letters and poems.'

I look at the floor.

Dear José, I have heart-breaking news. For several days the city has been under siege. Elena, impetuous as always, was in the university quarter with Durruti and the others...

He gives a little cough. 'By your face, I know you have found them. I am a poet. I read faces like a palmist, a hand.'

What do I feel? A little guilt but also disappointment that I will have to part with the fragment of a story that I have only just begun. Despite poring over the letters for the last few days, I have only been able to decipher a few sections. The pages I've glimpsed are written in Catalan by a woman in Madrid named Sofia. The recipient is named José.

'Are you José?' I ask.

He observes me for a few seconds. 'Today, yes, I am José.'

I walk over to the coffee machine. 'Would you like a coffee?'

'Thank you. Black, one sugar.'

He sighs heavily. 'So you understand Catalan?'

I give a snort. 'Well, I can read it better than I can speak it.' I wait by the coffee machine while it warms up. 'I'm sorry to have looked at the letters but they landed in our orchard and I didn't think anyone would ever claim them. I had no idea where they'd come from.'

He shakes his head sadly. 'It's a foolish thing. I was in my brother's old orchard. It is beyond the small path at the bottom of your field. I go there sometimes for a little peace. I simply fell asleep and when I awoke my Pandora's Box was open and the contents had taken flight.'

I pour the coffee and join him at the kitchen table.

'I like this table,' he suddenly says. 'It is made of oak and hand-turned.'

I smile. 'Yes, it's from a small family firm in Barcelona.'

'So, you kept these letters in a box?' I ask.

'Last week was the anniversary of a terrible event. Like a fool I opened the box, reliving memories that have scorched my soul for decades.'

There's a scraping at the back door and Minky's sodden and startled face appears at the pane. I'm rather glad to see him. He enters the kitchen and shakes himself down.

'I'm so sorry to hear that,' I say feebly.

'Are you?' he replies. 'What can you possibly know of such suffering?'

I bite my lip, wishing I had better Spanish. My words sound so wooden.

'Let me get the letters.'

I jog up the stairs and remove the transparent file from my desk. José is on his feet when I return.

'What do you know of the Spanish Civil War?'

I pass the folder to him, which he places in front of him.

'I've read some books on the subject. Anthony Beevor's *The Battle for Spain* and several others.'

'Have you read *Homage to Catalonia* by your countryman, George Orwell?'

I nod.

'He was a fool. What did he understand of democratic socialism?'

I take a glug of coffee, wondering whether I've inadvertently opened my own Pandora's Box. Perhaps I should have pretended not to have seen the letters at all.

'I'm afraid I'm no expert in these matters. I fear many young idealists fought in the war without fully understanding the politics at play.'

He opens the file in front of him. 'Thankfully my nephew helped me recover nearly all the other lost pages, but we couldn't get access to your orchard so I decided to pay you a visit.'

'Well, I'm glad you did and I'm happy to return the pages I found.'

He takes a last sip of coffee and places his beret on his head. 'Thank you for your kindness. Now I must be off.'

He picks up his stick and slowly walks over to the front door. I take his raincoat from the banister and help him into it.

'Before you go, can I just ask one thing?' I ask.

He hesitates at the front door and nods.

'The letter I was partly able to read talked about someone called Elena. Who was she and what happened to her?'

A little grin suddenly plays on his lips. 'She was beautiful and a would-be revolutionary. Elena was the sister of my girlfriend, Sofia.'

Then his smile curdles and he frowns. 'She was killed in crossfire on the nineteenth of November 1936. It was during the bombardment of Madrid by Franco's forces.'

I feel suddenly miserable. 'How old was she?'

'Twenty-three.'

He opens the front door. Tears well from a swollen sky but the wind has abated.

'Would you tell me more about that time?' I ask, startling myself.

José takes the black umbrella from the porch with a shaky, translucent hand and regards the sky with a contemplative expression.

'I feel we may meet again.'

He walks slowly away with a faltering step, as if in great pain, across the gravel and through the gate without glancing back.

The afternoon brings milder weather. The Scotsman is shooing the strays away from the front garden as I potter on to the front porch. The sun has now appeared and perches high on a ribbon of white cloud, shedding honeyed light on the silvery leaves of our old olive tree on the front lawn. I remember the time when this verdant grass was nothing more than a patch of parched terrain dotted with old abandoned chicken coops and bales of barbed wire. Our pond was formerly home to an ugly *cisterna*, a cement water tank filled with flotsam, moss, insects and dead rats. The facade of our old *finca*, now partially covered with tentacles of dark green ivy, was pitted with holes and loose mortar. The Scotsman strides towards me, beaming.

'That's put paid to their antics!'

I give him a quizzical look.

'I've put pepper all over the plant pots to keep those pesky strays at bay.'

'Do you ever give up?' I ask.

'No, this is war.'

I stroll out onto the gravel and stare up at the house.

'Do you ever think back to the days when we first bought this?'

'Frequently,' he replies. 'I can remember seeing the sunken roof and barred windows and thinking we'd be mad to take on the project.'

'We've certainly come a long way.'

He sighs. 'Yes, but there's still lots to be done. I want to get the old stone sink up on the patio and get the little outhouse built.'

'We should think about getting Stefan up to have a look at it.'

Stefan is Catalina's brother, and our local builder. When we originally bought the house, there were some dilapidated outhouses at the rear of our property that our builder cleared. We'd now like to use the space for a barbecue and dining area as well as a small outhouse in which to keep the washing machine and freezer. All in good time or as the Mallorcans say, *poc a poc*, little by little.

There's a commotion going on by the lawn. I snap out of my reverie to hear the Scotsman cursing and clapping his hands together in fury.

He is standing by his beloved plant pots which have been spilled onto their sides. Three mischievous feline heads – black, white and tabby – pop up from the bushy shrubs at the side of the lawn.

'They did it on purpose! They haven't just peed in the pots; they've deliberately overturned them all. I was keeping an eye on the blighters, but all of a sudden I heard a thud and have just caught them red-handed,' he blusters.

I try to stifle a grin. 'Well, you weren't very kind putting pepper in the pots. It's poetic justice.'

The Scotsman turns them upright and scrapes up the soil with his hands.

'This isn't the end of it,' he growls. 'I'll have their whiskers yet.'

I watch as Boris the white kitten yawns and does a little somersault on the lawn, perhaps in celebration of winning round one.

TWO

DONKEYS AND DON QUIXOTE

A hearty fire of wild amber flames crackles in the hearth of our *entrada*, while rain tumbles down outside. Friends back in England sometimes find it odd that our entrance hall serves as a general sitting room but it isn't an entrance hall in the British sense of the word. For one thing old Mallorcan houses are generously proportioned and the lofty ceilings are often vaulted or beamed, giving the room a rather grandiose feel. When we renovated our *finca* it made sense to knock down the wall that divided the roomy *entrada* from a pokey dining room and kitchen that lay towards the rear of the property. We created a large open space and installed French windows that open out on to the front patio to let in more light and added an old traditional Mallorcan hearth to give the room character.

Tonight we are entertaining our great Mallorcan friends Juana and Pep, who with their teenage son, Angel, have become part of the family. It was quite by chance that we met Pep some years ago at the local Sóller football pitch while Ollie played in a match. Familiarity comes at a price though, because Pep does not mince his words and is always happy to show us the error of our British ways.

He and Juana sit in un-matching chairs in front of the hearth nursing glasses of *herbes*, the local Mallorcan liqueur. Alan is mumbling darkly over the coffee percolator in the kitchen while I place some chocolates on the coffee table at their side.

'A wonderful dinner, if I may say so,' compliments Pep with a small smirk. 'Although, one day you might venture towards a starter without a salad base.'

Ollie is sitting like a cross-legged little elf on the rug and flicking through some playing cards. 'She was a rabbit in her last life. She'd live on lettuce if she could.'

'Per favor!' exclaims Juana. 'What's wrong with you men? Always complaining about us and yet totally inept when it comes to cooking!'

Pep's eyes bulge. 'Inept? Who, *cariño*, prepares the suckling pig every Christmas?'

She taps the arm of her chair. 'If you couldn't do that much when your own father reared them at home, I'd throw you out!'

Alan potters over, a cup of coffee in his hand. 'I still haven't got to grips with that wretched machine, you know.'

Pep explodes with laughter. 'You bought that new coffee-making contraption a year ago! Don't tell me you still can't work it?'

'It's very complicated, Pep,' I say, sitting on the floor next to Ollie. 'You have to press a big green button and let the coffee pour into the cup. Mind-blowing stuff.'

Alan pulls over a chair. 'Aye, well you might laugh, but it's got a mind of its own.'

Pep observes me on the floor. 'For goodness' sake, when are you two going to buy a sofa?'

'It hasn't been a major priority,' I retort.

'Maybe not for you, but it matters to your guests. I mean these wicker chairs should be on a beach, not in the *entrada*, and much as I enjoy talking down to you it would be nice to have a level playing field from time to time.'

Juana reaches across and thumps Pep on the leg.

'No, it's true,' sighs Alan. 'We keep saying we'll find time to buy one. It must be done.'

'But it has to be the right one,' I counter.

'Absolutely,' agrees Juana.

Pep gets up and walks over to the window. 'Can you believe this rain? I thought we might have some respite after last month.'

'Yes, it's not a normal October but, then again, it's good for the garden so I'm not complaining,' Alan replies. 'By the way, Pep, have you seen the algarroba tree near the front gate? It's covered in beans.'

'Yes, but don't get excited, *mi amigo*, those beans are practically worthless.'

'I wasn't thinking of selling them,' he laughs.

'Good, because you can't give them away these days. I was up at the local *cooperativa* and they're re-selling them for only twenty cents per kilo. Can you imagine?'

'Terrible,' laments the Scotsman. 'To think of the labour involved, too. I was watching a couple only the other day beating the beans down with long sticks. It looks like back-breaking work.'

'Algarrobas are only good for pigs. *No vale la pena.*' They're not worth the effort, Pep adds.

Juana gives Alan a quizzical look. 'What do you call them in English?'

'St John's bread tree or carob.'

'That's where we get the word carat from for measuring the purity of gold,' says Ollie as he creates a tower of cards on the rug. 'It comes from the Arabic word, *kharrūb.*'

'Clever *chico*,' says Pep. 'The carob seed always keeps the same weight so it's a useful measure for small objects like jewellery. Did you learn that in school?'

Ollie rolls his eyes. 'Don't be ridiculous. You don't learn anything useful at school.'

'You'll be an entrepreneur one day,' giggles Pep.

'Maybe I'll just find a rich woman and do nothing.'

'In your dreams, sunny boy,' scoffs Juana. 'Anyway, you could be a vet. You've got enough livestock.'

'Actually, we're thinking of getting some donkeys. You wouldn't happen to have a good contact?' I ask.

Pep hits his forehead. '*Madre de dios*! Cats, hens, goats and now donkeys. Are you completely *loca*?'

I turn to him. 'What's mad about buying a couple of donkeys? They've always been one of my favourite creatures ever since my aunt Minny bought me a toy donkey called Pepito while on a holiday in Spain. I might have only been five, but I've loved them ever since.'

Pep sniffs loudly. 'All this emotion. I think I'm going to cry.'

Juana hisses at him. 'Shh... you oaf! It's a lovely story. Carry on'

'Well, there's not a lot to add except that when we moved here Alan promised that one day we could have some donkeys.'

Pep regards Alan with amusement. '*Mi amic*, you only have yourself to blame.'

Alan shakes his head. 'You know what she's like. Once we acquired that small bit of land by the orchard I knew she'd have some crazy scheme up her sleeve. I thought she'd forgotten all about the idea.'

'But wait a minute that land is for the cattery, isn't it?' he asks.

I nod. 'Yes, but with a fence there'll be plenty of room for two donkeys. I want to name them Minny and Della, after my favourite maiden aunts.'

'Isn't that a bit ominous? Those were the names you gave your hens and they were carried off by a genet,' snorts Pep.

'Maybe, but I'd like to see a genet trying to make off with a donkey. Besides, I want something to honour the memory of my mad aunts and they both adored donkeys. I've also heard it's best to avoid buying males.'

'*Si*, you don't want machos. They can be vicious,' adds Juana. 'Minny and Della, those are nice names.'

Pep plonks himself back down onto his seat, patting the cushion to make himself comfortable. '*Pues*, if you're serious, I do know a man.'

'Not Antonio from Can Vespa? His donkeys always get sick,' warns Juana.

'Hush,' says Pep. 'No, I'm thinking of Jacinto. You know, we call him *como dice* – how do you say it – the donkey whisperer.'

'You mean horse whisperer!' the Scotsman cries good-naturedly.

'No, this man is a donkey expert. He talks to them and knows their innermost feelings.'

'Really?' I ask. 'I'd love to meet him.'

Alan groans. 'Oh, Pep, I'm not sure this is such a good idea.'

Ollie is grinning. 'I must see this!'

'That's settled,' says Pep. 'I will arrange a meeting. This man is most unusual.'

'*Si,*' says Juana diplomatically, 'He's a little *raro*.' In other words, strange.

Ollie gives a big yawn, a cue for us all to drain our glasses.

'Here's to the donkey whisperer!' I say.

The others chink their glasses and then rise.

'Time for bed,' says Pep. 'Tomorrow will be a wonderful sunny day, just you see.'

We follow Pep and Juana onto the porch and wave them off in the drizzling rain.

'Donkey whisperer indeed!' exclaims Alan. 'Pep really is a wag.'

'For once I think he's not spinning a yarn.'

'Seriously?'

I give him a slap on the shoulder. 'Well, there's really only one way to find out.'

As I set off for Sóller town I have to admit that Pep was right, it's a beautiful sunny day. Living as we do in the craggy north-west of the island, a hop and a skip from the imposing Tramuntanas, the views are spectacular on a bright, clear day. One of the greatest attractions of living in the rural Sóller Valley is the close proximity of both mountains and sea even though the island's capital of Palma is only forty minutes away by car. I jump into the driver's seat and am only just through the gate when I glimpse a little black face staring back at me in the mirror. I give a small, involuntary scream and stop the car. Damian the stray has somehow got himself a free ride. I open my door and a nimble streak of black fur leaps over my arm and makes a getaway over our nearest neighbour's wall. I watch him scrabble up the branches of some purple bougainvillea before disappearing from view. The *finca* next door is owned by Wolfgang and Helge who live in Berlin for much of the year so the shutters are fastened tightly and crisp leaves have invaded the front terrace, sitting in defiant huddles like unwanted squatters under the eaves of the porch. I settle myself once more in the driver's seat, wondering whether Alan's preoccupation with the strays has some basis. I have hardly driven twenty metres along our winding old track when my neighbour Rafael leaps out in front of the vehicle. Whatever next?

He is dressed in gym gear and his dark, curly hair has been clipped so short that he resembles one of his newly shorn sheep.

'Hey! *Vecina*, where are you going?' Rafael always likes to keep tabs on the movements of his neighbours.

'I'm off to town to do some shopping – and what about you?'

He props a muscle-bound arm against the side of the car. 'I go to the gym. When you do the Athens marathon?'

'In November.' This is like a red rag to a bull.

His face lights up. 'Ha! Only another month or so and then you try the hardest marathon in the world.'

I give him a pert smile. 'Hardly the hardest.'

'It's true,' he remonstrates. 'It's all big hills and much sun. Think what happened to that English runner, Paula Radcliffe.'

'Thanks, Rafael, I'm feeling better by the second.'

He jumps up in the air and deftly pulls a fig off a nearby tree and begins tearing it in half.

'You know, the man who did the first marathon in Athens is now dead.'

'Well he died about two and half thousand years ago so it's rather old news, Rafael. Anyway, the whole Pheidippides running from Marathon to Athens story is probably apocryphal.'

'No, I think it's true. He died a hero.'

I turn off the engine. 'Perhaps.'

Dark green leaves tumble to the ground around him as he plucks another fig. 'I hope you're training hard. I don't see you running much these days.'

'That's because I'm going late at night with Tina the traffic warden. She doesn't knock off duty until nearly nine.'

'Tina the traffic warden? You're kidding me. She was the number one women's tae kwon do champion in Sóller. You'd better not upset her.'

He takes a bite of the fig and dissolves into giggles.

I start up the car. 'Don't worry; I don't intend to get into a fight with her. We spend too much time chatting.'

The wonderful thing about running with Tina is that we don't race along and therefore have a chance to catch up on local news. We take our time in true Mallorcan *poc a poc* manner. I often wonder whether I'd ever have run with the local traffic warden back in London but of course that's a ludicrous thought. In our square in Pimlico traffic wardens were the enemy; the people who slapped fines on our cars and revelled in writing out a ticket even when we were only a matter of minutes over the due time. Tina is different. For one thing her dazzling white smile would light up the deepest mine shaft and, although conscientious at her job, she plays it fair and square. She doles out tickets to hardened offenders but shows leniency to those of us who occasionally slip up. Tina and I first met at the town car park where I had sought her help with a faulty ticket machine. She had shown infinite patience and good humour as we repeatedly inserted coins, only to find them falling out of the bottom slot without issuing a ticket.

She had shrugged cheerfully. 'It's *roto*. You go free.'

That broken machine marked the beginning of a friendship. Soon our habitual greeting of *'Hola!'* in the street graduated to long chats and finally runs together. Our route is normally a big loop around Port of Sóller and gives us ample time to catch up on life and gossip while we run.

I carry on along the track and finally past the home of Pedro and Silvia, our neighbours at the mouth of the track. Opposite their *finca* on the right-hand corner is the white chalet which belonged to Margalida; Silvia's mother and my beloved elderly neighbour who died a few years ago. The house has remained unoccupied, although Pedro and Silvia's cleaner pops in most weeks and the garden is kept neat and orderly. Every day I see Margalida's tabby cat prowling forlornly about the plant pots and shrubs at the bottom of the steps leading up to the *finca*'s front door. It's as if he's the custodian, carefully inspecting each plant to ensure that it is thriving and maintained in the manner his owner would have wanted. Margalida's favourite old jacaranda tree sits wearily by the garden wall, its wide green leaves remaining stubbornly in place despite autumn having taken its hold on the valley.

Once on the road to the town my mood lightens, especially at the thought of a double espresso and a moreish croissant at Café Paris. I have some food shopping to do but like to reward myself with a little treat first. I find a parking space in the Gran Via and stroll towards the town centre. Many of the houses in this part of town are large Gothic affairs created by prosperous Sóller merchants, who having emigrated to France in the late eighteen hundreds to make their fortune selling oranges and olive oil returned to the valley with their pockets full of gold. I pass the recently opened British-owned L'Avenida Hotel, an elegant contemporary hotel that seems to attract an affluent brigade of visitors. I reach the post office and see Tina standing outside in her traffic warden get-up. She kisses me on both cheeks.

'Free for a run tonight?'

'Sure. What time do you knock off?'

She grimaces. 'Eight-thirty. Is nine too late?'

'If it's dark, we can always wear head torches.'

She laughs. 'That would be funny! I'll meet you at the Monumento roundabout.'

A minute later she is tickling a couple of toddlers and chatting breezily with their mothers. Every town needs a Tina. In Café Paris, I see Senyor Bisbal huddled in a corner with a chum. This hardy veteran in his eighties might appear stooped, shabby and, at best, understated but is in fact one of the wealthiest men in the valley. He has a finger in every pie and has invested in bars, restaurants and construction companies that stretch as far as Palma. He has a coterie of elderly retainers that do his bidding, usually assisting with irrigation and maintenance of his land. Today he has one of my favourite old companions with him, whom I've nicknamed 'Barney Blue Eyes'. A half-chewed *puro* is forever cemented to his lips and a black beanie hat seems glued to his head. He is tiny and hunched with a small wizened face like a wrinkled prune and thin, delicate hands. There is something endearingly vulnerable about his large watery blue eyes and diminutive frame. In marked contrast, Senyor Bisbal is tall and wiry with a thatch of strong white hair and intense almond brown eyes. José greets me from behind the counter, and a couple of minutes later places an espresso, glass of water and croissant in front of me. I exchange nods with Senyor Bisbal who soon rises to his feet and ambles over to the bar. I hear the spring of the till and imagine he's paying for his coffee but no, I am the recipient of his generosity today.

'I've paid for your breakfast,' he says in a quavery voice.

I remonstrate but he holds up a large leathery hand and indicates with a stubborn chin that there's to be no argument. I thank him and watch as he returns to his companion – Goliath and David passing the time of day together. The door whines and in steps Antonia, the owner of Hibit, the local computer shop. She raises her eyebrows at José who immediately sets about making her a *cortado*, a small coffee with a dash of milk. She pulls out a chair.

'Can I join you?'

'By all means. Funnily enough I was going to pop by later for some new ink toner.'

She shakes her head and lights up a cigarette. 'Forget the toner. We can't get any from Palma until next week.'

'That's a pain.'

'You're kidding me! We have the same printer as you. We're going crazy waiting for supplies. Why does life have to be so complicated? Anyway, how's work?'

'Fine, except that my MD's asked me to stay at a haunted house next month. The owner needs some PR.'

'Sure, I bet he does. No wonder. Who wants to stay with spooks? Don't go without a big crucifix.'

'Good advice, Antonia. You think that would ward off any bad spirits?'

'Who knows but you can always use it to thump the ghost over the head.'

She drains her coffee cup. 'Listen, Albert's manning the shop, so I'd better go. He's got to head off for a computer job in Palma.'

She stubs out her cigarette and scuttles out of the cafe, leaving me to pore over a copy of *Ultima Hora* left on the table. When I do take my leave I give a wave to Senyor Bisbal and José, musing on my good fortune to have had a free breakfast and read of the daily newspaper. As they say, the best things in life are free.

Greedy George, my thoroughly roguish client, owner of Havana Leather and based in New York, is bellowing down the telephone receiver. Whenever he calls me from the Big Apple he seems to think it necessary to shout. He has cultivated a cockney twang, which he thinks sounds cool and trendy, and likes to sport the latest Armani gear even though it looks a little incongruous on his bulky frame. If I close my eyes, I can visualise him jabbing a stubby finger animatedly at the receiver as he speaks and pushing a fretful hand through his ultra-cropped spiky grey hair.

'So look, guv, the thing is I've got this mate who wants a bit of PR and I said you'd give him a call.'

I hold the phone from my ear. 'What sort of business does he have?'

He gives a loud cough. 'He's opening a Chinese restaurant.'

'Oh, that sounds like a winner!' I snigger. 'In Chinatown, no doubt?'

'Don't get all snooty with me, guv. Listen, it's not just any old Chinese. It's going to be a really upmarket joint based in Mayfair. It won't be serving the usual naff old fare. I mean their signature dish is going to be pigs' cheeks.'

'Mmm... that'll be a cheeky little number.'

'Yes, well, Miss Sarky, if I told you my mate was a Chinese multimillionaire, you might change your tune.'

I sit on the stone wall beside the pond, distracted by the pirouetting baby frogs plopping into the sparkling water. They'll soon be gone for the winter and I'll no longer have my amphibian choir serenading me below the office window.

'Are you listening, you dozy woman?'

'Yes, I'm all ears. Now don't you think this is more Rachel's cup of tea?'

'Not so fast. Rachel told me that until you'd merged the company you'd be handling my account and that goes for any of my mates.'

'I doubt she said that.'

'Well, Mr Chan has invited us to a pre-opening tasting next month so that's that.'

I stand up and wander over to the porch. It sounds like destiny has decreed that Mr Chan and his piggy chops will feature on my next London trip.

'By the way, did you get my release about your new Chicago store?'

'Yeah, yeah, all in hand, guv. Our PR agent over here said she *lurved* it. Mind you, she's as thick as a brownstone wall so don't get excited.'

'I rarely do. Anything new to report?'

'There is just one thing. It's about donkeys.'

'Donkeys?'

'How much do you know about donkey hide gelatin?'

'Are we heading towards George joke territory?'

'No we're not, Mother Superior. I'm talking about a Chinese medicine.'

'Sorry, George, I've never heard of it. What has this got to do with Havana Leather?'

'It was Dannie who told me about it. She said it comes from a rare black-skinned donkey in the mountains of east China.'

I take a deep breath. Dannie Popescu-Miller, one of my other New York-based clients, is the owner of Miller Magic Interiors and possibly a latent vampire, being related to Vlad the Impaler of Romania. The idea of these two convening over donkey gelatin is too wearying to think about.

George is chirruping on. 'It just so happens that Dannie takes this gelatin donkey whatsit as an anti-ageing cure.'

'You surprise me. That accounts for her milk-white skin.'

'No, guv, don't get confused,' he guffaws, 'that's because she's a vampire.'

'Very droll, carry on.'

George is enjoying himself. 'So I asked my Chinese mate about this stuff and he says it's fantastic. He takes it every week. Better than that though, he thought this rare donkey hide might be good for an exclusive new product range for Havana.'

I don't like the sound of this one little bit. 'They wouldn't need to kill the donkeys?'

He's quiet for a moment. 'Course not – the hide would merely be a by-product from donkeys that are already dead.'

'Would they be dead because the Chinese have already killed them for the gelatin?'

'Don't be stupid.'

'How sure are you?'

He exhales loudly. 'Oh don't go all Mother Theresa on me. Look, my mate's hardly going to handle murdered goods is he?'

'Do you know what they do to cats in China?'

'I don't give a monkeys', guv. They can eat them for all I care.'

'You're disgusting.'

'Coming from you, I'll take that as a compliment. Anyway, gotta run. Invited to some benefit do with Bill Clinton tonight. Tickets cost an arm and a leg.'

When he's gone, I consult the Internet and discover that it's true – there is a rare donkey hide gelatin. This immediately starts me fretting about the welfare of the black-skinned donkey. Perhaps it's quite opportune that I'll be meeting Mr Cheeky Chan. I have a few pertinent questions I'd like to ask him.

It's nearly eight-thirty in the evening. The darkening sky is marbled with fine, wispy streaks of grey cloud that envelop the higher peaks of the Tramuntanas so that they appear like small, pointy sails floating in a serene and bottomless sea. Orlando and Minky are curled up on a chair in the *entrada* while Inko sits adoringly at Ollie's feet. Hunched over the kitchen table with a bright desk light at his side, Ollie studies a typed text. After some minutes he pushes back his chair and puffs out his cheeks.

'This is such a load of old rubbish. I mean, compared to Shakespeare it's hopeless.'

I sit down next to him and look at the paper. 'You know this book was voted one of the best works of fiction ever written.'

'Give me a break.'

'It's true. *Don Quixote* is the best example of writing from the Spanish Golden Age. Just think, it was written by Miguel de Cervantes way back in the early sixteen hundreds.'

He picks up the paper. 'But what's so great about it? This bit is all about Don Quixote thinking a bunch of windmills are giants. That's so ridiculous.'

'Yes but then things in Shakespeare could seem silly to a Spaniard. I mean, Puck turning Bottom into a donkey in *A Midsummer Night's Dream* is a bit odd.'

'Yes but that's all about magic, so it makes perfect sense.'

'Then there's mad old King Lear running around a heath thinking his friend Gloucester is his daughter Goneril with a white beard.'

Ollie remonstrates with his hands. 'Of course he does because he's going bonkers.'

'Ah, but so is Don Quixote. He's living in a world of fantasy, thinking he's some amazing hero, helping the less fortunate and vanquishing imaginary enemies. He's obsessed with chivalry.'

I jump up and consult the bookcase. 'I've got two copies of it somewhere. To my shame I've never quite finished it.'

'For once you've done something sensible,' he retorts.

A moment later, I find an English translation of it on the bottom shelf. 'I must revisit this.'

Ollie groans. 'Don't expect me to read it. It's bad enough having to do a comprehension in Spanish about one section. Then there's this annoying old man in the story called Sancho Panza who rides on a donkey.'

'Ah yes, he's Don Quixote's squire. Isn't his donkey called Rucio…?'

There's a sharp tap at the front door. Pep is standing on the porch in the dark. I switch on the outside light and greet him.

'Turn it off! I have Jacinto at the gate. He prefers natural light.'

I flip the switch off. 'You've brought the donkey whisperer? Already?'

He leans in closer. 'Look, I passed his field this evening and he offered to pop round to say hello.'

I look over his shoulder. 'You could have rung first.'

He gives me a disarming smile. 'I wanted it to be a surprise. You know how spontaneous we Mallorcans are.'

I jog into the kitchen and release the catch for the front gate. Ollie follows me outside.

'It's a donkey!' he hisses in my ear.

'Perhaps it's Sancho Panza and his Rucio.'

Ollie shoots me a withering look. 'Don't even go there, mother.'

The gate opens slowly and an elderly man walks into the courtyard, followed by a chestnut donkey. Pep leads us down the front steps of the porch to meet them. He slaps the diminutive figure on the back.

'This is Jacinto.'

Ollie and I hold out our hands. He reciprocates the gesture. '*Encantado*,' he says. In other words, he's delighted to meet us. 'And what is your name, *chico*?' he asks, turning to my slightly awed son.

'I'm Ollie,' he replies shyly.

After a moment he gestures towards the donkey and smiles. 'This is Rosa. She is a magical donkey, Ollie.'

A small grin plays on Ollie's lips.

'This donkey can understand everything we are saying,' the old man continues in a low, husky voice. 'Every word.'

Ollie finds it hard to keep a straight face. 'Really? *Increíble*!' Incredible.

The man bends close to the donkey's ear and whispers something quite urgently. The animal looks up and gives a little whinny.

'She says she likes you and would be happy to live here.'

I give Pep a pointed stare. '*Si, pues*, as Pep probably explained we're not quite ready to buy a donkey yet. We have to sort out the field first.'

Pep skims the air with his hand. 'Jacinto understands all this. I have explained. Don't worry.'

In the half-light, Pep's donkey whisperer resembles a little goblin with his short compact form and cropped grey hair. He is wearing a pair of faded brown trousers and a hand-woven tunic. Despite the cold, he has on a pair of open-toed sandals. He leans close to the donkey.

'She'd like to be properly introduced to you and your son.'

Ollie and I come closer, finally putting out our hands to stroke the soft, warm fur. Rosa gives a demure nod of the head and seems quite happy to be fondled. She juts her neck towards Jacinto. He mutters something to her.

'Now she'd like to see the house.'

I step back. 'The house? You don't mean inside?'

'Just the *entrada*. She is curious.'

Rather unhelpfully, Pep just shrugs sheepishly and indicates with his hand that we should head towards the front door.

I'm relieved that the Scotsman is at his Spanish language class in Sóller. I fear he wouldn't be too pleased about entertaining a donkey in the house. The donkey clip clops up onto the porch and, as if on cue, turns to Jacinto and brushes his ear. The old man mutters something to her and then allows her to step into the house. Minky and Orlando, wrapped up together on a wicker chair, give a start when they see Rosa lunging through the doorway. For a second she stands there before bending her head and performing a delicate and sure-footed about turn. I give a sigh of relief. She walks calmly back down the steps and rather gracefully trots over to the far wall of the courtyard, which overlooks the orchard and field below. With head raised she wiggles her long ears and gives a little grunt as if clearing her throat. Jacinto scuttles over, appearing to converse with her in a low voice while animatedly pointing to the Tramuntanas beyond. Rosa shakes her ears and whinnies as she contemplates the moon peeping up from behind the dark mountain peaks. For a brief second I almost forget that Jacinto's companion is in fact a donkey until reality takes a hold. Is the man stark raving mad? Long streams of ghostly white breath rise up from the donkey's nostrils and for an insane moment I almost fancy she's having a sly cigarette. I resist the temptation to catch Ollie's expression in the gathering dusk, knowing that he'll be surveying the scene between Jacinto and Rosa with his usual cynicism. Pep appears fairly pleased with himself and has an inane grin plastered on his lips.

'Thank you for coming,' I say as Jacinto walks slowly over to the gate with his donkey.

He shakes my hand goodbye. 'Rosa likes this place a lot. She thinks her daughter would too.'

'Her daughter?'

He smiles sweetly. 'Of course. If Rosa came to live with you, her daughter Bella would have to come too.'

'I might have to change their names. Would they mind that?' I ask.

He smiles. 'What would you call them?'

'Minny and Della, in memory of some special aunts.'

He leans towards the donkey and mutters a few words. The donkey waggles its ears.

'She says that would be OK. She'd like to be called Minny.'

Pep is suddenly at my side, a large *puro* now glowing between his fingers. 'You know donkeys get lonely. Jacinto's right. You'd need to have two.'

I give him a knowing look. 'I'm sure that's the case but for now we've rather a lot to sort out with securing the land before we can introduce any donkey to it.'

Jacinto gives me a crooked smile. '*Muy bien*. Rosa says she looks forward to meeting you again. *Adeu*!'

Pep kisses me on both cheeks and with a surreptitious wink follows Jacinto and Rosa out of the gate. I give a little wave as they head off.

Ollie leans towards me. 'What a joke,' he whispers. 'That donkey didn't have a clue what we were saying.'

The small party, now silhouetted against a silvery moon, stops in its tracks as Rosa turns her head and silently trots back towards us. She fixes her gaze on Ollie and then buts him gently with her nose. He totters back and gives a gasp.

Jacinto roars with laughter beyond the gate. 'Be careful, Ollie,' he calls out. 'As I told you before, Rosa understands every word you say.'

Stunned, Ollie stands on the spot and watches as the donkey, with a quick snort, makes a second departure through the gate. The sky is swaddled in a blanket of inky cloud and the high-pitched cry of the screech owl echoes from the higher branches of the algarroba tree. I give a little shiver.

'Let's go inside.'

'Wow, that was weird,' Ollie says, as we retrace our steps to the house. 'Do you believe all that about Rosa understanding what I said?'

'I'm really not sure what to think,' I reply, 'but one thing's for certain, I shall never look at a donkey in quite the same way ever again.'

THREE

TOADS AND TOADSTOOLS

It's a crisp autumnal day towards the end of October and the front porch is clogged with small mounds of dry, fragile leaves that leap up in fright at the slightest gust of wind. Sitting quietly in the courtyard, cold and feverish with dew, is our Mini Cooper. For several years, in fact from the time we arrived on the island, we drove a hire car on an extended lease. This was borne out of apathy as much as loyalty to cheerful Jordi at the car hire firm in the port but we finally took the plunge and bought one of our own. Of course the purchase wasn't by design. As is the custom, things just happen here in the valley and are rarely motivated by vigorous action or intent. Our film director friend, Victoria Duvall, had decided to sell her sleek little black Mini Cooper and, knowing my love of her car, offered us first refusal. Despite some initial resistance from the Scotsman, who for some reason felt his six-foot frame might be a tad constricted at the wheel, the deal was done. It was only when he practically had to rest his head on the dashboard to fit into the driver's seat that I took heed of his misgivings. A happy solution was eventually found when we rolled back the driver's seat as far as it would go, so that his knees no longer met his nose. Naturally this meant that no one could ever sit behind his seat but, as a three-person household, it was a hardship we learned to bear.

The front door swings open and Alan hurries down the front steps while Ollie follows up the rear, as always with his arms flung out as if he's about to do a free-fall parachute dive. It took me some time to realise that this strange phenomenon was due to the enormous rucksack of school books, a veritable mobile library that he carries like a hapless Atlas supporting the world on his back every day. Why he cannot keep some of his books in his classroom locker is beyond my understanding but he assures me that he likes to keep his belongings with him at all times.

'Late again,' frets the Scotsman as he clicks into his safety belt.

'Oh, calm down,' replies Ollie as he dumps his load on the back seat. 'It's only school.'

How times change. At his age the very thought of missing the morning bell and having to face the dreaded headmistress, Miss Wulff, on the front steps of my school used to fill me with terror.

Ollie leans out of the passenger window. 'You don't feel like making any more chocolate muffins today, do you?'

'Have we run out? Well, I suppose I'd better because the kids are over tomorrow.'

Ollie narrows his eyes. 'Remember to keep my bedroom door shut at all times.'

For the last few years I have held an informal English class for a group of local children more by accident than design. What began as a favour for my friend, Francisca, whose young daughter needed a few English lessons, has now blossomed into a regular weekly fixture in the calendar for six boisterous eight-year-olds and me. Ollie is none too happy when I raid his room for puppets and old toys for use in my games and has pinned a

KEEP OUT notice on his bedroom door, in both Spanish and Catalan.

I watch as the Mini Cooper shudders into life, slowly exiting the gate and trundling along the track, leaving a trail of white smoke in its wake. Ollie waves from the window until, as the car passes Rafael's front door, he is lost from view. The air is cool and yet scorched with the smell of bonfires. I tilt my head and see that at different points in the valley early morning bonfires are burning. As soon as October arrives, the ban on bonfires is over and pyromaniacs across the valley can rub their hands in glee. I slip over to the pond and see Johnny the toad gawping at me from his favourite haunt, a semi-sheltered ledge jutting from the pond's wet and mossy wall. A jungle of vines extends its tentacles along the rough old stones that form an overhang above the pond, their tendrils stretching down to kiss the water's edge. I yawn and potter over to talk to him. Johnny, my friendly, wise-cracking American toad and I have many a conversation, perhaps imaginary but always memorable, for me at least. Given that he is a native Mallorcan toad some might question my giving him an American accent but it seems to suit his sometimes defiant and confident demeanour. He fixes me with his glassy eyes.

'So, how's it going? Off for a run?'

'Any minute.'

'Be careful. The sky's not looking too good. Could be a downpour.'

I look heavenwards. 'No, it'll be fine. There are just a few clouds.'

He puffs out his throat. 'Suit yourself, but don't come crying to me when you're soaked through. So what's happening about that crazy cattery idea of yours? Giving up on it?'

I tut. 'Of course not. We're just waiting for some revised plans for the new building from England and then we'll get cracking.'

He blinks. 'Pity. The last thing me and the boys want around here is any more cats.'

As if in agreement, several loud croaks sound in unison from the rocks and lily pads.

'I'm afraid I've no idea where all the strays are coming from,' I sigh.

'Geez, you put up a welcome sign for cats on the porch and wonder why they keep on coming.'

'Don't be silly, they can't read.'

'I can and I'm only a toad.'

'But you're not real…'

Someone shouts from the gate. Johnny gives me a wink. 'See ya later, travelator.'

He plops into the dark water. I run over to the gate where Jorge the postman stands patiently, his long tresses swept back over one shoulder.

'I've got some books for you. When do you have time to read them all?'

I pull the *mando* – an electronic gadget which activates the gate – from my pocket and let him in. He strolls past me and, swinging his shoulder bag down on the front step, hauls out a large parcel. It has a Spanish frank.

'These are the books I ordered about the Spanish Civil War.'

He waits until I've torn open the package. Four dog-eared tomes tumble into my hands.

'They're *segunda mano*?' he says with slight disapproval.

'A few of them are out of print so I was lucky to even get them second-hand. This one is by Josep Massot i Muntaner. He wrote a lot about how the war affected Mallorca.'

He shrugs. 'As an Argentinian, I don't know much about what happened here during that time. We've had enough of our own problems.'

I nod. 'Yes, the world is a troubled place.'

He laughs. 'It may be troubled but I'm off *seta* picking tomorrow with my girlfriend, so I'm happy.'

'How is Beatriz?'

'*Bien,*' he says. 'We've been together for some time now. She's even managed to stop me looking at other girls so much.'

'Good. Long may it last.'

'Yes, this is true love.'

He holds a perfectly sculpted hand to his heart and grins. The man's the devil in an angel's guise. He takes up his postbag and leans forward to grasp my arm.

'Strong muscles for a woman. This running is doing you good.'

He gives a wink and saunters off. A few minutes later I am puffing along the track en route to the port.

Heavy droplets of rain fall from the sky like coins from an upturned purse, hitting my skin with such force that I mistake it for hail. The road back from Port of Sóller is already bubbling with water and cars swish by in a blur of red and white lights. Two cyclists in voluminous red cagoules wobble by, their faces streaked with rain, and then a *moto*, on which I see the familiar bulky form of Gaspar, the newspaper delivery man. He slows down when he sees me, waving with one hand while trying to steady the bike with the other. He pulls over and removes his huge helmet.

'You're a bit wet.'

'Yes, Gaspar, that's the problem with rain. I'm trying to get some training in before Athens.'

He grins from ear to ear. 'Ah, the marathon! I'm going to wave you off from Palma Airport. Just give me the date.'

'That's so kind of you, but it's really not necessary.'

He shakes his head. 'I'm coming and that's that. You've taken me out running enough times so it's the least I can do to give you a little *ànim* for the trip.'

I smile weakly. I'm not sure if Gaspar waving me off at the airport will be the sort of *ànim*, spirit, I'll need. It's true that I have taken him out for some gentle runs in the past but he soon tired of them. The draw of our local *pastisseria,* the cake shop, proved too much for him in the end.

He regards the sky with some chagrin. 'I think it's getting heavier. Of course I'd give you a lift home but I have to deliver the papers.'

I pat him on the back. 'Don't worry, I'll run like the wind and will be home in no time at all.'

He struggles back onto his bike and pushes his helmet down. '*D'acord*. Don't forget to give me the date you're leaving. *Adeu*!'

Squelching back up the track I notice a small brown parcel poking out of the postbox by the gate so I grab it and make haste to the porch. Taking the key from my pocket, I'm about to enter the house when I hear a strange plopping sound. There, hopping about in swirling muddy water on the front patio are dozens of frogs. I slosh over to the pond wall only to discover that the overflow pipe has become blocked, causing water to gush over the rim. Dunking my arm into the slimy depths, I finally manage to clear the blockage – old weeds – with a small stick. Although the overflow begins to function, I fret about how the frogs will clamber back into the pond before the cats get scent of them. There's only one thing for it. I'm not sure what methods are used in the annual frog catching competition in San Fernando in the Philippines, but mine are fairly basic. I begin lunging at the frogs as they sit quietly puffing out their lustrous little chests. Twice I nearly catch one, but the little rotter leaps into the air with elasticated legs a second before I manage to nab him. There's a loud croaking from the pond and there sitting in the same overhang as before with a smug grin on his face is Johnny.

'You haven't got a clue, have you? That's no way to catch a frog!'

I'm in no mood for mockery. My Lycra running gear is soaked through. I've already abandoned my trainers and socks and am paddling around in the icy water barefooted.

'It's impossible,' I snarl.

'For a loser like you maybe but I bet Ollie could do it.'

I could swear his slimy little shoulders are heaving up and down with convulsions of laughter. Of course he's right. Ollie is a proven frog-catcher of great dexterity.

'Now listen up, what you have to do is sidle up to the frog in small moves but pretend you're not remotely interested in him. Got it?'

'Oh for heaven's sake, I've got a pile of work on my desk. Perhaps I'll just leave them to the cats.'

He observes me coldly. 'That's nice. Well, if you want amphibian blood on your hands...'

'Shhh!' I wipe the rain from my face and begin a new strategy. Creeping up slowly behind a baby frog with my eyes averted I wait for a second and grab it from behind. I plop it back in the pond with relief.

'Bravo! See, it works.' My mottled brown tormentor is fixing me with a triumphant stare. 'You've only got about another twenty to go.'

Half an hour later I make my weary way into the house, have a hot shower and brew up some tea. The brown parcel catches my eye on the table. Carefully undoing the old string that binds it, I loosen the brown paper and find inside a small leather-bound volume of Catalan verse entitled, *Oda a la Guerra – Ode to War* – by someone called Michel Ripoll. It is dated 1948 and the publisher is French. I'm mystified. I take it upstairs to the office and with some difficulty translate the first poem. The five stanzas are sad and stark, relating to the Spanish Civil War. It talks about the death of a woman but I can't quite understand the final verse. With some frustration I place it down on the desk and get down to some work. A few hours later, there's a knock at the front door. I skip downstairs and see my old friend, Neus Adrillon, on the porch. This elderly, feisty lady was a close friend of my former neighbour and surrogate grandmother, Margalida. Last year I'd helped Neus deal with a troublesome English neighbour and we've been great friends ever since. I like to think that Margalida brought us together, that something positive came out of her passing. She hobbles into the *entrada* and gives me a hug. As usual she is breathing heavily, as if she's just run up Ben Nevis in her pompom slippers.

'I walked all the way down to the orchard gate so that I didn't need to disturb you,' she says wheezily.

'But I only have to press a button to open the front gate, Neus.'

She pushes her bushy white hair back from her face. 'I prefer the old manual gates that you push, not these new electronic ones that slide open. I always think they might rebel one day and squash me to a pulp as I walk through.'

'Thanks, Neus. That's a brand new neurosis to add to my list.'

She gives a big throaty laugh and without invitation walks into the kitchen and sits down at the table. She turns in her chair to observe the patio beyond the back door.

'What a fine view you have of the Tramuntanas from here. An artist's dream.'

'Yes, shame I'm useless at drawing. Fancy a coffee?'

She smiles. 'No, just a glass of water will do.'

'So how's life?'

She gives a sniff. 'I've been a little lonely. It's difficult now with Eduardo in Barcelona but he's got a steady job. God has been good to him.'

Neus has two sons living on the island but one has recently taken up a new engineering post on the mainland on a two-year contract. I get the impression that she relied on him the most. Still, she lives in a comfortable terraced house only five minutes' walk from our *finca* and is surrounded by a caring local neighbourhood and many friends.

'What about Jaume in Santa Maria?'

'He's a good *chico* too, but he and his wife are so busy with work and the children. I only see them at weekends.'

She pulls out a rosary and turns the crucifix towards me. 'Well, at least I have my constant companion. He always listens to me.'

'So do the rest of us. Don't forget your friends.'

She smiles. 'That's true, but he's with me every second of the day.'

I fetch her a glass of water. 'Have you ever heard of a poet called Michel Ripoll?'

'*Segur*. He's well known in Mallorca.' She chuckles. 'The old rogue's even older than me. Michel's grandparents were two of the earliest Sóllerics to emigrate to France in the mid eighteen hundreds. They opened a grocer's in Sète and did very well.'

She rubs her eyes and yawns. 'Michel's father, Mateu, was born over there and married a French girl called Francoise. He even fought in World War One.'

'So is Michel still living there?'

She laughs. 'Oh no. After the war, about 1920, Michel's parents returned to Sóller with him. He must have been just a toddler. His grandparents built an enormous house in the town.' She gives me a knowing look and rubs her fingers together. 'They had money.'

'So this Michel is quite old?'

She yawns. 'He must be ninety or more. I rarely see him about now. He lives with Ignacio, his nephew, and family. They've been good to him ever since the troubles.'

'What troubles?'

She tuts. 'The war, of course.'

'Which war.'

'Pah! Which war, *reina*? There is only one that matters. The Spanish Civil War.'

I still find it amusing that *reina*, queen, is used so regularly as a form of endearment in Mallorca. I suppose it's the equivalent of saying 'duck' in Leeds.

'Did Michel fight in the Spanish Civil War?'

She pulls a face. 'He became one of them. A Republican. It was hard for the family. He was a good-looking boy, full of idealism, but he got in with a strange literary crowd in Palma who filled his head with nonsense and before you know it he'd gone off to fight in the war.'

I'm gripped. 'What happened to him?'

She sighs. 'I don't know much more. Some terrible things happened to his family because of him but they were honest, God-fearing Catholic Nationalists and tried to understand and forgive.' She makes the sign of the cross and fidgets with her rosary.

'Terrible things happened here during the war. There was a man in Sóller who spent the entire war down a *pozo*, you know.'

'A well?!' I laugh.

'Oh it sounds funny now but it wasn't at the time. Many Republicans had to go into hiding to avoid imprisonment, or worse. Most of us were Nationalists but we'd still help them because they were neighbours.'

'How odd. So even though you supported different sides you still remained friends?'

She shakes her head. 'It was complicated. To be honest, when the civil war broke out most of the hostilities came down to long-standing feuds and old enmities between families. The war was often just an excuse to settle old scores. All you had to do here in Mallorca was denounce someone as a Republican sympathiser and they'd more than likely be carted off by the Nationalist governing power.'

'How terrible to live in such a climate of fear and uncertainty.'

She shrugs. 'We all coped somehow. In the rural areas we just kept our noses clean and didn't get involved with the politics. The Mallorcan philosophy is to live and let live. Anyway, why do you want to know about Michel?'

'I happened to come across one of his books.'

She looks surprised. 'That's lucky. I wouldn't imagine many of his books were still in print. Perhaps in France but not here. He lived in Paris for many years after the civil war.'

'Did he marry over there?'

'No. We were told he never recovered from a broken heart.'

She gets up. 'All I do know is that he didn't come back to the island until the 1960s, by which time he was a celebrated poet in France but he nearly always wrote in Catalan. My brother had a few of his books. Lord knows what happened to them.'

She rises to her feet. 'Anyway, I've got to get off home. An old *tío* is taking me out to dinner tonight.'

I express surprise. Neus being taken out by some bloke on a date?

She slaps my arm. 'On a date? At my age? No, *reina*, Bernat and I are old school friends but I haven't seen him in years. He was recently widowed and has kept a bit to himself. I know what it's like to lose a partner as you know.'

'So did he just contact you?'

She shrugs. 'I bumped into him in the market and he suggested we catch up over dinner.'

'What are you going to wear?'

She tuts and hobbles over to the front door. 'The same old things as always, although I'll have to do something with my hair. I'll use the stuff in that bottle you gave me. I keep it for special occasions.'

'It's only conditioner, Neus. You're supposed to use it every day.'

'*Que va*! What a waste!'

She stands on the porch surveying the sky. 'Well the rain's nearly over but it's been good for the *bolets*. Are you planning on mushroom picking?'

I smile. 'Actually, Carolina Constantino from the museum is taking me out to identify wild *bolets* next week.'

'Ah well, you're lucky. She's a fungi expert, like her father. He wrote a book on the subject, you know?'

'I do.'

I kiss her on both cheeks and we walk slowly to the gate together. She pauses for a second to catch her breath.

'A funny thing I've remembered about Michel.'

I wait.

'When he returned to Mallorca, he'd sometimes call himself José.'

'José?' I say in some surprise.

'*Si*, it was strange. He once threatened a man in a bar for calling him Michel. We all thought the war had maybe turned his mind. Poor devil.'

She shakes her head and with some caution steps on to the track, her eyes fixed on the stationary gate.

So the mystery thickens but now, at least, I'm fairly sure who left me the book of verse. Why, though, and is there a hidden message? I turn back towards the house, deep in thought, wondering whether I might expect another visit from José, or Michel, one day soon.

It's a crisp, blustery day and the sky is thick and velvety despite the early hour. I creep out of the front door avoiding the wailing cats planted on the top step and start up the car engine. The headlights penetrate the thick undergrowth by the side of the gate, casting long, ragged shadows around the stone walls. A small rat scuttles out from behind a dark rock and darts across my path as I head out of the gate. I watch as it scrambles up a bank of grass, its wriggling, tawny body illuminated with momentary light. Aside from wee beasties lurking in the long grasses and the early birds swooping overhead, the valley is silent. I catch a glimpse of my watch face in a shard of moonlight. It is six o'clock. Has the sun overslept? Surely someone somewhere must be stirring soon? The car rattles along, past the sleepy *fincas* belonging to Rafael and

Silvia and Pedro, and out onto the country road. There's not a soul in sight, windows are tightly shuttered and heavy wooden doors are barred against the world. I head towards the Sóller tunnel and am comforted to see that a few yawning workmen are walking slowly along the road, their cigarettes glowing fiery red in the darkness. Nearing the Museu Balear de Ciències, the Balearic Natural History Museum, I flash my indicator to a road devoid of cars and park up near its front gate. Nothing stirs but, as in the best spy movies, a dark car just beyond mine purrs into life and the lights flash twice. I squint to make sure it is Carolina Constantino, director of the museum, before locking up my car. I jog over to the passenger side and jump in.

Her big brown eyes light up and she gives me a gigantic smile. 'Up for a little *bolet* and *fong* hunting?'

Bolet is the Mallorcan word for mushroom, the Spanish equivalent being *seta* and *fongs* are fungi or *hongos* in Spanish. 'Yes, I think so – even at this crazy hour.'

Carolina and I met a year ago when I became interested in Myotragus, the ancient mouse goat that was peculiar to the *Baleares* and which roamed the island up until about 3000 BC. I subsequently became a member of the museum and visit the new installations and exhibitions whenever I can. Knowing that I have a love for *bolets*, although unfamiliar with all the different species, Carolina has invited me to come out for a morning's mushroom hunt. As a fungi expert, she promises to introduce me to some rare varieties here in the hills.

We drive off, taking the broad and winding road that leads to Lluc monastery and eventually Pollença in the north of the island. As we head into the hills a few cars totter out on to the road in the direction of the town, few seeming inclined to follow us up the steep hill leading to the Tramuntanas. Carolina is already warming to her theme. As the daughter of Carles, a well-known mycologist on the island, she has spent her childhood surrounded by fungi, eventually training in the science herself. Although I have been out before hunting for edible *bolets* with Catalina and her aunt, Maria, who runs the popular local Ca N'Antuna restaurant, I have never been on a fungi fact-finding trip. Carolina has promised to show me a selection of typical Mallorcan *bolets* – the edible variety – and also some of the more toxic *fongs*.

'Of course,' says Carolina, 'the most dangerous fungi are the *Amanita phalloides* which funnily enough you can find here in Sóller as well as in Menorca.'

'How poisonous is it?'

She shrugs. 'It causes death in about eighty per cent of those who ingest it.'

'I should maybe avoid those, then?'

Carolina titters. 'Most of the fungi you see are to be avoided. Out of the thousand or more varieties on the island only about 150 are edible and some 200 are highly toxic.'

'It's like trying to find a needle in a haystack. I wonder why anyone bothers.'

She tuts. 'That's part of the fun of it, identifying the fungi and finding the edible ones.'

We turn up the dark hill, still the only car on the road. 'Where is everyone?'

'The clever ones are still in bed. As for the *caçadors de bolets*, the mushrooms hunters, they'll already be in the hills.'

A small creature darts in front of the car. Carolina gently presses the brake and turns her head to watch it hurtle into some leaves at the side of the road.

'A pine marten,' she says. 'You have to watch out for sheep and wild goats on this road too.'

A strip of penetrating forestland forms a jagged silhouette in the headlights as we sweep by. To the right of me, enormous trees rise up, shoulder to shoulder, in the sudden light then disappear in the smudgy darkness. We climb higher and soon reach an area of open forestland. Carolina takes a left and we bump over rocks and clumps of wild grass until we reach a wide track.

'Here. This will do.'

She kills the engine and jumps out of the car. Both of us are dressed in woolly fleeces and jeans and have come equipped with walking shoes and torches. Carolina rummages about in the boot.

'OK, let's take these wicker baskets and small knives.'

'Is it always best to use baskets?'

'Mycologists collect the fungi in open baskets to prevent them breaking and also so that the spores aren't lost so easily during the walk.'

The air is chilled and peppery with a strong aroma of garlic. I search about me in the half-light and see clumps of bushy rosemary, thyme and, sure enough, wild garlic. A light breeze ripples through the trees, shedding leaves that dance and twirl to the earth. I feel the soil.

'It's quite moist here. Is that good?'

Carolina nods. 'The conditions should be perfect given that we had a plentiful rainfall in September and a warm start to October. Come on, let's try our luck.'

We walk up a long, winding track for some three kilometres, finally taking a right-hand turn into a leafy area of forestland. The sky is almost edible, stained magnolia and daubed with swirls of dark rose light so that it resembles raspberry ripple ice cream. I look up hungrily.

'We don't need our torches any more,' says Carolina. 'Come and have a look at this.'

She is squatting by a pile of pitted stones, but on closer inspection I see that they are not stones at all. They are *bolets,* edible fungi of some kind.

'*Esclata-sangs,*' she yawns. 'You must have eaten them before. They are also called *rovelló* and they can sell for twenty euros a kilo or more.'

I inspect the wide funnel-shaped cream heads tinged with orange and red, recalling how delicious they taste fried with garlic and olive oil. Carolina picks a crop of them, being careful to cut rather than pull them out of the ground, and gently places them in her basket.

'Why do you always use wicker baskets for gathering?' I ask.

'It lets the mushrooms breathe. Otherwise they might ferment.'

We push on through the undergrowth until Carolina holds up a hand.

'Look, these are interesting. *Bolets de femer*.'

'Doesn't *femer* mean manure?'

'*Si*, heaven knows why they call them that!' She laughs and holds up one of the inky-coloured mushrooms that are shaped rather like a tulip flower.

'Can you eat them?'

'When they're young, and as long as you don't drink alcohol with them.'

'Gosh, it's like Russian roulette.'

We walk on, pulling stray brambles and long, trailing vines from our path. I stumble upon a crop of whitish-grey, flat-headed mushrooms.

'Oh those are *blavas*, they taste good. See how they always grow close to conifers.'

I take in my surroundings, drinking in the woody smells and fresh fragrance of pine. Carolina taps my arm. 'See these? They are *verderol* and fairly toxic. In Spanish they're called the gentleman's mushroom.'

'They're not very attractive, are they? A bit greeny looking.'

She places some samples in her basket and wanders on until she sees a small group of spindly, yellowy fungi. 'Now, this type is good. They're called *camagroc*. I knew they were here by their smell. They have a very distinctive fruity aroma.'

I sniff the air. 'Yes, it's quite pungent. Are they good to eat?'

'Yes, but best not to eat too many at once,' she replies.

I'm dazed by the sheer number of varieties in one wood and impressed that Carolina can identify them so easily. It would take me a few lifetimes.

She observes her watch. 'Come on, let's return to the museum. I want to show you some other fungi that we've collected. It's nearly nine o'clock and the sun is up.'

We carry our wicker baskets along the narrow forest tracks, the ground springy beneath our feet. Once back at the car we retrace our journey, arriving at the museum by ten. Stiff-legged, we make our way into the central office where a huge array of fungi has been laid out.

'You know every Monday evening we invite people to come in with mushrooms they've found and we help identify them. Some varieties are quite fascinating.'

I point at a strange-looking fungi which, dare I say it, resembles a breast, being whitish with a bright pink tip.

'That's a *llenega*, I guess what you'd maybe call 'wax cap' and over here is *pets de llop*, wind of a wolf.'

I pick up the white little mushroom, shaped like a globe. 'You do have odd names for your fungi.'

Carolina pushes her long, dark hair behind her ears. '*Pues*, it makes it more interesting, don't you think?'

'I suppose it does. What's this one? It looks like a little chocolate cupcake.'

She pulls a face. 'I don't think so. It's a *bolet peziza*. They tend to grow in humid zones. These over here grow in sand dunes. We have about forty different *bolets* that grow in sand.'

The door opens and Cati, one of the museum's staff bears a small tray with two coffees. I thank her and plop a sugar in my cup.

'Ah, just what the doctor ordered,' I say, taking a sip.

Carolina clicks her teeth and says with a smile, 'I'm sorry we don't have anything to eat. Maybe you can have a croissant when you get home unless of course you might like to sample some *bolets*?'

'Yes, I could try my chances with the lethal *Amanita phalaoides* perhaps. I might be one of the lucky twenty per cent who survive it.'

'It would be like eating that Japanese fugu pufferfish, you know, the one that can kill if it's not prepared properly?' laughs Carolina.

I drain my coffee and, with a wink, get up to leave. 'Exactly, so if it's OK with you I might just opt for that croissant at home.'

I jump into the Mini and am just about to start the engine when my mobile phone rings.

It is Ed, my neurotic but exceptionally talented chum in London. He is ringing me from work, which for him is a small office within the labyrinth of the BBC in White City. Ed and I have known each other for donkeys' years, in fact ever since our days as students at Leeds University. When we all waved goodbye to student life Ed carried on in academia, having achieved a first-class degree in English. With a doctorate in his grasp, he joined the BBC and never left. He is a true British eccentric and a genius, which I fear the BBC has never fully appreciated. Despite his enormous brain power he is utterly incapable of the simplest practical chore, has panic attacks on public transport and is a disaster in forming relationships. Aside from all that he is the most loyal and endearing friend I could ever wish for.

'When are you back in London?' he drawls.

'Next month.'

He gives a loud tut. 'Well that's a bore. I wanted to introduce you to a new woman I've met on the Internet.'

'Oh no, Ed. I just don't think I've got the stamina.'

He gives a sniff. 'Don't be horrid. This one is different. She's called Irina and she's from Russia.'

'From Russia with love,' I sigh.

'Oh very funny,' he grunts.

Every six months Ed finds the new potential love of his life through dating sites on the Internet. They habitually turn out to be complete nutty fruitcakes, neurotics or spongers.

'Thanks to her, I've joined a poetry group in Islington. I feel inspired to compose again.'

'Good for you,' I say. 'I've just met a poet, funnily enough. He's called José.'

'Perhaps we can swap poems?' he says brightly.

'I'm not sure. He's a little rarefied.'

'How do you know him?' he persists.

'It's a long story – I'll share it with you one day. Now I've got to go for my breakfast. I've been out mushroom picking this morning and I'm ravenous.'

'Mushroom picking? But you could be poisoned! Wild fungi can be deadly. Think of the toxins! Are you mad? And at this hour of the morning?'

I give a sigh. 'Bye bye, Ed.'

I survey the kitchen table with amusement. It looks as if a band of possessed chimps have been doing battle with an armoury of chocolate biscuits, squash, pencil shavings, crumpled paper and felt-tip pens. My six little cherubs, Tina, Mateo, Sara, Tofol, Marga and Iván have just skipped off down the track with their parents after my English class with them, and have left me to clear up the debris. I retrieve the dustpan and brush and am clearing up the mess when there's a buzz at the gate. Catalina swings into the drive with headlights blazing. She saunters up the front steps, jangling her car keys.

'Well, lazy woman, it's a Friday night so I thought I'd pop by for a glass of wine. You just finished your kids' class?'

She stalks into the kitchen and giggles when she sees the table.

'Give me that brush!'

She throws off her jacket and in a matter of minutes has the kitchen looking spotless.

'Now get me my wine.'

I pull a bottle of cold cava from the fridge and pop off the cork. We chink glasses.

'So what have you been doing with the kids today?'

'Oh, playing with puppets and reading *Wind in the Willows*.'

'The story with talking animals? We studied that in my English class at school.'

'That's the one. The kids love Toad of Toad Hall the best because he's so impetuous and silly.'

She laughs. 'Yes and he crashed his car, no?'

'You've got a good memory. I'm impressed.'

'What a week!' says Catalina. 'You know I haven't stopped. We've had so many visitors in Fornalutx.'

Despite the summer being over, the valley is still popular with hikers and cyclists who prefer the cooler autumn climate. With a small team of helpers, Catalina somehow juggles the cleaning and laundry changeovers of about twenty holiday rental properties each week that are in her charge.

'Are you working this weekend?'

She sighs. 'Only Saturday but that's enough. So, how's your week been?'

I tell her about Michel the poet and Neus's words on the subject. She nods.

'I've heard of him vaguely but I've never read his poetry. Can I see the book?'

I take it from the bookcase in the *entrada* and hand it to her. She takes a sip of cava and begins studying the first poem. I open a packet of salted almonds and place them in a bowl in front of her.

'This is not very cheerful. Mind you, calling a book '*Ode to War*' is a little odd, no?' she titters.

I give a shrug. 'I suppose if you fought in the Spanish Civil War you wouldn't have many happy memories.'

'That's true. This last verse says that he is forever tormented by loss. It must have been a terrible time,' she says soberly.

'I didn't understand that last stanza,' I reply.

Catalina reaches for a nut and accidentally drops the book on the floor. She picks it up and wipes the cover on her jumper. 'Ah, what's this?'

She reaches down and picks up a small newspaper cutting. 'This fell out of the book. Have you seen it before?'

In some anticipation, I lean over her shoulder to see it. The paper is yellowed and the writing is tiny.

Catalina pushes her glasses back against the top of her nose and scrutinises it carefully.

'It is a newspaper called *La Voz* in Madrid and it's dated 7 March 1939. It is a death notice. Some woman called Perez, I think. It's hard to make out the first name. My eyes aren't sharp enough. It says she is from the family of Perez in Salamanca. That's a nice part of Madrid.'

'I wonder who she was,' I say, puzzled.

Catalina takes a handful of nuts and grins. 'Well, she died a long time ago so don't lose sleep over it.'

I take the tiny fragment of paper from her and hold it to the light. I finally make out the Christian name. 'Oh no. It's Sofia. The name is Sofia.'

She looks at me blankly. 'So what?'

'José's girlfriend was called Sofia. If it is the same Sofia, it means she died right at the end of the war. How dreadful.'

Catalina drains her glass and frowns. 'Who's José?'

'He's Michel. For some reason he gives himself two names.'

'I don't know,' she smiles. 'It all sounds a bit too complicated for me. Now I must get back to make dinner for Ramon and the twins or there'll be hell to pay.'

She gives me a peck on both cheeks and sweeps out of the house like a wild woman, banging the front door and honking loudly as she swerves across the gravel and makes her exit through the gate. I sit staring at the cutting. If the civil war began in 1936 and ended in April 1939, it meant that both Sofia and her sister, Elena, died during the conflict. I think of how devastating this must have been for their family. Were the girls supporters of the Republican or Nationalist cause, or perhaps neither? I slip the cutting back between the pages of the book and carry it upstairs to my office for safe-keeping. I try fruitlessly to piece together the few fragments of the story that I have, knowing that in reality only my elusive poet holds the key. I stand at the open window listening for my frogs and chirpy toad, Johnny, but as it's October they've already left for the winter. Water tinkles from the wide mossy ledge above the pond and the baleful cry of a hound resonates across the valley. I think of Michel alone with his thoughts and his memories. Forever tormented by loss.

FOUR

PIGGY IN THE MIDDLE

Monday 8.15 a.m., the club, Mayfair

A vacuum cleaner droning from an upper floor seems incapable of drowning out the discordant Irish ballad wafting down the central stairwell. I stand on the third-floor landing listening to Bernadette's painful rendition of 'Three Lovely Lasses from Bunyan', wondering when she might need to take a breath. I've been a member of this Mayfair-based club for women for a few years now and joined originally because I needed a pied-à-terre in London when I moved to Mallorca. It's wonderfully eccentric and full of characters, and that applies to the members as much as the staff. Bernadette is the club's Irish housekeeper, a larger than life personality.

I make a hesitant move towards the top stair and grimace when a sharp pain shoots up the back of my leg. The day after completing a marathon is always the worst, but despite the discomfort I know the best thing to do is keep the limbs moving.

'Cooeee!!!'

I look upwards and see a moon of a face smiling down at me. The eyeshadow is a bright, pearlised green, the hair a puffball of henna and lacquer.

'Mother of God, you look like an old woman!' She emits a wild, hysterical cawing, her body bent over the mahogany rail.

'Don't mock the afflicted,' I wince.

'God love her,' she says to a nearby wall. 'That'll learn her for going off and doing these stupid things in November. You must have caught your death of cold running around Athens at this time of the year.'

I exhale deeply and stagger on to the third stair. 'Well, Bernadette, at least I finished the race and raised a fair amount for charity.'

She gives a loud scoffing sniff. 'You'd probably have raised more at a bring and buy sale, you daft apeth!'

'You're a tower of strength, you know?'

More manic laughter and then a feather duster waggles at me from above. 'You take care now, girl. Watch them stairs. We don't want to be calling an ambulance, do we?'

After a long and arduous descent, I hobble out of the red-brick building and walk slowly down Curzon Street and across Berkeley Square into Mayfair in the direction of my PR agency. When I reach the office I contemplate taking the stairs but finally opt for the lift, deciding that I've suffered enough physical pain this morning. Sarah, one of my senior staff, is bustling about in the main office when I make my entrance. She comes over to give me a hug.

'Well done! Rachel told us you made it. Hope you've got your medal?'

I dump my bag on the reception desk and fumble about in its depths until I unearth my small metallic trophy. She takes it from me and loops the orange ribbon around her neck.

'Wow, that's cool. They say the Athens marathon is the hardest in the world. Is that true?'

I shake my head. 'No, I reckon it's Boston or, come to think of it, Antarctica.'

She opens her mouth wide. 'Don't tell me there are lunatics willing to run in those sorts of temperatures?'

I laugh. 'I'd rather like to do it one day and run all seven continents.'

She giggles. 'You are seriously deranged.'

'Yep. There's a lot of truth in that. Now then, how's the ship?'

She pushes out her bottom lip. 'Well we're still afloat and clients are flooding in. Rachel's fixed up for you to meet quite a few while you're over.'

She scoops up the big, leather-bound diary that always sits on the reception desk. 'You've probably got most of these appointments in your diary, except Greedy George who's booked you in for lunch today with his Chinese restaurant chum.'

'I groan. 'Oh no. Not Mr Pig Cheeks?'

She grins. 'That's the one. You've also got a meeting this afternoon with Charlie Romstead, the artist, and Marcus and Pippa Darley this morning.'

'That's right. They're the mad hatters, aren't they?'

'Yes, Rachel thinks you'll like them. They're pretty outrageous. Well, the wife is.'

The door swings open and in walks Rachel, dressed in a black wool crêpe suit and turquoise pashmina. I check out her black suede shoes with their killer heels, wondering not for the first time how on earth she walks in them. She must have been a stilt walker in her last life. She throws her black leather gloves on the reception desk and fixes me with an enormous grin. 'So, tell us about Athens!'

'It was fantastic, although it's probably the hardest course I've done.'

'Any difficult moments?'

'Only before I left Mallorca. Can you believe Gaspar, our paper delivery man, came to see me off at Palma Airport?'

She picks up some mail and scrutinises it. 'Sweet,' she says crisply.

'It was sweet, although hugely embarrassing. He came with his friend Pau and they unfurled a massive banner while I was standing in the easyJet queue, with my name and the words "GUANYADORA DEL MARATÓ D'ATENES!" in huge red letters.'

Rachel is mystified. 'What does that mean?'

'Winner of the Athens marathon!'

'That was a bit of wishful thinking.' She smirks.

Sarah puts her hand to her mouth. 'That is embarrassing! What did everyone in the easyJet queue make of it?'

'They were sniggering, of course. Thank God I had speedy boarding so that my humiliation was fairly short-lived.'

They both laugh out loud.

'You're the limit,' says Rachel. 'Anyway, let's have a coffee and a catch up. We've got to pop over to Chelsea at eleven to see the Darleys.'

'Darrrrlings!' corrects Sarah. 'That's what we all call them here.'

'Why?' I ask suspiciously.

'You'll find out,' Rachel replies cryptically.

11 a.m., The Chelsea Mad Hatters, King's Road

Rachel hops out of the black taxi behind me and pushes a tenner through the driver's front window. He nods his head, tears her off a receipt and drives away. We stand outside the bow-fronted window of The Chelsea Mad Hatter's, inspecting the merchandise.

'Nice hats,' I say. 'Very *osé*.'

'Yes, the Darleys like to be different. *Harper's Bazaar* uses their products all the time for fashion shoots. The shop's got a great reputation.'

'So this is its tenth anniversary?'

She sweeps her long hair back over her shoulder. 'That's why they came to us. They want to do something special this year; some kind of anniversary event.'

'Who does their window dressing?'

She shrugs. 'I've no idea but it's pretty kinky, isn't it? All that rubber and black feathers.'

The front door suddenly flies open, releasing a sharp peal of sound. It reminds me of the bell I used to have on my scooter as a child. A tall, spidery creature in black with the palest skin I've ever seen steps out and surveys us both with a quizzical smile. The hair is fair and lank, the eyes China blue and the nose extraordinarily crooked.

'Welcome, good friends, enter if you dare!'

Rachel is completely unfazed. 'Marcus, how are you? Can I introduce the marathon runner herself?'

He leans forward, jutting out a sharp, bony chin, enthusiastically grasping my hands in both of his. His fingers feel like live, cool eels and I can't wait to shake them off.

'*Enchanté*, mademoiselle,' he lisps.

'Delighted to meet you,' I say. 'What a glorious front window display.'

He follows me over. 'Yes, indeed. Bruno is a genius. He's been dressing our windows from the day we opened.'

'Marvellous,' I simper. 'Does he style other shops?'

He clasps his chest as if I've stabbed at his heart. 'Heaven forbid! That would be the end. No, he's all ours.'

'You're very lucky, then.'

Flattening out a crease in his black frock coat, he huddles closer, adopting a confidential air.

'The truth is, Bruno isn't quite all he seems.'

There's a pause for effect. I eye Rachel nervously but she's looking completely blank.

'Bruno works as a drag queen in Soho by night and as our creative director by day.'

'Well, fancy that!' gushes Rachel.

'Do you like gay shows?' asks Marcus, eyeing me intently.

'To be honest, we don't have that many in the Sóller Valley.'

He raises his eyebrows. 'How odd. Never fear, we'll arrange for you and Rachel to visit Bruno's club one night. It's a thrill ride.'

He walks over to the door, his legs springy like thin pieces of elastic. With his back turned, I give Rachel a steely glance. She throws out both hands in a gesture of innocence and mouths, *'What?'* Inside the shop, it's hard to find one's bearings. The amber lighting is dim and individual sheets of perspex are suspended in long curls from the black ceiling, zigzagging around the shop to form a bizarre internal labyrinth. On each vertical sheet hangs a hat, attached by nylon threads and under-lit by tiny, coloured bulbs. Marcus watches me carefully.

'It's a work of art, as you can see.'

'Mmm. Absolutely.' I daren't look at Rachel.

'The idea is to follow the perspex route all around the shop. That way you get to see all the new merchandise. Fifty different designs.'

Rachel nods knowingly. 'Yes, it's a clever device and quite captivating.'

'What's that strange noise?' I ask with some concern. 'It's like a trapped bird flapping its wings.'

'Flight of fancy, perhaps?' suggests Marcus with a superior leer. 'What you are experiencing is son et lumière – a sound and light show within a shop space.'

I wonder if I've skipped right onto the pages of *Alice in Wonderland*, and am further convinced of it when what appears to be the Queen of Hearts steps out from behind a door at the back of the shop.

'Ah! This is my dear wife, Pippa, queen of hats.'

A tall woman steps forward. She is wearing a full-length, black velvet gown, and plum in the middle of her chignon bun is a bizarre little gold concoction with a short veil and long, thin black feathers, which dangle over her forehead like the legs of a monstrous spider.

'Welcome to paradise, darrrrrrling,' she drawls.

Between her fingers, a slim cigarette holder glistens like a bone. She ruches her lips and plants a kiss on Rachel's cheek, extending a pale hand in my direction.

'The athlete returns from Athens, carrying the torch of victory!'

'Yes, well, I'm not sure about that, but at least I finished it,' I say limply, remembering the sheer exhaustion I felt on completing the arduous course.

'Come, let's have some coffee in the back parlour.'

She beckons to her husband, who sweeps ahead of us through the narrow door and begins arranging chairs around an oval mahogany table. Rich ruby curtains are drawn back from the elegant windows and the walls are covered in a fine cloth that has the appearance of damask. The room is mercifully light, which means that I can take notes.

'Where's the coffee?' bawls Pippa.

A draped entrance reveals a girl of slight build carrying a massive silver tray of cups and saucers.

'This is Isabelle. She is the daughter of a duke.'

The girl says nothing, merely positions the tray carefully on the table and takes her leave silently back through the drapes. Marcus pours out steaming coffee from a massive silver pot and proffers milk. I shake my head and take my cup gratefully. Perchance one stimulating sip will wake me up from what must surely be some insane nightmare. No such luck. I place the cup down in front of me with some disappointment.

'So, what sort of event have you in mind?'

Pippa rests an elbow on the table and inclines her head towards me. 'We want to do something fun, mad, unexpected and full of surprises.'

'Yes, an event for the media and all our loyal clients of course,' says Marcus.

Rachel takes a gulp of coffee. 'A sort of hat show?'

Marcus scratches his nose thoughtfully. 'Or a spectacle of some kind.'

Pippa pushes a miniature croissant towards me. 'You must try one. I made them myself.'

I take a small bite and am amazed to find it delicious. 'Excellent! So you make hats and cakes?'

'And babies!' She gives a manic screech and is joined in jovial laughter by her husband. 'We have five now. Rachel's met all our cherubs.'

I swivel round to examine Rachel's face. A kind of rigor mortis has set in.

'Rachel loves children,' I smile. 'Always bear her in mind for babysitting duty.'

She gives an involuntary little yelp. 'Urgh! I mean yes, absolutely, time permitting.'

Pippa jumps up. 'Actually, I must show you something.'

She whips a frame off a sideboard and inspects it. 'Here.'

I take one look at the image in the frame and wonder if the Darleys really are raving mad. The picture is of a human stomach with what look like stitches sewn across it.

'I had a major tummy tuck after having all the children so we photographed it for posterity. I can show you what it looks like now if you like?'

She begins pulling at her robe.

'No!' I cry in horror. 'I think I've got the idea. Do show the image to Rachel.'

'I've already seen it, thank you,' says Rachel rather stiffly, giving me a warning glance. Pippa returns the frame to the sideboard.

'I find aesthetic surgery rather addictive. Don't you?'

'In truth, I don't think it's quite my bag.'

'Nonsense. You'd love it. Kiss goodbye to wrinkles and lines and welcome in the new you.'

'One day, maybe,' I smile cheerfully.

Rachel lowers her face and pretends to be writing notes. I polish off my croissant and decide that it's time to make a speedy getaway. Before we leave we'll have to come up with a ridiculous, totally impractical idea to keep them at bay.

'Now, I've had a thought about your tenth anniversary event,' I announce.

A lean smile crosses Rachel's face. The others are full of anticipation.

'Do tell, we're all ears,' she purrs.

'How about holding a spectacular Mad Hatter's tea party with a twist at some stunning and voluptuous venue, such as The Dorchester? Perhaps you might engage your Bruno as master of ceremonies, a sort of mad 'drag' hatter with some of his drag queen acquaintances modelling hats.'

Silence. Rachel is quite obviously beyond words.

'Ingenious,' say the Darleys in unison. 'A Drag Hatter's Tea Party?'

'Why not?' I say perkily.

'Why not indeed?' replies Marcus in ecstatic delight.

12 noon, in a taxi

Rachel is worryingly quiet in the back of the taxi.

'What's up?' I ask warily.

'Oh, let me think about that,' she says, her voice frayed. 'Could it be that you've just bated the insane Darleys with possibly the most absurd and laughable idea in the entire universe? How long have you been cooking that one up?'

I look out at the boxy and bijoux Chelsea houses that flit past the window. 'Those houses must cost an arm and a leg.'

'Don't change the subject,' she grunts.

'Look, if you'd wanted me to say something sensible you should have briefed me better. Talk about being thrown into the lion's den.'

She whisks a hand over her face. 'If I'd told you before how loopy they were, I'd never have got you into a taxi.'

'Possibly,' I reply. 'The truth is I just dreamed the idea up on the spot. Anyway, I'm sure Bruno the window-dressing drag queen will hate the whole concept and nip it in the bud.'

'I'm not so sure,' she sighs.

The taxi driver careers up the main run towards Hyde Park Corner, only braking when he sees a slab of cars ahead. I look at the queue of red buses stacking up opposite The Lanesborough Hotel and try to think back to the last time I actually travelled on one. Strong gusts of wind are rattling the trees on the edge of the park and kamikaze leaves skip across the road, oblivious to the snarling traffic. Rachel suddenly sits up and wallops me on the arm.

'Sod it! Why not? The Darleys are so off the wall that it's probably completely right up their street. I mean, the fashion media might even go for it. It's stupid enough.'

'I'm curious to meet this Bruno,' I grin.

'Yes, so am I.'

'Do you think we should pay him a visit?'

'You mean go to the nightclub he works at?' she says incredulously.

'Of course.'

She throws her head back and laughs. 'Well, it'd be nice to have a night on the town.'

'It would beat babysitting for the Darleys,' I bait.

'Yes, I'll get you back for that one!'

The taxi lurches into a slot outside the office.

'Can you believe it? It's twelve-thirty already,' says Rachel with an evil smile. 'Haven't you got a delicious Chinese lunch to go to?'

1 p.m., China Dreams, Mayfair

Greedy George sits by the window of China Dreams staring out at the Rollers parked up along Curzon Street. His cheeks are bulging with egg fried rice and – dare I even say it – morsels of pigs' cheeks. Liu Chan, as wrinkled and baleful-eyed as an ancient Basset hound, is thrusting his chopsticks in my direction and telling me to get stuck in.

'You won't get fat if don't eat,' he gives a thin, reedy little laugh.

'The thing is that I eat far too much as it is, Mr Chan,' I smile.

George slaps a cream damask napkin against his mouth and coughs heartily.

'Don't be wet, guv. Go on, get it down you. Best pigs' cheeks in London.'

'True,' nods Liu Chan, passing a fretful hand over his thin grey hair. 'My grandfather was best seller of pigs' cheeks in Beijing and I learn his special recipe.'

A young waitress with delicate ivory skin and exquisitely sculpted lips arrives.

'Granddaughter,' says Liu Chan, stabbing at his back teeth with a toothpick. 'Name Aaliyah.'

The girl nods shyly and gracefully removes the clutter of white porcelain dishes from the table. George sits back in his chair and sighs contentedly.

'Good to see you using chopsticks, guv. I can't be bothered with all that tosh.'

I inspect the beautiful bone sticks carefully. 'It's sacrilege not to try.'

George raises his eyebrows. 'Well, did you know that in China they throw away about forty-five billion disposable chopsticks every year, which is the equivalent to twenty-five million trees?'

I frown. 'I'm sure that's not true.'

Liu Chan gives a frail shrug. 'Maybe, but here we use only bone and metal. We don't waste chopsticks.'

'Good for you, Mr Chan,' I add.

'You say that but...' Before George can finish I give him a hearty kick under the table and a warning look.

He flinches in pain. 'Anyway, Liu, I was telling guv about donkey hide gelatin.'

Liu Chan gives me a broad smile. 'You take to stay young!'

'Well, that appeals but I worry about the poor donkeys used for it.'

'No, they OK,' says Liu Chan dismissively. 'Maybe we get nice hide for George to make wallets?'

I digest this information carefully. 'You know, I don't think it would be legal in the UK.'

'Bollocks!' exclaims George.

'Donkey already dead,' says Liu Chan.

'But how?' I ask.

The old man drops his head and begins laughing silently. His bony fingers play with the fringe of the starched tablecloth. 'Maybe,' he says mirthfully. 'The donkey fall off a hill!'

He and George find this very funny. I sit po-faced and glance slyly at my watch.

'I hope you'll think hard about this new range, George. There are lots of other animal hides commonly available.'

'That's the point, guv, I want something new and sexy.'

I rise and thank Liu Chan for his delicious pig-cheek fare. In truth the new restaurant is extremely plush and the food excellent, though I do find the pigs' cheeks an acquired taste.

'Off somewhere nice?' smirks George, as he orders himself a Cognac.

'To see a man about a painting.'

'Have fun, but remember, guv, all artists are tossers.'

4 p.m., Fitzroy Square

I stand outside the enormous white-terraced property of Charlie Romstead, a society painter whose wife, Alicia, is the daughter of a marquis. Rachel has agreed to help Charlie with his forthcoming exhibition called 'A Chink of Light', a title apparently inspired by the island of Ithaca, where the couple have a home. Much as I know Rachel has worked hard to secure new clients such as this, I do worry that at a time when we're supposed to be trying to offload the company, we're taking on new work. So frantically busy is my Scottish managing director that today I've reluctantly agreed to sit in for her at a meeting with the artist. At the weekend Rachel and I will be off to visit the Claverton-Michaels' at their Sussex stately home, and then she is off to New York to help publicise a new line of Miller Magic cutlery for our client, Dannie Popescu-Miller.

Despite having jammed my finger against the bell three times, there's no reply. My mobile rings. It's my old friend Ed.

'Hi Scatters, have you got a second?'

I pull my woollen jacket up around my ears. 'Make it snappy, Ed. I'm about to have a meeting.'

'Irina and I are having a bit of a problem.'

Ed having a problem with one of his Internet babes, now there's a surprise.

'About what?'

'Well, she's invited me to some Russian White Ball and wants me to dress as a Cossack.'

'Novel.'

'The thing is the Cossacks backed the Nazis in the last war, so I'm disinclined to dress as one. I'd rather go as Grigori Rasputin. I wondered if you'd make her see reason.'

There's a shriek in the background and a new voice fills the void. 'Hello, I'm Irina. You Ed's good friend, yes? He cannot come to Russian White Ball as Rasputin! The man was a peasant and a charlatan!'

'Hello Irina, well, perhaps he could go as a tsar?'

'He doesn't want to go as tsar, either,' she says tetchily. 'You tell him, OK?'

Ed returns to the receiver. 'Sorry about that. We've reached a bit of an impasse. I don't want to go as a figure from imperial Russia. What shall we do?'

I ring the doorbell again, this time with a degree of irritation. 'My advice, Ed, is to go as Stalin or possibly a Russian doll or maybe find yourself a new girlfriend. *Adios*!'

I shove the mobile phone in my pocket and observe the austere front door. I fret that Charlie Romstead has forgotten the appointment but am suddenly aware of a banging coming from the floor below. I walk back along the front path and peer down the basement steps. A window overlooks a small patio, and standing flat against the glass like one of Ollie's suction toy lizards is a bespectacled male. He catches a glimpse of me and begins thrashing at the panes. I walk gingerly down the steps, concerned that I might have discovered a resident lunatic – perhaps Fitzroy Square's very own answer to Bertha Mason from *Jane Eyre*. His muffled yelps bounce against the glass pane. 'I'm locked in! Alicia has locked me in!'

I shout against the glass. 'Your wife? Why?'

'Because she's a bitch!'

I nod sagely. 'Ah. Can I let you out?'

He shakes his head miserably. 'She wants me to finish the canvas.'

He observes my troubled expression and, like a hammy mime artist, strides to the centre of the room, gesturing dramatically at a half-finished painting languishing on an easel. He returns to the window.

'We'll have to meet another day. OK? Sorry.'

I shrug and nod. He stands dejectedly on the other side of the glass and pulls a face like a Pierrot.

I retrace my steps and wearily hail a cab, wondering whether anyone sane is still left in this mad city.

Saturday 6 p.m., Frithington Manor, West Sussex
On a strip of frosty grass an elderly couple dressed in tweeds bicker in loud, cut-glass accents. Rachel stands nearby in a designer donkey

jacket, sniffing the air and feigning nonchalance. I think it's the first time I've seen her wearing trainers, albeit some cool Italian brand. An icy breeze ripples through the apple trees at the edge of the paddock, kissing my chapped lips and cold cheeks. Not for the first time this morning, I question why I'm here at all and hope that we'll all be heading back to the warm house soon. Meeting a potential client is one thing but suffering an entire weekend in their company is quite another. Rachel has embraced the whole country house party theme with vigour, insisting on trekking out to see the furthest terrains and the livestock. Together we have strolled around the walled topiary garden in the rain and got lost in the freezing decorative maze until rescued by the gardener. Had we not been viewing the Claverton-Michaels' land in near sub-zero temperatures, I might have found it a vaguely entertaining experience.

I take the heavy old binoculars from around my neck to study the facade of the house. Frithington Manor sits like a hefty and frumpy old dame amidst conifers and large oak trees in a rectangle of land that has been manicured with studious precision. To its rear are sprawling red brick outhouses, chicken coops and farming paraphernalia, with verdant fields and rolling countryside beyond. The house itself is rather unprepossessing and grey with Gothic pretensions. In a feeble attempt at sauciness, a coquettish folly of a spire decorated with turquoise fish-scale tiles sits aloft a tower on one wing. A row of stone gargoyles glower down at the front porch from a marble arch, and the path running up to the grand front portals is mossy, its ox-blood tiles chipped and broken. Rachel is calling to me with some urgency. Lowering the binoculars, I discover my MD on her haunches, tugging at the prosthetic leg of Rupert Claverton-Michaels. I stride through the thick tufts of grass to reach them.

'Is everything all right?'

Rachel throws me an exasperated expression. 'Does it look like it? Lord Claverton- Michaels has got his foot stuck down a rabbit hole.'

He winces in pain. 'Oh do call me Rupert, for heaven's sake. There's no good pulling my leg, girl. The damned foot has got trapped under a rock.'

'Stop being such a baby!' shrieks his wife, who is bending over him with an impatient air. 'Just give it a good wrench, Rachel. His leg won't come off.'

Rachel observes the metallic object uncertainly, the full horror of what might occur suddenly crossing her features. I have to hide my face to mask a bout of nervous giggles.

'Oh come here!' Clarissa Claverton-Michaels bellows and pulls hard at her husband's leg. It finally comes free and we all breathe a collective sigh of relief. He sits on the grass, rubbing his thigh.

'That was painful. Why do you have to be so brutal about everything?' he moans.

'Because we haven't got all day,' she snaps.

'You should try having a false leg,' he says mournfully.

'Half a leg,' she hisses. 'Besides, you've had more than thirty years to get used to it.'

'It must be frustrating,' I say. 'Can you bend the knee?'

'Not really,' he sighs. 'This latest prosthetic limb has taken some getting used to.'

'Always moaning. And it cost an arm and a leg too,' puffs Clarissa.

Rachel bites her lip and turns away.

'Is it a war injury?' I ask.

'Northern Ireland. During the Troubles. Damned explosion blew off my leg below the knee.' He pauses. 'Never saw it again.'

'Of course you wouldn't, you silly sausage,' tuts his wife.

'I've just been reading about the Spanish Civil War,' I say, for want of anything better to add. 'The injuries and amputations were horrific, particularly on the Republican side.'

'Served them bloody well right too,' opines Rupert. 'Damned reds. Spain was crawling with them – Ruskies, Trotskies, Marxists and other undesirables. Without Franco, where would Spain be now?'

'Well, that's a complicated question.'

'In dire poverty and overrun with Commies, that's what. England could have been next.'

I laugh. 'That seems a little far-fetched.'

'Not at all. In untold chaos, Franco was the stern but loving father.'

'Some might say he was the father of genocide.'

Clarissa blows her nose. 'Do shut up both of you. War's such a frightfully dull topic. So, do you two feel you've had enough of a spin 'round the terrain for today?'

I nod enthusiastically, my teeth chattering. 'Yes, it's been a wonderful walk but maybe we could head back now.'

'Quite,' sniffs Rupert.

Rachel and I proffer our hands but he rolls onto his side and, using his stick for support, struggles until he is finally back on his feet. The darkening sky is thrown into sharp relief by the amber light now flooding the manor. Lady Claverton-Michaels pulls a small apparatus from her pocket and speaks commandingly into it. There's a loud hissing sound.

'Fix some cocktails in the drawing room, Fenton.'

There's a whining and crackling. 'Yes, ma'am.'

She stashes it away in her jacket.

'I could do with one of those,' I grin.

'Yes, but unless you've got staff there's not much point,' tuts Rachel.

'True,' old Claverton-Michaels says ruefully. 'Problem is you have to pay the buggers.'

The oak-lined hallway is as cosy and warm as a goose-down duvet and in the flamboyant drawing room a roaring fire crackles in the grate.

'Just pull off your wellies out here,' Lady Claverton-Michaels instructs us. 'God, I need a stiff Martini Dry.'

Never has a drink sounded so good.

'Would you like me to send in Bertie now?' asks Fenton, the butler, a tall willow of a man.

'No, leave him in the kitchen. He might snap at the girls.'

I catch Rachel's eye.

'Who's Bertie?' she dares to ask.

'Just our old boxer. He's a little fractious these days so best not to tempt fate.'

We settle around the fire in large comfortable sofas and are soon attended to by the tall and discreet butler. I take the glass with its tinkling ice and nearly choke when I take the first sip. The gin is lethally strong.

'Bottoms up!' says old Claverton-Michaels and knocks his back in one.

Rachel and I sneakily exchange grins.

'Another round, Fenton,' yawns Clarissa.

'We never did finish the story of the ghosts,' I say.

'Oh it's all a load of old tosh isn't it, Fenton?'

The butler falters at the doorway and gives a small, dry cough. 'Probably, ma'am.'

'Have you ever seen or heard anything strange?' I ask him.

He fixes his dark, hesitant eyes on me and then gives a pert smile.

'It's a big, old house, ma'am. One's imagination can run wild if permitted.'

He takes his leave.

'Exactly,' says Clarissa. 'Fenton's been with us for ten years and never reported seeing any ghosts. It's just ridiculous tittle-tattle between the chamber maids and cook.'

'Roddick, the gardener, will tell you all sorts of nonsense too,' laughs her husband. 'He says there's a woman in a Victorian gown and hat that walks around the gardens.'

'No, she's Edwardian,' corrects his wife with some impatience.

'Victorian,' he growls. 'Ask Roddick yourself.'

'I've had a fun idea,' says Rachel suddenly.

Her cheeks are glowing with the warmth of the fire and the contents of her drink, no doubt.

'Say we held a public open day on the first of April and put out word that ghosts stalked the house. I reckon the media would love it.'

'It might drive everyone away,' mumbles Rupert.

'No, it won't,' she laughs. 'Best of all, we can hire some models or actors to dress up in historical garb and make ghostly appearances at intervals.'

'Absurd!' squeaks Clarissa. 'But it does sound like fun. That would be one in the eye for Rolling Meadows.'

'Is that the name of the new attraction that's just opened nearby?' I ask.

She gives an indignant sniff. 'It's an appalling place, like a giant hamster run full of enormous, coloured tubes that people have to climb through. Why anyone should want to visit such a place, I can't imagine.'

'It's called an adventure playground for all ages,' adds her husband. 'What a joke!'

The butler returns and offers us each a replenished glass. 'Dinner will be served at eight, ma'am. Perhaps the guests might like to freshen up before then.'

'Great idea,' says Rachel. 'Could we take our glasses with us?'

'Of course,' he says tautly.

Rachel and I take our leave and after five minutes of getting completely lost along several long, dark corridors eventually make it to our suites.

'I'm glad you're sleeping next door,' I whisper.

Rachel giggles. 'Listen, probably the only thing you've got to worry about is that mad old boxer dog they've got tethered in the kitchen. I hope they don't let him off the lead in the night.'

'I really don't care. I shan't be venturing out in the dark.'

We creep into my room, a high-ceilinged affair with lavish mahogany furniture and exposed wooden floorboards. The windows are arched and the panes etched with lead. Heavy plaid curtains extend to the floor.

'These rooms are a bit creepy. Did Rupert say this wing is Queen Anne period?'

'Apparently, but the furniture's a bit of a jumble of epochs.'

We sit chatting and finally polish off our drinks.

'I'm feeling quite tipsy,' Rachel laughs.

'Probably the only way to cope in this place,' I mutter.

'Too right!' she gets up and sashays over to the heavy oak door.

'See you in your glad rags in half an hour.'

Sunday 4 a.m., Frithington Manor

I awaken with a start. Something is scratching at the door. Is it a mouse? The salivating Bertie? I lie beneath the heavy flannel sheets and eiderdown without moving a muscle, my ears alert to every sound. Silence. I am about to turn over when I hear a rustling at the door. I sit bolt upright and fumble for the bedside light. A clear moon grins at me from a granite sky through a chink in the curtain. There it goes again – a rustling sound, then a small thud. Was I imagining it or had something or someone just tried to turn the door handle? My ears buzz, my pulse races and yet I feel as cold as ice. I rest my head on the pillow trying to rationalise my fear. Bertie. Wretched hound. He must have got free of the kitchen. I turn to the locked, heavy wooden door, knowing that even the canniest dog in the world would never be able to open it, and finally drift off to sleep.

9.a.m., Frithington Manor

There's a knock at the door. I'm already awake and staring up at the ornate ceiling, contemplating the day ahead. I jump out of bed and, yawning, unlock the bedroom door. Fenton peers discreetly over my right shoulder.

'A pot of breakfast tea, ma'am.'

'That's very kind of you, Fenton. Thanks.'

He glides across the room and, clearing a space on a small side table, sets the silver tray down.

'I do hope you slept well.'

He begins tugging forcefully at the curtain pulleys as if he were milking a cow. Finally, light pours into the room.

'The bed was very comfortable. The only thing was the dog. Bertie came snuffling round my door in the night.'

Fenton, as stiff as a corpse, silently observes the fields beyond the glass pane before turning slowly and heading for the door.

He gives a small cough. 'That's quite impossible, ma'am.'

'What is?' I ask distractedly as I fumble with the elaborate tea strainer.

'Bertie couldn't have come to your bedroom last night.'

'Why not?' I say.

A small, sadistic smile plays on his lips. 'Because, ma'am, Bertie spent the entire night in his kennel in the grounds.'

Without offering any further explanation, he dips his head reverentially and exits the room.

FIVE

HOME FOR CHRISTMAS

A brilliant white sun dazzles my eyes as I lean out of the office window in search of life. Sitting at my desk for the last three hours I have become acutely aware of the silence which for a weekday morning is unusual. The pond is quiet without Johnny and the melodious frogs, which I imagine are living it up at some raucous amphibian winter resort, leaving the fish, their silent companions, to flit about in the murky and chilly depths below. Boris and Damian, our black and white strays, are huddled in the front garden by the olive tree and now regard me expectantly, perhaps mistakenly anticipating some morsel of food to drop like manna from my window. In the modest orchard, which is situated on a wide terrace running directly above our front garden, I see Fernando, our new neighbour, cutting back weeds. He is dressed in a sloppy old jumper and jeans and stops often to wipe his brow. Catalina has just telephoned to say that she's on her way, having been delayed due to some unspecified drama at one of the holiday *fincas* in her charge. Fernando puts his hands on his hips and turns to face the mountains. Out of the corner of his eye he spots me at the window and gives a hearty wave. We're not close enough to speak but I give him the thumbs up. He makes a gesture as if he's drinking a coffee so I beckon him over and reciprocate the mime. After some confused hand signs, he gets the message, nods his head and disappears from view. I amble downstairs and open the front gate. A moment later he jogs into view, having climbed down a stone wall from the terrace above and jumped onto the track.

He gives me a hug. 'Are you offering me a nice *café* on this frosty morning?'

'I certainly am, Fernando. Any excuse not to get down to work.'

He chuckles and follows me into the kitchen.

'And where is the senyor?' he asks.

'Oh, coming back from Sóller. He popped out for some seeds.'

He shakes his head. 'That man is so dedicated to his garden. He puts us all to shame.'

I pour him a coffee and watch as he plops three sugars in his cup and stirs it vigorously.

'Sweet tooth?' I ask.

He pats his stomach. *'Si, un poc massa.'* A little too much.

I take out some chocolate gingerbread biscuits, an early Christmas gift from a local German friend. They're shaped as stars and squat little snowmen and dusted down with icing sugar. Fernando looks with delight at the tin, which sports distinctive German branding.

'German biscuits? I've heard they make the best bread and cakes.'

He pops one in his mouth and closes his eyes in delight.

'I lived in Bonn for a year before I went to university and I put on eight kilos because the food was so good,' I explain.

He chomps on his second biscuit and grins. 'I'm not surprised. Well then, you're lucky to have German neighbours.'

'Yes, and Helge is an excellent cook. They're not here as often as we'd like but they say they will be for Christmas.'

'Maybe they'll bring you lots of goodies?'

I laugh. 'You never know.'

The door swings open and the one-woman tornado sweeps in, throwing her bag and keys down on the kitchen table. 'Hey, what's going on? You having a fiesta without me?'

Fernando gets up to greet Catalina.

'I saw your father the other day. He says you're swamped with work.'

'*Si, si,* always busy,' she replies, then turns to me. 'You make me a coffee or I have to lick your spoon.'

I give her a dark look and go off to get a cup.

'So, what was the drama this morning?' I ask.

She grabs a biscuit from the box and breaks it into two before stuffing it into her mouth. Fernando and I wait patiently.

'You won't believe it, but I nipped over to one of my holiday properties to greet the guests arriving from the airport and I see water pouring everywhere, out of the front door and into the garden. I nearly died!'

We observe her in horror.

'So I get in and find that the water tank has burst in the attic and these poor English guests are coming in just one hour for their two-week holiday.'

I pass her the coffee cup. '*Que pesadilla!*' What a nightmare.

'*Que susto!*' What a shock, says Fernando, not to be outdone. 'What did you do?'

She shrugs and helps herself to another biscuit. 'I call my brother Stefan, Pep, the plumber and the owner of the *finca.*'

It's a distinct advantage in Catalina's line of work to have a builder for a brother.

'What happened?'

She waves her hand dismissively through the air. 'The boiler and pipes had burst with age but my brother and Pep fixed everything. Now the house must be dried out. The owner of the *finca* was crying when I called her but what could I do? Anyway, I rang round, found another *finca* for the English people and they are happy.'

'You do have some stressful moments in your work,' I say.

'All the time there's something,' she replies. 'It'll be Christmas in just over a week and the *fincas* are all getting full. So many visitors.'

'You won't have much of a festive break, then,' titters Fernando.

'*Es la vida.*' She turns to me. 'Anyway, crazy woman, you all organised for Christmas?'

I sip at my coffee. 'Well, Alex is going to be home for Christmas so Celia's happy.'

My nephew Alex is now studying in London but has promised my sister, Celia, who lives in the nearby village of Fornalutx, that he'll return for the holiday. Ollie dotes on his cousin and is ecstatic at the prospect.

'This year we're thinking of joining Pep and Juana up at Es Turo for Christmas lunch.'

She nods enthusiastically. 'Why not? Sometimes it's good to have a rest from cooking.'

'That's what I thought. Celia fancied a break from the sink, too. What are your plans, Fernando?'

He pulls a face. 'The whole family's coming round so I'll be preparing the pig the night before and the house will be in chaos.'

I laugh. 'Catalina's got it sussed. She has Christmas lunch at Ca N'Antuna, her family's restaurant, and since her aunt's a professional chef, she can't go wrong.'

'True, but we all have to muck in. Sometimes there can be too many willing cooks.'

Catalina gets to her feet. 'Llorenç is coming with the wood later. He says he's very busy with orders.'

At this time of the year, Llorenç is hugely in demand because everyone in the valley stocks up with firewood for the winter.

By the end of the season his back must be as stiff as a haunch of Serrano. Catalina potters off to get the ironing board while Fernando stretches and yawns.

'I'd better be going. If I don't get that orchard cleared today, the *dona* will be after me.'

He kisses me on both cheeks and heads towards the door. 'By the way, I'll bring a sack of almonds down later. They're just ready.'

'Wonderful! One day you'll have to take me almond picking.'

He throws his arms wide. '*Hombre*! Why didn't you ask before? I always need extra help. The season's passed so you'll have to wait until the end of August now.'

'Fine, no rush.'

Whistling, he saunters across the courtyard and through the open gate. I remove a small block of wood that I've wedged in it to prevent it from closing. Moments later, there's honking and both the Scotsman and Llorenç arrive in convoy.

'Open up!'

I poke my tongue out at Llorenç, who is giggling at the wheel. I've rarely seen him in sombre mood. Alan gives a toot behind. I release the gate and both cars tumble in.

Llorenç jumps out of the front seat of his white van and gives me an impish smile.

'*Pues*, don't just stand there, *mujer*, where's my coffee?'

Calling me *mujer*, woman, is chancing his arm and he knows it. 'This isn't a cafe you know, Llorenç. Some of us have work to do.'

He slaps his thigh cheerfully. 'Messing around on a computer? You call that work?'

Alan strolls over to the van and shakes his hand. 'What do *mujeres* know about men's work, Llorenç? I spend my life toiling in the garden and what thanks do I get?'

'It's true, Alan. Women have no idea how lucky they are to have men around.'

I observe them with amusement. 'I'll get you both a coffee, just to stop you talking.'

They exchange winks.

'Anyway, as you're both so hard-working, I'll make the coffee once you've unloaded all the wood. Just give me a shout.'

They look defeated. 'A coffee would warm us up for the task.'

'Once you get cracking, you'll be as warm as toast,' I smile sweetly.

Catalina appears on the doorstep with a broom. 'Oh and when you've finished, can you sweep up all the leaves on the porch?'

'Is there no end to our torment?' moans Alan.

'That depends on how badly you want that coffee,' she sniggers.

Greedy George is huffing and puffing at the end of the line. 'Look, guv, we always pull off a stunt at Christmas, you know that.'

'A stunt is one thing, but making a mockery of religion is asking for trouble.'

He snorts loudly. 'That's your prissy Catholic upbringing coming out. Look, what's wrong with taking a donkey through the streets of St James's for a little Christmas photocall?'

'Forget the donkey, it's the contemporary Mary and Joseph on its back that I'm worried about.'

'They'll look fab. We'll have Mary in a virginal blue, vintage designer dress and Joseph as Santa holding a sack of Havana Leather Christmas goodies.'

I shudder. 'It's a grotesque parody and I am not going to be a part of it.'

'Suit yourself, guv. Rachel thinks it's quite fun. She reckons the media will lap it up.'

'Fine, well you can work on the idea with Rachel and, if it all goes wrong, don't come crying to me.'

He chortles to himself. 'Anyway, Liu Chan's placed an order for my Chinese donkey hide. I'll have some prototype products made up once it arrives. I'm thinking of wallets and small leather products with a twist.'

'The twist being that it's illegal hide?'

'Give me a break, guv. Domestic animal hide is legal. Period.'

'Are you absolutely sure this hide is from donkeys that have died naturally?'

'What? You're worried they were murdered in their sleep?'

'Something like that.'

'I haven't a clue, guv, but Liu Chan loves animals – seahorses, black bears, rhinos, tigers, you name it. He won't use anything else in his Chinese medicines.'

'You really are sick, George, you know that?'

'That's me!' he chuckles. 'Anyway, I'll keep you up to speed on the photocall, guv. Rachel will show you the error of your ways.'

I thump the phone down in some irritation. What is Rachel playing at supporting such a tacky idea, and what's the deal with the Chinese donkey hide? I hope for George's sake that Liu Chan's donkey trading is legitimate because if not I'm going after them both.

Alan pops his head round the door. 'George waving his jester bells again?'

'Sometimes I could quite happily strangle him.'

He smiles. 'Well, here's something that'll cheer you up. The final revised plans from Chris, the English cattery manufacturer, have just arrived.'

'That's exciting. Let's see them.'

He pulls up a chair and spreads out the various technical drawings on my desk. 'It's a much more modest affair than we originally planned, but more manageable, and the wooden structure is strong enough to withstand the harshest gales and rainstorms.'

I study them carefully. 'What about the security aspect?'

He points to one of the plans. 'This is the safety corridor around the individual pens. If our feline guests tried to do a runner, they'd only get this far.'

'Ingenious. So how many cats could we house?'

'About ten, which won't bring in many euros at first but hopefully it'll end up paying for itself and then we can help out the local vets.'

Our idea is to use a portion of any profits raised from the cattery to help finance a neutering programme for the stray cats, which have become a significant problem in the Sóller Valley. Our two local vets would need financial help with carrying out such a plan so a contribution of this kind might greatly support their efforts.

'Well, let's fix up a meeting with Stefan. He needs to see the plans and revisit the plot.'

He folds up the sheets of paper. 'OK, I'll talk to Stefan. By the way, any news from Rachel about potential mergers for your PR business?'

I lie back in my chair and twiddle a pen. 'Apparently there are three companies interested so I've agreed to meet one of them in January when I'm back. It's a massive corporation so heaven knows why they'd be after our little outfit.'

He shrugs. 'Maybe they're looking for some niche luxury clients or want to start up a high-end retail goods division. You never know.'

'We live in hope.'

He gives my shoulder a squeeze. 'I'm off to my Spanish lesson and then I'm meeting Pep to pick up some of his horse manure.'

'That sounds like fun. Just make sure that, if you put it in the Mini, none of the manure spills out from the bag.'

He mumbles something and disappears. I hear the car engine rev into life and then there's silence. I work for another hour and finally stretch and amble towards the kitchen to make a coffee. Glancing out of one of the upstairs windows en route to the staircase, I see a strange sight. Michel, my enigmatic Catalan poet, is waiting at the gate holding our white stray in his arms. His stick is propped up against a wall. I wonder how long he's been standing there.

I release the front gate and watch as he gently places the cat on the ground and takes hold of his stick. He walks stiffly across the gravel, a determined if painful expression on his visage. I greet him on the front steps.

'Michel, how good to see you.'

He cocks an eyebrow. 'Who's Michel?'

I wonder if this is a game. 'José, perhaps?'

He nods and walks past me into the *entrada*.

'May I?' He wafts his stick in the direction of the kitchen.

Painstakingly slowly, he removes his thick winter coat and places it carefully on the back of a chair. He has no hat with him today and his hair is wispy and white like a softly spun web. He pats it down against his scalp and taps a long, arthritic finger impatiently against the table. I offer him a coffee, which he accepts unsmilingly.

'I want to thank you for the poetry book you left me.'

He looks at me with some irritation. 'Thank Michel, not me.'

'If you should meet him, please pass on my thanks.'

I make myself a coffee and stir in some sugar.

'You know, around 1850 my grandparents left Sóller to seek their fortune in France. They were pioneers. My family had a grocery business and my grandfather was a young man with big ideas.'

I take a seat at the table, wondering where this might be leading. He pauses for a second to sip his coffee and turns to face me.

'What do you know about the emigration of Sóllerics to foreign climes?'

I sit up, feeling like a child in a school history lesson.

'Just that Sóllerics traded oranges with France and many emigrated over there from the mid nineteenth century.'

'You're missing some important details,' he says impatiently. 'Sóllerics first went to Central and South America. It was later that they emigrated to France and other European countries. Their departure changed the face of the town forever.'

'Was it a good thing in your opinion?'

He throws his hands wide. *'Quien sabe?'* Who knows. 'All I would say is that it brought immense wealth to some in the valley and good things came about like the train and tram, for example.' He gives a little chortle. 'And let's not forget the creation of the Bank of Sóller, where many émigrés stashed their new-found cash.'

'So your grandparents did well in France?'

'My grandfather worked hard and in fifteen years had a successful business with shops in Sète and other ports, such as Marseille, but then his brothers wrote with news of a terrible plague that had hit the oranges in Sóller and that was the end of the citrus trade for a while.'

'How terrible. When was that?'

He frowns. 'It was in 1865 but my grandfather was clever; instead of oranges, he began importing Spanish wines and Negrita Rhum, the dark and strong liquor from Martinique, to supplement the dried fruits he sold.'

The sketchy details of the story I'd gleaned from Neus had whet my appetite to learn more.

'So when were your parents born?' I probe.

'My father, Mateu, was born in Sète in 1880, the youngest of six. He married my mother, Francoise, a young French girl and the daughter of a village mayor, in 1911.'

I'm amazed by the clarity of his memory. 'How do you remember all those dates?'

He sighs. 'Every key date of my life and that of my family is engraved on my soul.'

I stir my coffee in silence. He lapses into a reverie of his own for a few minutes and I feel uncertain whether to speak. Suddenly, he blinks and resumes his story effortlessly.

'My father was a committed Francophile. France had been good to him. His shops flourished and his success was well catalogued back in Sóller. To be honest, there was also a little envy. You could smell the dank odour of poverty on the streets in those days.'

'It's so hard to imagine, given how prosperous Sóller is today. Tourism has created so much change here.'

He shakes his head a little sadly. 'For me, change is just one more step towards the other world.'

'And where is that world?'

With a trembling hand, he dabs at his rheumy eyes with a handkerchief. 'I'll let you know when I get there.'

I give him a smile and, despite himself, he chuckles.

'Are you bored yet? Tired of hearing the witterings of a crusty old fool in his nineties?'

I look at my watch and wink. 'I'll give you another minute.'

'So my father and his brothers and sisters worked happily developing the family business in Sète until World War One. Mateu was adamant that he must fight with the French against the Germans, despite being already in his thirties. My mother wept, thinking he would be killed but obviously he survived or I would never have been born.'

'Did many Mallorcan émigrés fight in World War One?'

He tuts. 'No, not many. It wasn't our war. Spain was neutral. Our own was to come soon enough, though.'

'So, when did you return to Mallorca?'

He scratches his forehead and regards me for a moment. 'Could I disturb you for a biscuit or some nuts?'

I leap up from my seat. 'You're hungry? Of course.'

He carries on with his story while I hastily put together a snack of Manchego cheese, Serrano ham, tomatoes and oat biscuits.

'I was born in 1918 so I was only small when we returned to Mallorca to a big fanfare from the family. My father and mother accompanied my grandparents who wanted to live out their days in Sóller. They were frail and both in their nineties so my father built a huge house for us all in the town and that's where I grew up, just off the main *plaça*.'

I return to the table and place a plate and cutlery before him.

'What a feast!' he exclaims, with the innocent delight of a child.

'Did you have any siblings?'

Michel frowns and, with a stiff hand, places some cheese on an oatcake. '*Si*. An older brother named Joaquin. He is no longer alive.'

He nibbles at the food, munching thoughtfully. 'I like these oat biscuits. I met a Scottish boy who joined the International Brigade during the Spanish Civil War and he gave me some.'

'They were the foreign volunteers, like George Orwell, who fought against Franco, weren't they?'

'Mostly idealistic fools,' he mumbles.

'Did you keep in touch with the Scottish boy?'

His face drops. 'He was killed in action.'

'Tell me about your childhood in Sóller.'

'In many ways it was idyllic. We studied at the local school and harvested olives and almonds with our parents, depending on the season. Every summer we returned to France to see my mother's family and that's where I met Sofia and her sister, Elena.'

'How come?'

He exhales deeply. 'Sofia's father was a wealthy entrepreneur from Madrid and he and my father had done business in France together for many years. His wife, Maude, was from a wealthy family in Barcelona. They and my parents became close friends and so we children became close too. They would leave Madrid for France every year just to spend their summer holidays with us. We spoke in Catalan and Castilian Spanish together.'

He sighs. 'Then everything changed and the Spanish Civil War began.'

'It must have been a terrible shock.' I say.

'Maybe not to my parents, because trouble had been brewing for some time, but for my brother, Joaquin, and me, yes – we were too young to understand politics. Besides, living in the *Baleares* gave us distance from what was going on in the mainland.'

'Didn't Spain have a fairly feudal system, with rich landowners and a powerful aristocracy at that time?'

He shakes his head sadly. 'Things were very bad. From the twenties until the early thirties the country was under the thrall of the dictator, General Miguel Primo de Rivera, a bit of a bumbling fool who tried to run the country as if it were a military camp.'

'What about the king?'

'That was Alfonso XIII. He was weak and booted out not long after old Rivera, but I am getting ahead of myself. When the Second Republic was formed in 1931, things seemed to improve for a while but there was growing unrest among the right-wing factions. There was an election held in February 1936 and the popular front, the Socialists, came into power and defeated the right-wingers.'

'The beginning of real democracy?' I ask.

'No, it was the beginning of a short-lived democracy because the right-wing Nationalists under Franco were livid and sprung a military coup exactly five months later.'

'So was your family pro Franco and the Nationalists or the left-wing Republicans?'

He puts down his knife and fork. 'If only life were so simple. My parents were devout Catholics so in theory they should have backed the Nationalists but they also had Socialist values and were admirers of the newly appointed mayor of Sóller, a Republican chemist called Josep Serra I Pastor. The poor devil was only in office a matter of months when he was arrested just for being a Socialist and put in a concentration camp.'

'When was that?'

'In September 1936, not long after the Nationalist rebels seized power in Mallorca. I was only eighteen at the time but I remember my family talking about his arrest with anger and fear.'

I get up to stretch my limbs. 'Did you keep in touch with Sofia and her family in Madrid?'

'Of course, we were long-distance sweethearts. We sent postcards to each other and letters but things became difficult.'

'Why?'

'Distance was one reason but another was that her father was a prominent Nationalist, a Fascist and close friend of Franco. This was dangerous for him, given that the city was controlled by the Republicans, and not good for me because of my political leanings at the time.'

'Were your family concerned that Sofia's father was pro Franco?'

He shrugs. 'They were not political animals. With Mallorca in Nationalist hands, they were quite happy to have a powerful friend in Madrid and willingly fell into line.'

He gives a bitter laugh. 'I did not.'

I look out at the mountains beyond the kitchen window. The sky has darkened and a ruby light caresses the higher peaks. 'So what happened to the mayor of Sóller?'

He rises and slowly begins to put on his coat. 'I must go because my nephew is expecting me but let me tell you this: the injustice suffered by the mayor of Sóller instilled a *ràbia*, a kind of madness, in me. It was then that I decided to fight against Franco and his cronies, albeit against my parents' wishes.'

He rubs his eyes and, taking his stick, totters over to the front door. We walk to the open gate together.

'So did the mayor come back?' I blurt out.

'Josep Serra I Pastor? Suffice to say that his wife and two young daughters waited anxiously for news of his return but the Fascists kept him imprisoned. December came and they prayed that he'd be back soon but he never made it home for Christmas.'

'Was he killed?' I ask fearfully.

'No, thank God. The son of Sóller returned, but after many years and many sorrows. That is all I have for you today.'

He gives a sad little nod and, balancing his stick between his legs, buttons up his coat before walking quietly away down the track.

It is Christmas Day and the sun sits like a squat orange in the sky, glowing contentedly and extending its rays to every nook and cranny in the *plaça* of Fornalutx. Pep and Juana are basking in the sun, stretching out their limbs beneath the table and enjoying a glass of the local *herbes*, liqueur. My sister, Cecilia, and nephew, Alex, who have shared an enormous Christmas lunch with us all at Es Turo, have returned to their home to feed the cats before joining us back at our *finca* in Sóller for an overnight stay. Ollie is savouring a double-scoop of chocolate ice cream and has a faint brown moustache forming on his upper lip.

'How can you eat that after all the food we've just had?' laughs Juana.

'Easy,' smiles Ollie.

'It's what we call the bottomless pit,' adds Alan.

'The sickening thing is that he eats like a horse but is as thin as a pin,' I remonstrate.

'Wait till he gets to Alan and Pep's age and he'll not be able to see his espadrilles,' sniggers Juana.

Pep gives a growl. 'Rubbish, women can't take their eyes off me!'

'Off your stomach,' I retort.

'That's a bit mean! Anyway, Pep, have you got all the Christmas presents you were after?' asks Alan.

'Pah! Angel gave me a tie. When do I wear a tie? She,' he points at Juana, 'gave me a pile of books about weight loss and a fancy wallet.'

'Didn't you like it?' I goad.

'*Si*, but it will hurt me to open it every day, so it's an unhappy gift.'

'What do you mean?'

'It's obvious, isn't it? If I open it, I must be spending money of course!'

'I had some seriously cool Christmas gifts this year and some new coins,' says Ollie.

'Old or new?' asks Pep.

Ollie rolls his eyes. 'Antique, obviously. I'm not interested in new coins unless they're in mint condition or limited edition.'

'In my day, we'd have been happy with an orange and a packet of almonds,' baits Pep.

'Yeah, right,' laughs Ollie.

Angel comes running across the square, carrying a bag of bangers and his father's car keys. He thumps Ollie on the back and dangles an arm over his shoulder. 'Got them, Ollie! I'd left them on the back seat.'

Ollie licks his spoon and clatters it in the empty bowl. 'Great! Can we go and play?'

Before anyone has time to answer, they run up the steps by the old church and disappear into the narrow stone alleyways. A few minutes later we hear some mini explosions.

'There they go,' says the Scotsman. 'Those boys are obsessed with bangers.'

'The bigger the better,' tuts Juana.

I sip at my *herbes* and see Neus hobbling towards us across the *plaça*. She nods shyly at Pep and Juana and we all rise to our feet and offer her Christmas kisses.

Pep rushes to get her a chair. 'You must be the wonderful Neus we keep hearing about?'

'I've told them that you're my confidante,' I grin.

She gives a little giggle and sits down heavily next to Pep. 'Nonsense! I'm just a busybody neighbour but we do have a good chinwag, don't we?'

'We certainly do.' I offer to buy her a drink but she shakes her head.

'So what brings you to Fornalutx today?' asks Alan.

'Well, I've just had lunch with Bernat in Sóller and am now on my way to visit an old cousin who lives up there near the church. Then I'm staying with my son and his family in Santa Maria later.'

'Busy day,' I say. 'Aha! So is Bernat the old school friend you mentioned a while back?'

She blushes. 'Oh hush, we're just friends.'

Pep takes a long puff at his missile of a cigar. 'Ah, do I feel a little romance in the air?'

'*Que va!*' exclaims Neus. 'We just like to reminisce together, that's all.'

Juana laughs. 'Good for you. Talking of reminiscing, seeing all the oranges in the orchards up here in Fornalutx has evoked such memories. My father used to produce many varieties of orange down in the valley.'

Neus smiles. '*Si, si*. My favourites are still the small *navelets* but *Valencias* are delicious too.'

'We have *perets* and *canonets* in our orchard,' yawns Pep. 'But in truth *navelets* are best because they are so sweet.'

'You know, few cafes use them to make orange juice these days because they're too small for the automated pressing machines. Here in Fornalutx they still use the old-style hand-pressers, using the little *navelets*,' says Pep.

'I suppose it's a case of trying to serve up drinks as quickly as possible,' I suggest.

'*D'acord,*' nods Neus. 'I often think of how we take ice for granted in drinks like *limón granizada*. Long ago, they used to transport the snow from the mountains to sell in the markets. Up in Puig Mayor, for example, a whole team of men would pack snow into a snow house constructed of rocks and seal it with a herb called *carritx*. Come the summer they'd strap up their donkeys and carry heavy loads of compacted snow down the mountain, through Palma and on to Sóller.'

'How long did that take?' I ask.

'I'd say the journey was about seventy kilometres there and back by donkey,' chips in Pep, 'and they did it all in twenty-four hours.'

I turn to face him. 'Blimey, that must have been tough.'

'I'm sure it was. Anyway, talking of donkeys, have you had any more thoughts about buying a couple from *mi amic*, Jacinto?'

'Absolutely,' I say. 'Alan and I just need to sort out a paddock area for them beyond where the new cattery block will go.'

The Scotsman gives a grunt. 'I don't want to think about it just now, especially on Christmas Day.'

'Why ever not?' grins Pep. 'This is an important time of year for donkeys.'

'True,' says Neus. 'Think of the poor, blessed Virgin riding on that donkey. It must have been very uncomfortable for her in the state she was in.'

Pep and Alan exchange winks. The church bell chimes, followed by several more explosions of firecrackers. The boys are obviously having fun. Juana drains her glass and slaps Pep's knee. 'Come on, time to go. Remember, we have my family over for dinner tonight.'

Pep groans. 'Not more food!'

Neus rises to her feet. 'I'm off. *Molts d'Anys* to all of you.'

'Many happy years to come for you too, Neus.'

I give her a hug while Alan slips in to the bar to settle the bill with the owner, Marga.

Pep waltzes over to the steps leading up to the church and begins hollering. Soon Ollie and Angel appear.

'*Venga*! We're coming!'

The boys protest heavily about having to depart but finally join us back in the *plaça*.

'Another great Christmas Day in the valley,' I say, 'and no washing up after lunch.'

'True,' says Juana, 'but what about tonight?'

Pep smiles cheekily at Alan, who is puffing slowly on his *puro*. '*Mi amic*, since we both have our families over for supper tonight, wouldn't it seem reasonable to ask them to clear up afterwards?'

'An excellent idea,' says Alan robustly.

'Dream on,' says a voice behind him.

Cecilia has just reappeared with Alex. They're carrying overnight bags and enjoying the Scotsman's discomfort.

'Just a joke,' says the Scotsman sheepishly.

'So it'll be you and me at the sink again?' quizzes Alex, giving him a pat on the back.

'Looks like it, but I'll make sure we have a few drams when they've all gone to bed,' reassures the Scotsman.

'Remember he's only twenty-two. I don't want him getting into bad ways,' chides Cecilia.

Alex rolls his eyes. 'Mother, stop fussing!'

The Scotsman claps his hands together. 'I've an unopened bottle of Lagavulin that might interest you.'

Alex gives him the thumbs up and makes a grab for Ollie but he wriggles out of his grasp and dares him to a race.

'Right, now I'm going to catch you both!' Alex shouts, chasing a gleeful Ollie and Angel all the way back up the hill to the car park while the rest of us follow behind at a very sedate and over-indulged pace.

It's Boxing Day and Rachel is full of bonhomie. I can hear her munching something while she talks to me on her mobile.

'Despite your worst fears the photocall went very well on Christmas Eve, save the odd drama.'

'Drama?' I say with some alarm.

'Hang on, let me just finish this mince pie.' A pause. 'What I mean is that the Virgin Mary was quite cool in a really great vintage Chanel dress and shawl but Joseph was a bit naff.'

'Did Greedy George really dress him up as Santa?'

'I'm afraid so but that wasn't the problem. The male model he hired was as high as a kite.'

'I don't believe it.'

'It was a bit awkward. He was swaying around on the donkey and dropping all the gift-wrapped Havana goodies from the sack he was carrying. George was pretty angry.'

I give a frustrated sigh. 'Serves him right for not vetting the model properly. I despair. What on earth did the media make of it?'

'It's a sad reflection on society that they didn't seem to turn a hair. I got the impression that they're used to dealing with coked-up models on photo shoots. Despite the embarrassment, the media didn't blame Havana for the episode and we got some fairly amusing diary pieces out of it and a picture in the *Express*.'

'Thank goodness for that. All the same, I'm still glad I had nothing to do with it. Was the donkey OK?'

'Oh yes, he seemed to be enjoying himself and left St James's with his owner, apparently for some donkey rural retreat.'

'So how have your yuletide festivities been so far?' I ask.

'Brill. It's been non-stop partying and tonight my parents are throwing a big 'do' in their Yorkshire village, which will be a hoot. What about you?'

'Nice and relaxed, with little fuss – just how I like it. And tonight we're off for dinner with our German neighbours, Wolfgang and Helge, who've just arrived.'

'You do know how to live it up in the hills.'

'Less of the sarcasm, MD.'

She sighs contentedly. 'Well, enjoy the break while you can. What date are you back in London?'

'Early January.'

'Ah, of course, in time for Dannie Popescu-Miller's visit. She's dying to hear all about your ghostly encounter at Frithington Manor.'

'You rotter! You didn't tell her about the snuffling at my bedroom door?'

She stifles a laugh. 'Of course. It's just up her street. She's already consulted her soothsayer, Tetley, about it.'

I groan. Tetley, the psychic guru and tea-leaf reader of my client, Dannie Popescu-Miller, is completely deranged but a huge influence on Dannie. Heaven knows what hypothesis she'll have come up with.

'Oh, and Greedy George was in hysterics when I told him.'

'Thanks, Rachel. You're a real pal. So how many more of our clients know the story?'

'That's about it. Don't forget you're seeing RTB Communications to discuss a merger when you're over.'

I sigh. 'Rachel, I do have a diary.'

'Sorry. I forget you're not always gaga. Anyway, happy Christmas.'

'Happy Christmas, Rachel, or as we say here, *Molts d'Anys*.'

SIX

A CHINK OF LIGHT

Tuesday 10.30 a.m., Mansion House, London
A brash, metallic building with a smooth and smoky glass facade glares back at an ice-cold sun. I stand outside the front portals, breathing hard on my black woolly gloves and scanning the address in my diary once more. This is definitely it. RTB Communications, one of the largest advertising and PR agencies on the globe, has invited me in to its hallowed headquarters to discuss a potential sale or merger of the company. I step into the vast lobby, my heels clicking on the black marble tiles, and survey the interior. A central atrium constructed of steel and coolness runs right up to a wide glass skylight at the top of the building. In the centre is a construction of steel rafters from which hang an abundance of foliage; ivy, strange exotic flowers and what looks like hemp. A waterfall is tucked away between towering walls of glistening black slate and the sound of wild, bubbling water and birdsong fills the lobby. I wander around this man-made, kitsch nature set, wondering whether the architect had perhaps OD'd on *Tarzan*

or *The Jungle Book* as a child. I try to imagine Mowgli swinging through the leaves and hemp ropes, before jet-propelling himself onto one of the fifteen or more floors running off the main atrium high above. A sharp voice suddenly kicks Mowgli into touch.

'Can I help you?'

It's the straight-backed, ponytailed receptionist, who earlier had been glued to a telephone.

'RTB Communications?' she sniffs. 'You'll need a security pass.'

I give her my business card and she scribbles down the details on a log while her dainty ponytail with its blue ribbon bobs from side to side.

'Someone will be down to collect you.'

I step away from the desk, the pass in my grasp, waiting like a lonely package to be retrieved by some benevolent secretary. Moments later, a lift door pings open and a smart twenty-something female strides towards me. She's wearing a tight grey suit and beckons me to follow her.

Gormlessly, I follow in her wake.

'And who are you?' I hear myself asking in a loud, clear, English-for-foreigners voice.

'I'm just Mr Fortescue's secretary.'

A secretary with no name.

We stand wordlessly, side by side in the metal lift until the door opens at the second floor. Miss No-Name whisks me along a corridor overlooking the atrium below and soon we are in a large, empty open-plan office. She indicates for me to wait and disappears.

I cast a glance at my surroundings. Why so many vacated desks? Do they all know something we don't?

A door swings open and out steps a chipper male in a sharp Savile Row suit.

'I'm Paul Fortescue. So sorry for the delay. The phones haven't stopped all morning.'

I squeeze his hand, which is cold and pulpy like a small frog.

'So where is everyone?' I ask.

A switchboard is moaning somewhere in the distance and a lone phone rings in the void.

He laughs. 'Good question. Anyway, let me get you a drink.'

We enter a lavish office with spectacular views over the city. He gestures towards some seats. 'Do take a pew and help yourself to coffee.'

I sink into one of the leather sofas flanking a table and pour myself a drink while he leafs through a sheaf of paper.

'So, as we discussed by phone earlier, we're interested in absorbing some specialist agencies such as yours. What's your view?'

He sits down opposite me with great gusto and greedily gobbles down a biscuit before pouring himself a coffee.

'To be honest, it all depends on how quickly I could be released if we did merge.'

He nods sagely and leans back.

'But we wouldn't want you to disappear. We'd like to offer you a board position.'

I shake my head. 'That's not quite what I see in my crystal ball, Paul.'

He gives me an alligator smile. 'Aren't you forgetting the financial rewards?'

I shrug. 'Crazy as it might seem, I don't think I'd be tempted by money any more. I prefer a simple life in the hills.'

He gets up and crosses the room to the window. 'I stare out at this sprawling city every day and do you know what I see?'

'Go on, surprise me.'

'I see thousands of people who've thrown away fantastic opportunities walking the streets with sadness in their eyes.'

I potter over to his side and look down at the small moving dots edging their way up and down the straight streets as if on a board game. 'You must have fantastic eyesight,' I snort.

'I'm speaking figuratively,' he answers flatly. 'Let me at least show you around your potential kingdom.'

He throws open the door and we march through the vacated department and up a flight of stairs to yet another large room, this time teeming with people. They sit in small rabbit hutches behind perspex screens, speaking furtively into telephone receivers or tapping away blindly at their computers. A sizeable office at the end of the room beckons to us. Inside it is bare and devoid of furniture.

'A lonely room looking for a big cheese to bring it to life,' says Paul. 'Tempting, eh?'

Paul takes me back to his office and rubs his hands together.

'There's no rush but my fellow directors would like to button things up soon if you think we're speaking the same language.'

We're absolutely not.

He smiles indulgently. 'Just take a look at this offer document and give it some thought.'

Against my better judgment, I take the fat envelope from his grasp. He seems relieved.

Before I know it I'm back down in Mowgli land, with the sound of water and squawking birds pounding my head. The receptionist is glued to her phone and barely acknowledges my presence when I drop the security pass back on her desk. I leave without saying goodbye and head off into the cool, brisk wind.

12.30 p.m., the office, Mayfair

Rachel is leaning back in her chair and munching on a cheese roll.

'I think you should give this Paul Fortescue a chance. I mean, you don't get the likes of RTB approaching you every day.'

'Yes, Rachel, but he quite obviously wants to tie me down to some long-term contract after the merger.'

She shrugs. 'You don't know that yet. This initial offer document looks pretty tempting.'

She yawns and looks out of her window.

'Another freezing cold day. What's it like in Mallorca?'

'Not much better but at least we get blue skies and spectacular views.'

'You're so lucky. Mind you, when we finally merge the company, I'll be off to not-so-sunny Yorkshire.'

'Still happy about that?'

Rachel flicks a pen against the desk. 'Marriage is all about compromise. I suppose I might miss the buzz of London.'

I take a sip of tea. 'That's what I thought. Then again, I do come back a fair bit. There's no reason why you can't do the same.'

'Exactly,' she smiles.

'By the way, remember we're meeting Dannie and Greedy George for dinner tonight at China Dreams.'

She laughs. 'I was considering leaving you to it.'

'Don't even think about it – and I refuse to eat any more pigs' cheeks.'

Rachel waltzes over to a filing cabinet and pulls out a file.

'Don't knock them. We've had some fantastic early restaurant reviews and the food journalists seem to love those piggy cheeks.'

'No accounting for taste,' I sigh.

'Anyway, what are you up to this afternoon?'

'I'm off to see a man about some coins in Holborn.'

She eyes me curiously. 'May I ask why?'

'Ollie's been struck by numismatology.'

'Is it contagious?' she sniggers.

'Only if you love coins. Apparently, the chap who runs this shop is a real expert. Ollie found him on the Internet and they've been trading coins.'

Rachel grins. 'I worry about that lad. Can't he get himself a girlfriend and join Facebook like every other kid of his age?'

'I'll keep with the coins for now, if that's OK with you?'

'Well, while you're spending your pennies, I'm off to see Rupert Claverton-Michaels about our little ghost event at Frithington Manor on the first of April.'

'I don't know who are worse, Rupert and his barmy wife or the mad hatters of Chelsea.'

Rachel arches an eyebrow. 'Aren't you forgetting Alicia and Charlie Romstead?'

'I'm yet to meet the gaoler's wife, but Charlie's obviously not normal allowing her to lock him up in his own studio.'

'You'll meet Alicia at his exhibition tomorrow night.'

'What's it called, A Chink of Light? How perfect for an imprisoned artist.'

Rachel snorts with laughter. There's a tap at the door and Sarah pops her head round. 'What are you two laughing about? Been on the bottle again?'

'I wish,' says Rachel, wiping her eyes. 'We were just saying how much we're looking forward to A Chink of Light.'

Sarah crosses the room and peers out of the window. 'See what you mean. It'll be great when the clocks go forward.'

Rachel and I exchange confused looks until the numinist's penny drops and we are left giggling like schoolgirls. Sarah observes us uncomprehendingly and then with a tut rushes out of the room to answer a howling phone.

7.30 p.m., Havana Leather

Dannie Popescu-Miller, flame haired and botoxed up to and beyond the eyebrows, is wearing a cropped black jacket with big epaulettes and matching trousers embroidered with tiny coloured crystals. Around her waist is a diamanté belt and, lying like a streak of blood across her lap, is a deep-red throw – cashmere, naturally. I inspect the apparel admiringly, instantly deciding that Dannie really should come back as a matador in her next life. Greedy George observes me from across the enormous table and gives a sigh.

'So, guv, you finally showed up! We've got to get going. Where you been? Ghost hunting?' He erupts into laughter and begins 'Ooooooohhhhing' loudly.

'George, don't be silly!' caws Dannie. She grabs my arm. 'Now, Rachel told us all about your ghostly encounters at this haunted English manor and we're dying to hear the story.'

I peck her on the cheek and take a seat.

George enjoys the moment. 'What I want to know, guv, is if you ran into any poor sod who'd lost his head?'

More guffaws.

'You really are a hoot, George. Sorry to disappoint, but I saw nothing at all.'

'But you saw a chink of light under the door and then you heard something?' asks Dannie excitedly.

'I didn't see any light. I just heard a scratching under the door, like a dog.'

'A hound from hell or perhaps a ghostly rodent?' shouts George in convulsions of laughter.

'Do behave, George. My psychic believes those from the other world were trying to get a message to her.'

'Yeah, like "Open the door, you dozy cow!"'

'I'd like to have seen how you'd have coped in the same situation,' I sniff.

'Wouldn't have bothered me. I don't believe in all that tosh, guv. Tell you what, why don't Dannie and I visit the place for a laugh?'

'The Claverton-Michaels' will be holding a ghostly event on April Fool's Day, if you can wait until then.'

'But we'd want to stay overnight,' says Dannie. 'We don't want to be part of a media circus.'

'I'll have to ask the Claverton-Michaels' but if they agree you'd have to behave, George.'

He gives a howl of protest. 'I like that! You know how good I am with the nobby crowd – always minding my Ps and Qs.'

'By the way,' he suddenly says, 'you haven't said anything about the brilliant donkey stunt I pulled off at Christmas.'

I shrug. 'That all depends on whether or not you hold with the adage "all publicity is good publicity".'

'What's that supposed to mean?'

'Tell me, Dannie, would you be happy with a headline in *The Sun* that read, "Almighty Coke Up" and went on to describe the drug-fuelled antics of a model you'd hired to promote your products?'

'Oh my!' coos Dannie, putting her milk-white hands to her cheeks. 'No I would not!'

'It was just a bit of fun,' says George sulkily. 'As usual the bleeding journalist made up most of it.'

'Actually, by all accounts it was fairly accurate,' I say with a smile.

'We still shifted a lot of products despite the problems with our coked-up Joseph on the donkey.'

I snigger. 'Just you wait till your donkey hide range hits the street. That'll prove a hit with Christians everywhere, especially if you can hire back that Joseph!'

'Give it a rest,' growls George petulantly.

Dannie perks up. 'Is that the donkey hide range you were telling me about, George?'

'Sure is,' he says. 'You'll meet my mate Liu later. He's the one getting me the black-skinned donkey hide samples.'

'How exciting,' yelps Dannie. She grasps my hand. 'You know I have used black-skinned donkey gelatin for years.'

'Really? And what does it do exactly?'

She pushes her face towards me. 'Feel the smoothness of my skin. That's thanks to the gelatin's anti-ageing properties. I use it as a blood tonic too.'

As Dannie is a direct descendant of Vlad the Impaler, better known by some as Dracula, that's probably not a bad idea.

'I suppose you know that Cleopatra was supposed to have used the milk of 700 asses for her daily bath,' she drawls.

'A bit excessive, wasn't it?' blurts George cheerfully.

'She was vain and wanted to keep wrinkles at bay. Of course it also preserves the whiteness of the skin, hence why I only use donkey milk skincare.'

'And there I was thinking you were a bit anaemic, Dannie, and needing to get your teeth into something,' says George.

'Like a steak or do you mean the other sort of stake?' she says coolly. 'Your little vampire jokes with me are ceaseless.'

'Just like to wind you up. I wouldn't want you to forget your roots.'

'Can we be serious for a moment?' I say with some frustration. 'My concern is that this breed of Chinese donkey might be endangered.'

Dannie laughs. 'Of course not! Donkeys aren't endangered creatures.'

'Then I wish they were. I don't like the idea of donkeys being killed for their hides.'

She crinkles her nose. 'They're just old donkeys that die naturally and have the gelatin extracted from their pelts. Don't worry about it. Anyway, why are you so hung up on donkeys?'

'She's about to add two of them to her Mallorcan zoo,' snorts George.

'How adorable!' exclaims Dannie. 'You could maybe go into the gelatin business yourself?'

'No, Dannie. I prefer living things.'

She shakes her head sadly. 'Really? Pity.'

George gets to his feet. 'So, anyway, shall we make a move? I told Liu we'd be at the restaurant by eight.'

I look at my watch. It's seven-fifty.

'By the way, don't make Dannie eat the pigs' cheeks tonight,' I plead.

George guffaws. 'She'll love them. Speciality of the house, Dannie.'

'Whatever you recommend, George.'

'Well, they also do fab stir-fried frogs' legs…'

I swipe him with my file. 'Don't even think of eating frogs in my presence.'

He rolls his eyes. 'I bet even Mother Teresa ate frogs' legs and probably the odd toad.'

'Don't be ridiculous,' I say with a weary sigh.

'By the way, guv, a mate told me that a whole population of toads exploded in Germany a few years back. Apparently they were attacked by crows and self-inflated to protect themselves and went poof! Splattered toads all over the show.'

Dannie breaks into a wide, pearly white smile. For the first time I notice how pointed her top incisors seem, like those of a wolf. 'My dear George, you really are the limit.'

I rise from my seat. 'Come on, Dannie, let's get going before George can dream up any more drivel.'

She gives a throaty laugh and follows me to the door. We are about to head down the stairs when she taps me on the arm. She has a strange gleam in her eye. 'You know, when I was a child my Romanian grandfather used toads for his incantations.'

'What? Was he a wizard?' asks George.

'Kind of. He loved toads of all shapes and sizes.'

'That's good to know,' I say.

'I loved them too, especially the way my grandmother cooked them,' she grins.

I give a little squeal.

'Only kidding!' she croaks and, giggling, makes her way down the stairs. George gives me a little prod in the back as we follow in her wake. I glance round and see that he's tapping the side of his head and pointing down at Dannie. At least he and I are agreed on that point. Dannie is completely loopy. Richard, Havana Leather's shop manager, waves us goodbye with an orange feather duster and we step out into the cold night in search of a taxi.

Wednesday 7 p.m., Mayfair

The gallery is buzzing by the time I arrive. Somewhat tackily a piece of old red carpet has been rolled out in front of the entrance and two hulks in black stand on either side of the door wearing bored expressions. Large posters flank the narrow entrance hall announcing the exhibition: 'A Chink of Light – One Man's Journey Through Rural Greece'. The image of a large pastel landscape boasting jagged hills, a smudge of sun and wild grasses could almost be Mallorca. Rachel and Sarah welcome me at the front desk.

'It's going well,' says Sarah excitedly.

'Having a few big names popping by has helped,' says Rachel.

I scan the room. 'Are there any still here?'

Sarah nods her head impatiently and indicates a woman in the crowd. 'Don't you know who that is?'

I narrow my eyes. 'She looks vaguely familiar.'

'Yeah, right. A little show called *The X Factor*. Ding, dong.'

Rachel sniggers. "If Plácido Domingo turned up, she'd recognise him.'

'Plácido who?' quizzes Sarah.

I groan. 'Arguably Spain's most famous tenor. Anyway, what's *The X Factor*?'

They both erupt into giggles.

'Put her in a home!' cries Rachel.

'Poor old thing I'll get you a glass of champagne, that'll perk you up.'

She wanders off in the direction of a waiter. I hand my damp coat and scarf over to a cloakroom attendant and put the numbered disc she hands me into my pocket.

'Don't lose that,' warns Rachel. 'You know what you're like.'

Sarah returns with a glass and thrusts it into my hand. 'Why don't you go and chat up Alicia and Charlie Romstead while we sign in guests?'

'Do I have to?'

She gives me a scornful look. 'They're dying to meet you. Now hop off.'

I remember the days when Sarah was a sweet, retiring girl – a few years in the office working with Rachel and she's turned into a sharp-toothed little piranha.

I weave my way through crowds of elegantly attired guests until I catch sight of Charlie Romstead. I'm pleased to see that his wife has liberated him from his cell in time for his own launch. He is surrounded by a bevy of businessmen and appears to be spinning some entertaining yarn. A well-preserved woman in her early forties is standing a few feet away, discussing Charlie's work in great detail to a prosperous-looking Indian couple. I wait patiently until the artist makes his excuses and comes over to greet me. He ushers me to the side of the room and speaks in hushed tones.

'Look here, I'm jolly sorry about the last time we met – or rather didn't. Alicia has a filthy temper and just wasn't happy with my work output that day. I aim to turn round a canvas every week, you see.'

I feel my brow furrow. 'What? That's ridiculous. It's hardly painting by numbers.'

He gives a nervous little laugh. 'Actually, it pretty much is but I get distracted easily. I'm a Tweeter so I'm always fiddling with the damned thing and, like half the world, following Stephen Fry, of course.'

He fixes me with an earnest little boy gaze and I immediately want to give him a good shaking and tell him to stop being so wet.

'So there's nothing to this painting lark, then?'

He chews at his thumbnail. 'I'm not going to say that to a critic but the truth is I can churn this sort of stuff out fairly quickly. Don't get me wrong – I'm a professionally trained artist, but I've found a style that everyone buys.'

'Why do you think that is?'

He shrugs. 'Most people don't want to hang controversy on their dining room walls. The guests here are comfortably off and like safe art. It's sad but true.'

'Don't you find that frustrating?'

He exhales deeply. 'Alicia and I have got three boys at bloody pricey prep schools so the commercial route's the way to go.'

The dragon appears, blowing fire over his right shoulder. She proffers me a tight smile and thrusts out a toned arm.

'I'm sorry I put the kybosh on your last meeting with Charlie but I had to teach him a lesson.'

I nod slowly. 'Do you work, Alicia?'

'Good heavens, no! I'm too busy being his personal promoter – and just as well, or we'd be living in a council flat by now.'

'At least I'd be free,' says Charlie mournfully.

'Don't be an oaf. You'd miss lunches at Scott's too much.'

'That's true,' he sighs.

'Come and have a look around.' Alicia fixes me with her steely eyes. We squeeze through the throng with difficulty. People stand around in small gaggles, drinking and laughing, and don't seem to be buying. Alicia catches my concerned expression.

'Don't be fooled. Most of the work's already been snapped up. We sold most of it before the exhibition opened. This event is just for PR hype really.'

'So why did Charlie choose the theme of Greece?'

She takes a sip of champagne. 'We have a summer house on Crete. It was a no-brainer.'

I stop at a picture of donkeys grazing near a deserted cove and turn to face her.

'I'm hoping to buy two donkeys. I'm mad about them.'

Alicia seizes me by the shoulders. 'I knew it! I could tell you were a donkey girl. We help run a sanctuary in Greece and have several rescue donkeys at our farm in Dorset.'

I'm beginning to wonder how many properties this not-so-impoverished artist in the basement and his wife actually own.

'I'm also a trustee of DDT, the Donkey Defence Trust, a fairly aggressive campaigning charity,' she says. 'Anyone caught abusing a donkey had better watch out.'

'Do you know much about donkey hide gelatin?'

'Absolutely. Can't stop its sale I'm afraid but we're monitoring its use.'

'What about selling donkey hide products?'

She looks suspicious. 'A strange question. Well, I suppose it depends on how the donkey died. Any signs of cruelty and we'd be on to it.'

'That's fascinating.'

'I must get on flogging the goods but if you'd like to talk further about this, let me know.'

We exchange cards and I watch as she darts off into the crowd to nab yet another moneyed victim.

While Greedy George and Mr Pig Cheeks are busy exploiting the donkey world, I've decided to cook up a little scheme of my own that might just knock their plans asunder.

Thursday 9.30 a.m., the office, Mayfair
Rachel sits in the boardroom, drumming her perfect talons against the table. It's yet another cold and dreary January morning and I'm longing to return to Mallorca. Even the constant droning of the traffic beyond the grimy window is beginning to get to me.

Today, our client Manuel Ramirez, the neurotic and hot-tempered owner of H Hotels whose head office is in Panama, is launching his first celebrity chef restaurant within H Hotel in Soho. Serge de Camp, who will be the star of the kitchen, is a sultry Gallic creature with designer stubble and an impressive culinary CV. He fronts a popular French food show and has a complicated love life, if we're to believe the tabloids. Sarah pushes open the boardroom door and deposits two Starbucks espressos in front of us.

'The girls are all down at H Hotel in Soho preparing the welcome desk and press packs, so I'll have to go and man the phones. No doubt Ray Drummond will be on the blower again.'

Ray Drummond is a seedy freelancer who is always selling salacious stories to the tabloids. He has been sniffing around Serge de Camp for a while, looking for a potential new scandal in his love life to sell to a newspaper.

'If he calls again about Serge, just give him short shrift,' says Rachel sternly.

'Of course, but he's ringing every day at the moment. He claims Serge has got three gay lovers on the go.'

I shrug. 'Whether he has or not, it's none of our business. Or his, come to that. If he becomes a real pain, put him through to me.'

Rachel gives her a cheery smile. 'Thanks, Sarah. You get on.'

I touch her arm. 'By the way, well done for the handling of the event last night. It was a brilliant success and Alicia was full of praise for you.'

Sarah blushes. 'Just doing my job, eh guv?'

She leaves the room with a bounce in her step.

'So what time are we meeting with my favourite paranoiac hotelier?' I ask.

Rachel yawns. 'At twelve. Poor Manuel has been so het up about this restaurant launch. Always tricky getting a celebrity chef involved. They're such a load of old queens.'

I laugh. 'But that's what hotels always do, drag in a celeb name to front the restaurant and hope it brings in the media and the punters.'

Rachel shrugs. 'Must work if they're all doing it.'

'It rarely does. Most of these chefs are complete prima donnas and fall out with the owners before the first year is out. Manuel and this French charmer already seem to be at loggerheads.'

'True, but I wonder if Serge de Camp knows that Manuel keeps a gold Kalashnikov above his desk in Panama?'

'Food for thought,' I say with a wink.

Rachel groans. I take a sip of my coffee. Not a patch on the espresso served in Café Paris in Sóller's *plaça*, but it's hot and wet.

'It's funny, Manuel doesn't call me in Mallorca as much as he used to.'

'That's because he's taken to pestering me instead,' protests Rachel. 'He seems to be in London all the time. I wish he'd stay in Panama, where he belongs.'

Rachel shuffles some papers together. 'I'm meeting Dannie in half an hour. Do you want to tag along or have you other plans?'

I give a moan. 'Well, I'm popping out for a quick coffee with my friend, Ed. He sent a distraught text this morning saying he has to see me.'

'What's new?'

'Yes, but this sounded more hysterical than usual. After that, I'm off to see Greedy George about his proposed rare Chinese donkey-hide range.'

She frowns. 'Is that all kosher?'

'Good word to use, Rachel. Actually, I'm not happy about it and I have a devious little idea in mind.'

'I don't like the sound of that.'

'I'll tell you about it one day.'

She nods her head. 'On your own head be it.'

I drain my cup and get to my feet.

'And now for Ed who's off his head. Wish me luck.'

10.15 a.m., Caffè Nero, Curzon Street

Ed is sitting dejectedly at a small table, his body slumped into a chair and his eyes wide with terror. I falter at the glass door, wondering whether I have the energy for his latest crisis. My better nature overcomes me and I head towards him. He rises like a spring from his seat and gives me a tight hug as if it will be our last.

'Calm down, Ed. What on earth is the matter? Please tell me you haven't dragged me out of the office to discuss Rasputin costumes.'

He sits down shakily and covers his eyes with his hands. 'God no! That's a mere trifle compared to what's happened.'

I unbutton my coat and throw it along with my woolly scarf over the back of a chair, moving his bulging black bag out of its way.

He throws me a wild look.

'Don't touch my MEK! For God's sake, pass it over to me!'

Ed's MEK – Medical Emergency Kit – is his lifesaver, a magic box full of lotions, potions, prescription pills and provisions that accompany his every move. Somewhat defensively, he grabs it from me and draws it to his chest.

I take a deep breath. 'Look, can I just up my caffeine count before you unburden?'

'OK, but be quick. Can you get me a double-choc muffin while you're up?

I roll my eyes. 'So much for the new dietary regime.'

He exhales deeply. 'I'm in a lot of trouble so I need sugar.'

I go off to the counter and return with a large espresso and his muffin. He looks disapprovingly at my cup. 'Call that a coffee?' Why don't you have a large cappuccino or shake of some kind?'

I ignore him and flip a small packet of brown sugar, pouring its contents into my cup.

'So, tell me all.'

He sighs. 'Where do I begin? Well, for some time I've been helping friends and colleagues out with their computer problems at weekends.'

He pauses.

'What's wrong with that?'

'Nothing, except that this morning I was carrying my boss's laptop in on the Tube...'

I interrupt. 'Why?'

'Because it had a technical hitch that I'd agreed to fix over the weekend. Anyway, one minute I had it with me and the next it had vanished.'

'What do you mean "it just vanished"?'

'I got off the Tube with my MEK and was just coming out of the station when I suddenly realised that I didn't have the other black bag, a small rucksack.'

'Oh. That's not good. What a shame you hadn't left the MEK on the train instead.'

He glowers at me. 'That would have been far worse!'

'Sure, I can just imagine the joy of a thief discovering the contents of the MEK. Nasal spray, yay! beta blockers, yay! Strepsils, yay!'

'Oh shut up! Anyway, my boss was incandescent with rage and said he had very sensitive material on his computer. He told me not to return to the office until I'd registered the loss with every lost property office and the police.'

'Have you done all that?'

He nods miserably. 'They haven't had anything handed in. The nice lady in the lost property office at the station said she could cry for me.'

'Hmm, not sure that would help terribly. How about turning this on its head?

'How?'

'Well, I'd return to the office, tell your boss you've done everything possible and say that there's nothing more you can do at this stage.'

His gloomy aspect melts my heart. 'Come on, he's probably got insurance and back-up discs.'

'He says he hasn't.'

'Then he's a fool. End of story. Now go back to work, keep your head down and pray.'

I stand up. 'I've got to go, Ed, but keep me posted.'

He rises slowly from his chair and wipes the muffin crumbs from his jumper. 'At least my love life's looking up. Irina's agreed that I can go as Rasputin to the White Ball.'

'Ah well,' I say, 'every cloud has a silver lining.'

SEVEN

THE WHITE GODDESS

A warm blast of air greets me as I step out onto the front porch. Skimming the tips of the mountains, the sky unravels like a bale of electric blue silk and the air is pungent with rosemary. We're experiencing what is known locally as *La Calma de Gener*, the January Calm. Jorge is standing at the gate with a fistful of letters. He waits patiently until the gate slides open and strides over to greet me.

'Isn't it a heavenly day?' He beams broadly, thrusting a whole lot of bills into my hands.

'Not any more, Jorge. Can't you bring me anything but invoices?'

He laughs. 'I have some news.'

'Don't tell me you're leaving the valley?' I say with some alarm.

'*Por favor*! *Of* course not. I'm getting married.'

'You're what?'

He smiles coyly and holds out his left hand. At first I think he's going to show me a ring, but in fact it's the little tattoo of a heart with the letter B etched inside. Jorge celebrates every new girlfriend with a tattoo. I hope this one lasts.

'Ah, so lucky Beatriz has ensnared you?'

He giggles. 'Don't say that! We're in love.'

'The whole valley of young, unattached women will be in mourning, Jorge.'

'I don't think so. Postmen don't earn much.'

I protest. 'That's a cynical remark.'

'But it's true. Most girls want security these days and I don't blame them. Beatriz isn't too worried because her parents have invited us to live with them. They have a big farm and could do with extra help.'

I give him a hug. 'I'm really happy for you both. Please fix a time with Beatriz to come over for a celebratory drink. So when did you propose to her?'

He's very bashful. 'It was on a full moon.'

'Very romantic.'

'Actually, it's less to do with romance and more to do with the power of the moon goddess.'

I smile. 'So, like the poet Robert Graves, you're a moon man?'

'Did he believe in the moon?'

'Absolutely. He wrote a book called *The White Goddess*, all about poetic myth-making based on the moon.'

He nods. 'Just like this poet, I, too, think of the moon as a goddess.'

'Then you must read his book.'

'Yes, as long as it's in Spanish.' He pauses. 'Beatriz's father has taught me a lot about harvesting during the right moon phases. He too believes.'

'How does the moon affect harvesting?'

'For example, he told me that this month trees that are about to shed their leaves should always be cut during a full moon and that if you're cutting canes to make roofs it should only be done during a waning moon.'

I wonder if Beatriz's father is pulling his leg. 'Are you sure about this?'

'*Por supuesto*. He has also told me that evergreen trees should be cut down during a new moon.'

'Thanks for the lesson in moon phases.'

He swishes his mane back and picks up his postbag.

'I must get back to work now. By the way, you and Alan will be invited to the wedding.'

'Really? How exciting. Thank you. When will it be?'

'June, so we have some time to plan.'

I accompany him to the gate. 'My congratulations again and please bring Beatriz over to see us.'

He winks. 'She has already asked about that. We'll fix a date.'

I walk back into the house and find Ollie sitting at the kitchen table, surrounded by his latest coin purchases. He gives me a cursory glance.

'There's a coin dealer in the States who's just emailed asking me to sell him those coins you bought in London. Can you believe it?'

I sit down next to him. 'Why, did you write and tell him about them?'

'Of course – it's good to get a second opinion and an idea of what they'd sell for in other countries.'

'What did he offer you?'

He shrugs. 'Around eighty dollars for all four.'

I laugh. 'Well, that's about double what I paid for them!'

He frowns. 'I'm not selling them, don't worry. I just like to know their worth.'

I tousle his hair. 'You're a little magpie.'

He sits back in his chair. 'D'you want to know something amazing?'

'Go on.'

'Well, yesterday I made nine euros at school.'

'How?'

'I waited till everyone in my class had eaten all their snacks at the end of break and then offered round chewing gum at a euro a piece.'

'How much did the pack of chewing gum cost you in the first place?'

'One euro – if you take that away from the ten euros I made, that's nine euros profit.'

I try to look severe. 'That's a bit cheeky. Surely you should have offered the chewing gum to your friends for nothing?'

He sighs impatiently. 'Are you nuts? No one in my class is stupid enough to do that. Anyway, now I've got enough to buy that Alfonso XII coin from Senyor Estades in Palma.'

I wish I'd been as savvy as my son at his age.

'How much is it?'

'It's twelve euros but he usually gives me a discount because I'm one of his best customers. It's pure silver, 1879. A real bargain.'

Alan walks in to the kitchen with a trug full of lemons in his hand and sets it down on the table.

I turn to face him. 'Did you know that Ollie inveigled ten euros out of his friends with a one euro pack of chewing gum yesterday?'

He claps his hands together. 'I know. Canny little devil. We could learn from him!'

He observes my cool expression and begins back-pedalling.

'Of course, this shouldn't become a habit, Ollie. Once is enough and besides it's good to share sweets with your friends without bringing money into it.'

Ollie laughs. 'Yeah right. What about free choice? I didn't make them buy the sweets and besides if that's how they want to spend their own money, why stop them?'

'He's got a point,' says the Scotsman limply, 'and that coin is rather special. He's been after it for ages.'

I take the trug over to the sink and begin washing the lemons. 'I give up with you two! Tell me, how are the lemons doing?'

He pulls out one of the kitchen chairs and sits down. 'They're coming on well but the Bermuda buttercup has been a pain this month. It's taking over everything in the field.'

'But it's so cheery. It's as if the orchards have been thickly spread with butter.'

'Oh, very poetic! Well, it might look pretty but it's a menace. You know it was imported from South Africa years ago and now it's completely taken over?'

'Still, once it's flowered it will die off until next winter – poor thing.'

He puffs out his cheeks. 'One less thing to control in the jungle. Anyway, at least we've got the five w's at the moment.'

Ollie looks up. 'What are the five w's?'

'How the Mediterranean climate's often described – warm, wet, westerly winds in winter.'

'That's cool. I'll remember that.' He packs up his coins in their special files. 'Right, I've done my cataloguing, so now I'm off to tennis with Juan.'

I tap his shoulder. 'Don't be late back because we've got Pep and Juana round for supper tonight and Angel is bringing along his new Labrador puppy.'

He looks worried. 'I've told Angel it'll have to stay on a lead. I don't want it upsetting the cats.'

I follow him into the *entrada*. 'Don't fret – we'll keep the cats upstairs.'

'OK.'

He nods and walks off to his room while I plod up the stairs to my office. I still haven't heard back from Ed about his drama with the missing computer, so I decide to give him a call. He answers the phone after two rings.

'Are you psychic?' he asks breathlessly.

'Not today. Why?'

'You won't believe it, but I've just had a call from Barbara...'

'Who's Barbara?'

'She's a lovely Liverpudlian who works at London Underground's lost property desk. Believe it or not, the computer bag was handed in.'

'With the computer inside it?'

'Yes, thankfully. I've just texted my boss and he's ecstatic.'

'That's fantastic news,' I say.

'The strange thing is that my poetry group urged me to make amends with a poem which I sent to my boss yesterday.'

'Not quite as satisfying as getting his computer back, though,' I say.

He ignores me. 'Anyway, he rang me in tears, saying it was such a beautiful poem. Quite frankly, he sounded a bit tired and emotional.'

'I'm sure.'

Ed is chirruping on. 'Suddenly it's as if a cloud has lifted and a moon is flooding the dark sky with light.'

'Excellent. Well, I'd better be going.'

'Do you want me to read you the poem?'

I hesitate. 'Why not just send it over on an email?'

He sounds a little wounded. 'If you'd prefer.'

'It's just that an old Mallorcan tradition says that in January poems should only be read during a waning moon.'

'Heavens, I never knew that! Fascinating.'

'Yes, isn't it?'

He leaves on a cheerful note, promising to email me the poem so that it's in good time for the next waning of the moon.

A fine layer of snow rests on the higher ridges of the Tramuntanas and a light icy breeze ripples the leaves of the lemon trees. Standing ruggedly in the field, seemingly unperturbed by the weather, is Stefan, our builder. He is holding the revised cattery plans from the cattery manufacturer in the UK, mapping out the area with a tape measure.

'What do you think?' I ask him.

He blows on his chapped hands. *'Bé.'* Good.

'Do you think we'll have problems with planning?'

He shrugs. 'I hope not. It's a much better plan than before, smaller and more environmentally friendly. The new design looks as though it will offer better insulation for the cats in winter.'

I nod. 'That's exactly what we thought.'

Alan is standing silently nearby, observing Salvador pecking at Goneril's shoulder as they take a marital stroll around the barren run. All of a sudden there's a flurry of feathers and hysterical squawking as Salvador retreats to the hen house, with Goneril hot on his tail.

'He does try his luck,' says the Scotsman, under his breath.

'Can you try to concentrate on the task in hand?'

He blinks at me. 'Sorry, it's just that I worry for the old chap being hen-pecked all day long.'

'If he hadn't goaded her, Goneril wouldn't have attacked him. He got what he deserved.'

'Women,' he mutters and, shoving his hands in his pockets, slopes over to Stefan.

'Chris, the cattery manufacturer, is keen to come over from the UK to discuss the plans directly with us. What do you think?'

Stefan smacks his lips together. 'I don't want you to have lots of expense, but it would be helpful. Could he fly over for just a day or two?'

Alan looks at me. 'He's quite happy to do that, isn't he?'

'Of course. He wants to view the land before ordering the parts, anyway. I'll give him a ring.'

'It'll save money in the long run,' says Stefan cheerfully.

'Hmm, I wonder,' growls the Scotsman. 'Can we get back to the kitchen now?'

Stefan follows him up the stone steps to the patio. The pool lid is rolled back, revealing murky green water. Its surface betraying the telltale signs of winter; floating leaves, bits of dead bracken and decrepit insects.

Stefan gives it a disapproving glance 'When are you going to switch to a saline system?'

'Hopefully in time for next summer,' Alan replies. 'It'll cost a bit. You think it's worth it?'

He shakes his head vigorously. '*Segur*. It's cheaper in the long run and much healthier for you and the environment.'

'Yet another expense,' sighs the Scotsman. 'Where will it all end?'

'*Es la vida*,' smiles Stefan. That's life. 'Now where's that coffee?'

We enter the warm kitchen and huddle round the kitchen table. The temperature has suddenly dipped and, despite a smouldering fire in the hearth, there's damp humidity in the air.

We sit and thaw out our hands on the warm coffee cups.

'It might be worth investing in a few dehumidifiers,' muses Stefan. 'Your house is in an area of deep orchards, so the humidity is always worse. It's money well spent.'

The Scotsman laughs. 'Yes, but your long-term solutions mean a lot of spending in the short term, Stefan.'

'That's why we have to work,' Stefan rejoins with a grin.

The telephone rings. With a frown, the Scotsman speaks into the receiver. 'Who? Oh, really? What? Me?'

He saunters over to the hearth, full of bonhomie. Stefan and I exchange looks.

'Maybe he's won the *lotteria*?' he says with a wink.

'I wish!'

A few moments later, the Scotsman joins us back at the table. 'You'll never guess who that was. It's been so long.'

'Surprise us,' I say.

'It was Focus Films. They want me to audition for an advert about winning the lottery.'

Stefan laughs heartily. 'That's funny!'

'Is it?' says Alan. 'Apparently, it's the same director who chose me for that bank advert I did a few years back. He says I'd be perfect for the part.'

'What's the part?' asks Stefan, draining his cup.

'A French butler.'

We both giggle.

'I thought you'd got bored auditioning for adverts?' taunts Stefan.

'Well, I had a minor falling-out with Focus over a shampoo ad but I seem to be back in favour.'

With a grin, I recall the time the Scotsman jokingly asked the age and physical attributes of the woman due to play his wife in a shampoo advert. The director was not amused and the Scotsman stopped attending auditions as a minor protest. It seems he's got over it.

'You two may laugh,' says the Scotsman. 'But with all these damned expenses for pools, humidifiers and catteries, this ad couldn't have come at a better time.'

Stefan yawns and rises from his seat. 'Must get on. Let me know when Chris can visit Mallorca.'

We accompany him to the front door. He hesitates and, pulling out a pen and scrap of paper, with a deadpan voice he says, 'Alan, you couldn't just give me your autograph before I go? When you're a big star, it might be worth something.'

Guffawing, he saunters down the steps before the Scotsman has time to think of a suitable reply.

Michel is sitting on a garden chair, swishing the crisp brown leaves around his feet with his stick. He seems oblivious to my presence. I feel a pang of nostalgia, remembering how as a child I used to love jumping on clumps of dry leaves, listening to them crackle and crunch as I flattened them. I can't for the life of me remember the last time I did that – something I must rectify. Michel stills his stick and looks out over the mountains with a wistful gaze and breathes in the air softly.

'Do you like to jump in puddles?' he suddenly asks.

'Yes, in *botas de goma*, what we call Wellington boots. I haven't done that for a while.'

A flicker of a smile crosses his lips. 'In the winter when it rains, I make it my priority to jump in every puddle I see, and in the autumn I crunch leaves underfoot, although not with the vigour of when I was young.'

I laugh. 'Maybe we can go puddle and leaf jumping together?'

'That's fine by me, but my jumps are more of a shuffle these days. With the stick, it becomes a game of risk.'

I sigh and rub my eyes, remembering that Rachel has a deadline on two press releases that I haven't checked. I also haven't got back to RTB about their offer.

As if reading my thoughts, Michel fixes me with his doleful eyes. 'I hope I'm not disturbing your work? I just happened to be walking by your lane and thought you might like another history lesson.'

Work can wait, and besides Rachel will probably have left for the day. I give Michel a smile. 'It's always a pleasure to see you. Let's not stay out here too long, though – it's very raw.'

He rests his hands gently on his lap. 'I just wanted to watch the mountains for a while. They're very mystical at this time of day with the moon creeping over the ridge.'

He gives a little cough. 'My grandfather used to say that when the moon crept up to the ridge you had to make a secret wish and it would come true.'

'And did it?'

He throws out his hands. 'I'm too old to remember.'

He grasps his fedora hat from the garden table and levers himself up. With one hand firmly gripping his stick, he waits politely for me to lead the way to the kitchen door. We enter the warm room and I notice that the fine, papery skin of his cheeks has flushed pink. He takes a seat at the table, the same chair he always sits at, and waits for me to bring him a coffee.

'Will I get to meet your husband and son today?'

'I doubt it. Ollie had to go straight from school to a tennis match in Deià. He and Alan won't be back for a while.'

'Another time, I hope.'

I turn on the lights, since it is growing gloomy, and make him a coffee.

'The last time we met, you were telling me about your anger over the arrest of the mayor of Sóller.'

He takes a sip of coffee and nods. 'It just so happens that around that time I had joined a literary and cultural club in Palma that was very left wing. I was hugely influenced by the intellectuals who ran it. I believed I was one of them, an inspired poet.'

'You obviously were.'

He finds that funny. 'No, it was years before I understood what it was to be a poet. This little club was a springboard for my actions during the war, though. When the civil war came, we committed as a group to fight the Fascists and Franco. As would-be poets we were furious that the Nationalists wanted to eradicate the Mallorcan language, which as you know is a Catalan dialect.'

'What do you mean eradicate it?'

He closes his eyes briefly. 'When the Nationalists assumed power they banned the speaking and learning of the Mallorcan language. Anyone caught using Mallorcan or Catalan could face severe punishment, or worse. It became an underground language and we would only use it in the home among trusted friends and relatives.'

'What about the schools?'

'Catalan was withdrawn from the curriculum and Castilian Spanish was taught. This is why so many locals today from the Franco era have poor written Catalan. The Catalan language only returned to schools well after Franco's death in 1975.'

I bring some serviettes and a plate of home-made chocolate muffins to the table. Michel is like a child at a birthday party. 'They look delicious.'

He holds out a frail hand and, with a slight tremor, puts one up to his mouth. He closes his eyes. After a while, he sighs.

'They're so good! You know, Sofia was a good cook. She used to bake cakes with her mother when we spent our childhood holidays together in France.'

'Were you much older than Sofia?'

'We were only one month apart. She was born in May, and me in June.'

He wipes his hands on his napkin and looks out at the gathering dusk.

'So what happened with your plan to fight the Fascists?'

He blinks and gives a little shrug. 'One night in early August, together with eight young men from my poetry club, I left Mallorca. I was too young to understand the arrangements but basically the boat we took in the dead of night was owned by Republican sympathisers. We had a miserable and terrifying crossing to Barcelona in stormy seas.'

'Did your family know you were going?'

He slaps the table, displacing some stray chocolate crumbs. 'Of course not! They knew nothing about my departure until some days later. My actions turned them against the Republican cause forever. They were grief-stricken and furious with me. My poor brother, Joaquin, took the brunt of their rage. He was a young teacher in Palma and totally apolitical and yet they blamed him for not keeping an eye on me.'

'That seems unfair,' I say.

He hangs his head. 'It was worse than unfair. Thanks to me, my brother was implicated and arrested.'

'By the Fascists?' I say, horrified.

'Yes. They felt sure he must have been party to my actions, even a sleeper for the Republican cause. My parents made contact with Sofia's father in Madrid, and thanks to his influence my brother avoided the death penalty.'

'So what happened?'

'Can I have another muffin?'

Somewhat impatiently, I pass him the plate.

'To cut a long story short, my brother was sent to a concentration camp on the island and then transferred to a prison on the mainland, while I ended up as a trainee with the Republicans. There were so many groups supporting the left cause and I ended up in the POUM, the Workers' Party of Marxist Unification.'

'Were you a Marxist?'

'Actually, factions within the left claimed it was Trotskyist because it was run by Trotsky's former secretary. I didn't care about the label. Like my comrades, I was just anti authoritarianism and the political control of the Catholic Church. We thought we were freedom fighters for the liberation of Spain.'

'And were you?'

'We were blind idiots, chasing a myth.'

He gives a shudder.

'I was part of a small military unit of POUM and, after very basic training, I was sent to protect borders and villages under threat from the Nationalists. We fought around Teruel, at first a Nationalist stronghold, and up towards Saragossa in the north.'

'Did Sofia know where you were?'

'I managed to get a letter to her in Madrid when I arrived on the mainland. She wrote back to me once when I was staying at a safe house in Barcelona. She told me her sister, Elena, had joined the Republican cause and had subsequently been thrown out of the family home by their father.'

He takes a bite of the muffin and chews thoughtfully. 'In September 1936 my unit was summoned to Madrid. I was ecstatic that I was going to be in the same city as Sofia.'

'What was the purpose?'

'No one explained. It was hot and unbearably humid when we arrived and we were billeted at a disgusting hovel in the university quarter. It was full of young fools like me, would-be heroes with old, faulty rifles, their heads stuffed with dreams of a better and more just world. We were given lessons in warfare, politics and weaponry.'

'Did you get to see Sofia?'

'I didn't realise it at the time but Sofia's sister, Elena, a student at Madrid University, had now become a Communist and was quite a warrior for the left cause. We met at a training session and she knew how to shoot a lot better than me! It was she who smuggled Sofia over to see me.'

'Smuggled?'

'Sofia's father was a prominent Nationalist and would never have let her meet me or her rebellious older sister. I was in the safe house, so Elena had to get Sofia there without being spotted. Sofia's family lived in a very wealthy zone of Madrid, known as Salamanca.'

'I stayed in a small hotel there once.'

'Then you'll know what I mean. Madrid was in Republican hands so it was dangerous for rich girls from Salamanca to cross the city especially at night, even if they did support the cause. There were curfews and the city was mostly in darkness and full of desperate people. A very sinister place.'

'What happened when you and Sofia met?'

He dabs at his eyes with his fingers, suddenly overcome with emotion. 'We talked for hours and even discussed marriage and how, when the war was over, we'd live a rural life in Mallorca. Remember we were both only eighteen.'

He gets up slowly and stretches his legs. 'News came in late September that Franco's troops were advancing towards Madrid and my unit was ordered to assist in the safe transfer of our political leaders to Valencia in Republican territory.'

'Did you get to see Sofia before you left?'

'Only briefly. She was terrified by the fighting and worried for me and her sister. You see, like my brother, she was not a politician or a fighter. She was just a sweet girl torn between us and loyalty to her father.'

'What happened to Elena after you left Madrid?'

He looks deflated. 'I will tell you more another time. I feel tired and sad. Too many memories are pricking my skull.'

I touch his arm. 'That's fine.'

He looks up. 'You know of the poet W. H. Auden?'

'Of course.'

'Well, I met him once in January 1937. He was a volunteer for the Republicans but he didn't do any fighting. I liked his poetry, especially the one called "Stop the Clocks".'

'It's too heartbreaking for me. I can't bear the last line when he talks of believing that love will last forever, but that he's wrong.'

He clenches a fist. 'But he was wrong. Love does last forever.'

I watch in silence as he wraps himself up for the walk back into Sóller.

A handful of stars have been flung across the sky and a full moon, a diva robed in white, steps out on to the night's stage.

Michel faces the sky. 'Have you read *Blood Wedding* by the poet Lorca?'

'A long time ago. Why do you ask?'

'You'll recall that the moon is portrayed as a vindictive and vengeful creature in that play.' He speaks softly, as if not wanting the moon to hear. 'But sometimes she can be kind.'

At the gate Michel squeezes my hand for a brief second, and then wanders off wordlessly down the track. I stand motionless in the dark, staring up at the stars, until I am distracted by the low rumble of an approaching car. The fierce headlights search out the walls, causing a tiny gecko to scramble for cover in the long grasses. Despite the cold, I wait until the Mini is parked and I see the grinning faces of Ollie and the Scotsman observing me from within. Tonight I need a dollop of their warmth.

It is Thursday morning and I am standing with Neus outside the gates of Ca N'Alluny on the outskirts of Deià village, erstwhile home of the English poet, Robert Graves. Every week I whizz up the mountain road from Sóller to Deià, azure or grizzly grey seas on my right depending on the season, for a punishing routine of pilates exercises in the village hall. Often I'll glimpse the great poet's house, recently opened as a museum, and tell myself to stop by on the way home but I always forget. It is thanks to Neus that I am finally here. For months she has been asking me to take her to see the 'house of the English poet' and finally I have succumbed.

It was back in 1929 that Robert Graves arrived in the unspoilt and tourist-free village of Deià – now mischievously dubbed by some 'Chelsea-on-Sea' – with his overbearing lover, American poetess, Laura Riding. Despite a ten-year interlude when forced to leave his beloved island for the duration of the Spanish Civil War, and later in World War Two, Graves resided in Deià until his death in 1985 at the age of 90.

I walk in to the small kiosk and buy two entry tickets. The young woman behind the desk gives me a little leaflet and explains the route we should take around the house and gardens. One wall of the kiosk holds a collection of Robert Graves' works as well as titles by his offspring, William, Tomas and Lucia. I pick up a copy of *King Jesus* and inspect a paperback of *I, Claudius*, along with various poetry collections. I'm tempted to linger but see that Neus is visibly excited and is already examining the flowers and trees in the courtyard. She beckons me over.

'I've always wanted to visit this house. When I was in my twenties, I heard a lot of talk about the famous stars from America who used to visit Robert Graves. It all seemed so glamorous.'

I laugh and, taking her arm, lead her up to a converted outhouse, our first port of call, where we are invited to watch a brief film about the poet's life.

'There's no one else around,' whispers Neus. 'It's just like our own private cinema.'

For fifteen minutes Neus sits spellbound, absorbed in the documentary. As soon as it's finished, she tucks her arm under mine and hobbles thoughtfully across the stone courtyard to the limestone house. She stops for a minute to catch her breath.

'What an interesting life Robert Graves led. You know, that film takes me back. I seem to remember publicity about his return to the island. I would have been in my early twenties then.'

'Apparently, his plane was the first civilian flight from Europe to land in Mallorca since the beginning of the Spanish Civil War.'

'Is that so? No wonder he was the talk of the town.'

'I imagine his reappearance must have signalled a return to normal life for many of the locals.'

She nods. 'Life here at that time wasn't easy. It would have been a comfort to know that foreigners were returning to the island.'

Before entering the old property, we look out onto the sprawling Mediterranean garden. Bursting with oranges and lemons and backed by grizzled mountains, it ushers the visitor back to a time when Graves, in old straw hat and peasant shirt, picked his own bitter oranges to make marmalade. The house itself peers over the mountain road in solitary splendour and, rather like the Tardis, its exterior does little to suggest the spacious interior and unexpected treasures that lie within. Neus steps into the stone corridor and gives a little yelp of delight.

'Isn't it authentic? Just like stepping into my mother's old *finca*. Look! They've even left his hat and smock on the coat stand.'

We wander about the rooms. It is indeed a relief to find that Ca N'Alluny, meaning 'The Far House', has not received plastic surgery or toe-curling embellishment. Faded stains remain on the old stone floor tiles, careworn laundry is piled in the hall and jars of marbles and pebbles, collected by the poet, sit on the bookcase in his study. On the poet's desk rests an old pair of spectacles amongst pens and scattered manuscripts, giving the impression that he has just popped out to the village for lunch and will return soon. We walk slowly upstairs to a long gallery, where there are examples of entertaining correspondence between Graves and the great literary, political and philosophical minds of that time. I'm amused to see a letter from Margaret Thatcher vying for space with the likes of Gertrude Stein, Siegfried Sassoon and the Queen's Secretary. Neus beckons me over to a glass cabinet.

'It says that Robert Graves was badly injured during the battle of the Somme and left for dead. Can you believe that?'

I nod. 'Far worse was that *The Times* actually announced his death and later had to make a correction at the poet's behest.'

She laughs and gives a loud tut. We leave the house and sit on a stone bench in the sun.

'So how many books did Robert Graves write?' asks Neus.

I pull a face. 'Good question. Well over a hundred, I think.'

'I know of his book *The White Goddess*, but I've never read his work. Remember I'm just a simple *glosador*.'

Neus is a beloved fixture of many fiestas where she chants *gloses*, traditional Mallorcan poems set to the rhythm of the *ximbomba,* an instrument that has the appearance of a terracotta pot with a goat-hide cover. By pulling a bamboo stick through the top a strange sound is emitted, rather like a distressed piglet. We have just celebrated the fiesta of Sant Antoni, when Neus and her fellow *glosadors* were in full swing.

'Where did the tradition of *gloses* come from?'

Neus laughs. 'Oh I can't say for sure but some scholars think it harks back to the Ancient Greeks. The tradition began in Europe at the end of the Middle Ages. My mother, who taught me the art of the *gloses,* said they began life as bits of comical advice or warnings at public events and fiestas.'

'Do they have any established form or rhythm?'

'Of course they do. They have metric structures and time-tested rhymes. They require a lot of skill. When I was younger competitions were held between *glosadors*, which were very amusing to watch. The *glosadors* were judged on wit and poetic improvisation and would poke fun at each other.'

'How?'

'*Pues*, an example goes something like this.'

Neus stands up and begins tapping her foot for a rhythm. What she emits is a cross between a song, poem and chant and it's very loud. The translation is something like this:

'*Save us, Saint Anthony,*
From the glosador*'s tongue.*
We use it like a painter
Who with the same colour
Paints both saints and demons.'

I begin clapping. 'Very good!'

She takes a little bow, suddenly conscious of a group of tourists nearby who are giving us bemused glances.

'Time to go, I think,' she says with a giggle.

We head back towards the gate. 'You know, *glosadors* are known by other names in different parts of Spain. For example, there are the *bersolaris* in the Basque Country and the *fistores* in

Galicia. They even have wandering minstrels in Rio de la Plata, called *payadores*.'

'Are there many female *glosadors*?'

'*Segur*. You have to remember that we have a long tradition of female poets and writers in Mallorca. Surely you've heard of Margalida Baneta mas Pujol, also known as Sor Anna Maria del Santisim Sagrament?'

'I'm afraid not.'

She looks disappointed. 'She was around in the seventeenth century and glossed many works by Ramon Llull. I hope you know who he was?'

'A medieval writer and philosopher, wasn't he?'

'The master of Catalan literature and a Mallorcan to boot. Mind you, there were talented female poets too as far back as the fourteenth century such as Reina de Mallorques, meaning "Queen of Mallorcans". No one knows for sure, but it's believed she was one of the wives of King Jaume III of Mallorca, either Constança d'Aragó or Violant de Vilaragut. Sadly, only one poem remains in existence.'

'Fascinating.' I say.

'The first line begins *"Ez yeu am tal qu'es bo e bel"*; in other words, "I love one who is good and lovely". I can't recall the rest off the top of my head. Then of course there was Maria Antonia Salvà i Ripoll, one of our most famous bards in the Catalan language. She only died in 1958.'

'Neus, you're quite a literary beast. I never knew.'

'There's a lot you don't know about me.'

'Such as?'

'That I was once a flamenco and folk dancing expert until my old hips gave up on me.'

I'm genuinely impressed. Who would have thought it?

I pull out my car keys, but not before popping into the kiosk by the front gate to buy her a copy of *The White Goddess*. It's not available in the Spanish language yet, so I hope she'll muddle through with a dictionary.

She flushes pink. 'Oh, how exciting. And so it's all about the moon?'

'Yes, how the moon has been interpreted through mythology.'

'I know a very good *glose* about the moon,' she says. 'Would you like me to sing it?'

Several tourists mill around the gate. A sense of British reserve overcomes me.

'Perhaps you can sing it to me in the car?'

She nods cheerfully. I pull out on to the mountain road, listening to Neus's raucous *glose* about *la luna perfecta*. Her words drift through the open window and catch the breeze, where I imagine them plucked by the moon goddess herself to whom all living things pay homage.

EIGHT

CLOWNING AROUND

February has arrived. Clouds of pinky white almond blossom drift gently across the valley and brilliant white snow settles on the higher ridges of the Tramuntanas. The grass is pricked with frost and a thin veneer of ice clings to the window panes. I potter over to the pond. It is some time since Johnny and the frogs left for the winter, perhaps to some amphibian-type Disney resort. It will only be another few months and they'll hopefully be back to serenade me night and day. A thick layer of weed covers the water's surface and it is only when I peer closer that I am able to see the golden fish darting about in the icy water. I get up, suddenly aware of the chill, and cross the front patio where a collection of strays are singing for their breakfast. I fill a large bowl with their food pellets and slip out onto the porch while our own felines slumber within, oblivious to my treacherous act.

Back inside, Catalina is pounding away at the ironing board, the iron spitting and spluttering in her hands like a furious beast. Occasionally, she'll dive for her mobile phone to give instructions to a plumber or builder that is trying to sort out problems at one of the rented properties she cares for.

'You want to see what I bought for the carnival?' she asks.

'Absolutely.'

The carnival, which marks the beginning of Cuaresma, Lent, is celebrated in most of the local villages during February, offering everyone the opportunity to don silly fancy dress outfits and to party until the small hours.

She props the iron on the board and strides over to the kitchen table, where she has left her wicker basket. Pulling out a plastic bag, she shakes a hideous mask of a crone at me.

'I'm going to look like a witch.'

'But isn't that the point?'

'*Pues, si*, but I don't want to look too bad or the *batle* will faint.'

'What's the mayor got to do with it? Anyway, you wait till you see Ollie's costume.'

She fumbles about in her bag. 'You like these?'

She attaches some long, purple plastic talons to her fingers and puts the mask on.

'It's brilliant. You'd frighten the life out of me.'

The Scotsman appears in the *entrada* and gives a start.

'God above, woman, what's that supposed to be?'

'I'm a *weeetch*!' yells Catalina.

He shakes his head and surveys her with a wry smile. 'You'll need a hat and a black cape.'

She pulls off the mask. 'I've got all those things, don't worry. I'm dressing the girls as little devils and Ramon is going as Dracula. How about you, Alan?'

He furrows his brow. 'I'm not quite decided. I was thinking of a bat.'

'A fairly corpulent one,' I mutter.

Catalina giggles. 'That's cruel. What about you?'

Alan gives me a prod. 'You're fairly good on ghosts or phantom hounds, so how about something along those lines?'

'Ah, *si*, the dog at the door. You really think it was a ghost?'

I give a sigh. 'Who knows, but I'm not looking forward to returning to Frithington Manor in April, I can tell you.'

'But you'll have Dannie and George with you next time. It'll be a good laugh,' says Alan.

Foolishly I had mentioned the idea of Dannie and George visiting the manor at the time of the April media event and the Claverton-Michaels' had loved the idea. It helped that Dannie was a big name in the States and that they were both fans of Havana Leather products.

'You know, Ramon believes in ghosts,' says Catalina. 'Once he was working in the kitchen of an old, abandoned *finca* when he heard a heavy banging from the next room. There was nothing there. Then in the kitchen he heard footsteps.'

'How eerie,' I say. 'What did he do?'

'What you think? He ran out and never went back!'

'That's a great comfort to me. Thanks, Catalina. I shall remember that when I return to the mad Claverton-Michaels' home.'

She saunters over to the coffee machine. 'We stop for a quick coffee?'

'Why not? By the way, any news of the dryer man?'

She exhales deeply. 'I called him again and told him that it is two months since we asked him to fix the machine. It's not healthy to have wet washing around the house.'

'What did he say?'

She shrugs. 'He says he will come next week and so I said you would denounce him if he didn't.'

Alan looks up. 'That's a bit heavy, isn't it?'

She places a coffee in front of him. 'No one likes to be denounced.'

'Did the whole thing about denouncing people begin with the Spanish Inquisition?' asks Alan.

'I've no idea,' she replies, 'but it's effective when people annoy you.'

I remember back to when we were renovating the *finca* and our tiler breezily mentioned that he had just denounced his brother at the local council. When I asked why, he said it was what you did when people didn't obey the law.

'I don't like the idea of denouncing. It took on a life of its own during the Spanish Civil War. Can you imagine your neighbours and friends betraying you to those in power to protect their own necks?' I ask.

Catalina resumes her ironing. 'The Spanish Civil War was something else. When locals denounce each other today, it isn't a matter of life or death. It's usually over planning applications.'

My mobile rings. It's Rachel.

'Have you got a second?' she trills.

'For you, always.'

'I've just had a call from RTB. They're very keen to talk to you.'

'Fine, but I've already told them I'm not back in London for another month.'

'OK, but Simon already has two other interested agencies lined up. He's impressive.'

Rachel and I have recently appointed Simon Rendall, a headhunting agent, to find us potential buyers for the company. He seems to have a myriad of contacts and is obviously keen to clinch a finder's fee.

'Anything else new?'

'Greedy George has received the Chinese donkey hide he was telling you about and is starting to work on some samples.'

'Damn it! I've got to do something about that.'

She gives a small shriek. 'Oh, don't get started on your wretched donkeys. Look, it's better we just don't get involved.'

'What if the donkeys are being killed for their pelts?'

'I'm sure they're not. It's probably just a by-product of farming.'

'You mean like those badger hair brushes George used to sell? He told me they were a by-product of Chinese farming, whatever that was supposed to mean.'

Rachel giggles. 'Do you remember that yarn he told the press about Chinese farmers clipping fur off their backsides as they ran about the fields?'

'Yes, you have to give him ten out of ten for creativity. Poor little badgers dying for their art.'

'By the way, have you finished the proposal for the Darleys' mad hatter event?'

'Yes, you'll love it.'

She giggles. 'I'll reserve judgement on that. Before I forget, Bruno, the Darley's window dresser, is desperate for us to see one of his Soho drag shows. Are you seriously on for that?'

'Of course. It can't be that shocking, can it?'

'Well, put it this way,' she says with a yelp of laughter, '*Rocky Horror Show* is probably a walk in the park compared to Bruno's drag show!'

I'm ambling back from the market with heavy bags, a good twenty minutes on foot from the *finca*, when I'm accosted by Rafael outside his house.

'Eh *amiga*! Why you not take the car?'

I look up. 'Have you seen that brilliant sky? Why on earth would I take the car on a day like this?'

He laughs. 'In other words, Alan is using it.'

I set my bags down and stretch my back. 'Yes, he's gone off to the nursery to pick up some seedlings, the rotter.'

He sits on the front step of his porch and shows me a toothy grin. 'Guess what I've been doing this morning?'

'Surprise me.'

He slaps his leg and breaks into inane giggles. 'I've been a clown.'

'You're always being a clown, what's new?'

He shakes his head with some impatience. 'No, really I've been a clown. I went to Palma to enrol on a clown course.'

It takes a little time for this to sink in. 'Are you really serious? This isn't one of your jokes?'

He stands up and thumps his chest. 'I wouldn't tell you a lie! I spend all morning learning to say "Hahahaha" and "Jejejejeje" and "Hohohohohoho" and they get us to dress up with a big red nose and enormous trousers and a curly wig.' He points at me and laughs manically. 'Now I have a big curly wig just like your hair!'

'Thank you, Rafael. I'll take that as a compliment.'

He pounds my back with his hand. 'You're like me! Always like jokes, *si*?'

'Sometimes, Rafael, but not always. Now tell me, why the sudden career change?'

He tuts impatiently. 'Don't be silly. I'm a baker. I don't want to be a clown! No, I do this to help with my stress.'

Now I am laughing. 'You? Stressed?'

He looks offended. 'Of course. I have all sorts of pressures in my life.'

'Such as?'

'*Pues*, let me think. Well, I have to do my shifts at the bakery, then get to the gym and sometimes the *supermercat*. Oh, and there's my girlfriend and sorting out where we go for dinner and I have to feed the sheep and do the washing. So many things…'

'Hmm. Sounds hugely onerous.'

'At least now I can relax a little with laughter.'

'I'm glad you've found some entertainment. Are there many others training to be clowns?'

'*Si, si*. Maybe twenty. Many people,' he says without any irony, 'are stressed like me.'

I gather up my bags. 'Well, I must be off.'

He grabs my arm. 'Hey, you know, maybe you should come along with me? You must get stressed with all this flying back and forth to London?'

'True,' I sigh. 'But my stress is nothing to yours, Rafael. Besides, I really think we only need one clown in our lane.'

I arrive in the courtyard to find Ollie prowling around the front garden on all fours, hotly pursued by Scraggy, Baby Boris, Damian, Tiger and Tortoiseshell. I watch him in some alarm.

'Please don't tell me you're going mad too?'

He turns his head. 'I'm being a cat whisperer.'

'Very droll.'

He sits up on his haunches. 'Seriously, it works. I've been whispering to Scraggy and the others and telling them to follow me, and look, they're doing just that.'

'It's got nothing to do with the fact that they're hungry and think you'll lead them to food?'

He dismisses me with a wave of the hand. 'Of course not. Anyway, when is Jacinto coming back with the donkeys?'

I battle up the steps to the porch with my bags. 'Can you give me a hand?'

He jumps to his feet and strides across the lawn. 'Maybe Jacinto can give me some tips?'

I offer him a bag. 'Look, we can't have any donkeys until Stefan creates an enclosure at the end of the field and we've got the cattery man coming over from England to sort out the cattery, which is a priority at the moment.'

'When is he coming?'

'Next month, so the donkeys will have to wait.'

He puffs out his cheeks. 'Someone's sending me a book about horse whispering.'

'Who is?'

'Joe Pentman, the coin dealer in the States who sells me stuff. He told me his dad was a famous horse whisperer and wrote a book all about it. Anyway, I bought two nice coins from him and he's throwing in his dad's book for free.'

I shake my head. 'Is there any end to your deal making?'

'Not really. Anyway, I've got to carry on reading *Don Quixote* now. Either he's getting madder or my Spanish is getting worse because in the bit I've just read he thinks a barber's basin is a mythical helmet. Do you think that makes sense?'

'I'm afraid so. Don Quixote was seriously deranged, possibly psychotic.'

'You think so? I'll tell my Spanish literature teacher that.'

I walk into the *entrada* and through to the kitchen.

'Maybe that's a bit harsh. Don Quixote was more of a clown.'

He dumps his bag on the kitchen table. 'No, I think you were right the first time. He was deranged.'

It's eight in the morning and I'm wandering around the orchard in a nightdress and Greek pompom slippers, a little present to myself on completion of the Athens marathon. Salvador is examining my apparel in some disgust and barely glances at my face when I replace his feed tray. Meanwhile, Goneril and Regan are having a squabble on the other side of the run while Cordelia sits sublimely on a pile of straw, dreamily contemplating the mountains. Well, that's what she appears to be doing. I rub my eyes and discover that I still have traces of heavy make-up from last night's carnival on my eyelashes and cheeks. My ghoul outfit was a great success at the village party in Fornalutx, but the black greasepaint Catalina smothered on my face stubbornly resisted removal before I went to bed. No wonder Salvador can bear to lay eyes on me. I yawn and stretch out my limbs. In the distance there is evidence of the last vestiges of snowfall on the higher peaks of the Tramuntanas, where small smudges of snow, like melting marshmallows, twinkle under the sun's gaze. Hovering beneath, a belt of soft white mist masks the forests of pines and oak trees so that the higher peaks appear marooned in mist like tiny islands floating in the sky.

Despite it being a frosty February morning, there is a hive of activity in the orchard – robins flit about the trees and bees hover close to the blossoming yellow mimosa and the early blossom of our solitary almond tree. New leaves and tiny buds are forming on our various fruit trees and the hardy squat palms glare up at the sun defiantly, as if unbothered by the wintry chill. The new orange crop is in evidence and the trees are covered in bright fruit and dark green leaves, while the lemons are just coming into season. The Scotsman has always had a penchant for cypresses and now, as I examine the craggy old stone wall at the back of the orchard, I see why. In just a few years since being planted, the long row of straight-backed, elegant wispy trees have begun to thicken and grow, creating a snug and verdant border to our land. At the foot of the stone steps that lead from the orchard up to the swimming pool and back terrace, a mass of spidery *Dimorphotheca* has seeded. Alan planted this South African daisy-like plant some months ago and now its purple and white blooms are spreading across the gravel like wildfire.

Walking over to a nearby lemon tree, my slippers drenched in dew, I manage to reach up and pluck off three enormous fruit. I carry them back to the kitchen and, after dumping the fruit in the sink, begin feeding the army of felines in and outside the house. I've barely put a cup of coffee to my lips when the telephone rings. Who can be ringing at this time of day? I hear the rich, deep timbre of Manuel's voice, more heady than a strong espresso.

'Manuel! What a lovely surprise – and on a Saturday morning too.'

He sniffs loudly. 'Can you talk?'

'My husband would say too much.'

'*Que?*'

'Just a joke. So, how are things with the new hotel? I thought the launch went well.'

He gives a profound sigh. 'You know, I am happy with the hotel and I like Soho. It's a good location. My problem is Serge de Camp. He does not like to accept instructions.'

'He's French and he's a chef. What did you expect?'

'I expect loyalty and respect for my authority.'

I often think Manuel Ramirez would have been perfect in a *Godfather* film.

'The easiest thing would be to show him your beautiful Kalashnikov in Panama.'

'You think he likes guns?'

'Well, I think it might help him to understand you better.'

He pauses. 'Maybe. I will think about this but I would appreciate your meeting Serge when you are back and perhaps underlining what I expect from him with the press.'

'What do you mean exactly?'

He sounds irritable. 'At the launch he spoke about the new restaurant as though it was his own concept when it is the brainchild of H Hotels.'

Oh dear. Egos are running wild.

'I'll talk to him, Manuel, but you must understand that he's a celebrity chef and that in turn gives a more human face to the hotel.'

He listens and gives a curt 'OK.'

'One other thing, Manuel. That irritating Ray Drummond, the sleazy freelance journalist I told you about, has been hounding poor Serge for some months now. He's like a sticking plaster.'

'Not still on about Serge's love life?' he growls.

'Apparently so. He's calling our office every day trying to sniff out information about him, which is becoming a little tiresome.'

Manuel is about to hang up when he is suddenly struck by one of his ideas of the paranoiac kind. 'This Ray Drummond is really bothering you?'

I flinch. 'He's a pain but we can handle him.'

A pause. 'Well, if he becomes a pest you must tell me. I will crush him like a little ant between my fingers.'

'Thanks, Manuel. That's very sweet of you but it's not necessary just yet.'

He gives a hollow laugh. 'Just say the word and you will never have to worry about him again.'

I put the phone down in some haste. Poor old Ray Drummond. He may be one of the most odious and irritating creatures on the planet but that surely doesn't warrant him ending up on Manuel's hit list... or does it?

It's a blustery evening as we arrive in the village of Santa Maria and park the car in a narrow side street close to the market place. Although we live only twenty minutes away by road, the terrain and ambience of this part of the island is quite distinct. Unspoilt and rustic in feel, the landscape is far less mountainous with gentle plains and long stretches of verdant fields and ploughed farmland. By contrast, Sóller is crammed with citrus orchards, bubbling *torrentes*, rivers, which flow into the azure sea, and the Tramuntanas are a constant dramatic backdrop wherever you are in the valley.

Tonight, Santa Maria is determined to celebrate the carnival in spectacular style and so has invited a *colla,* one of the island's human tower teams, to demonstrate the construction of a human pyramid of 150 people. These human edifices are known as *castells,* castles, and the participants as *castellers,* castle builders. Following the demonstration, *glosadors* from Mallorca and Menorca will be able to pit their wits and nerve against one another in a humorous poetry competition. Pep has decided to participate in the event and has invented some bawdy *gloses*, poems, especially for the occasion and much to our dismay. Although an amateur in the art, he enjoys dreaming up outrageous poems, full of double entendres, and making a spectacle of himself in public. Ollie and Angel have accompanied us, although they're far more interested in the human tower than listening to rival groups of poets and having to endure Pep's stage debut.

Pep slams the car door and stretches. 'I cannot believe that we all managed to squeeze into your Mini. It's the size of a shoebox!'

I give him a shove. 'You're lucky to have bagged the front passenger seat. Angel, Ollie and I were like sardines in the back.'

He lights up a *puro*. 'Yes, but you three are little. We *hombres* need our space, don't we Alan?'

The Scotsman gives an absentminded little chuckle and stuffs the car keys in his pocket. He observes his watch in the descending gloom. 'Come on, the event starts in ten minutes.'

'*Tranquillo*,' cries Pep, sauntering along with a smile on his chops. He holds a sheaf of papers in his hands, which rustles in the breeze. 'These are important,' he says with mock gravitas. 'My written pearls that will win me the Poet Laureate's crown.'

The boys run ahead, reaching the *plaça* well ahead of the three of us. Juana has perhaps wisely opted to visit her mother tonight. She admitted to me the previous evening that having to witness Pep making a goon of himself in public might prove too much for her.

The square is illuminated with strong white lights and the wooden stage has been erected in the centre and is already surrounded by a throng of people. Meanwhile, an even larger crowd of spectators is jostling for position around a cleared space, which has evidently been designated for the human tower demonstration.

Angel points towards it excitedly. '*Madre mio*! Are 150 people really going to take part?'

Pep shrugs. 'Of course. They have even bigger *castells* in Catalonia. You know I once saw at least 200 *castellers* forming the traditional tiered tower.'

I turn to him. 'Is it an event peculiar to Catalans?'

He nods. 'The concept of *castells* began some time in the late eighteenth century in Valls, near the city of Tarragona. The biggest human towers are created in the region and are quite breathtaking. It is said that the Catalonians began making the towers as a physical manifestation of Catalan national unity.'

'Blimey, that sounds a bit worthy,' I grin.

He throws out his hands. 'Well, it is a symbolic act. It is the creation of an edifice with strong foundations and infrastructure, built by and for the people.'

'I see your point. Maybe we should take the lead from the Catalans and start building *castells* in the UK for greater national unity?' I say.

Alan gives a snort. 'Somehow I can't see such death-defying acts catching on back home any time soon.'

There's a sudden hush and a man blows a whistle and makes an announcement in Mallorquin. We huddle closer to the action.

'He says the building of the *castell* will commence now,' whispers Pep.

A swarm of swarthy, well-built men rush to the cleared area and begin pulling together to form a close-knit ring. They are dressed in red shirts and white trousers and wear bright bandanas.

'Look, Ollie!' whispers Angel. 'The men are starting to make the first layer of the human tower.'

'This is the base,' says Pep excitedly, craning his neck to see. 'It is called the *pinya*, the pineapple, which is made up of the strong *castellers*, castle builders, who create a safe cushion for the others who climb on their backs to make the higher tiers.'

A pipe sounds and a loud band begins playing.

'They're off!' shouts Pep. 'See now how another group of men is quickly leaping onto the backs of those forming the *pinya*?'

'It's very complicated,' Alan yells back. 'They're so fast.'

'They're as agile as monkeys,' I gasp. 'How are they managing to climb so quickly?'

Pep grabs my arm. 'Quick! Look through this gap. Can you see that the *castellers* all wear black sashes round their waists? These are used as footholds for those climbing up to form the next level.'

Ollie is spellbound. 'Has anyone ever died doing this?'

Pep sighs. 'It's rare, but a young girl fell and died back in 2006. There are always risks but to be honest even if the tower collapses after it's been built, few people are ever badly hurt.'

Ollie gives a low whistle. 'You wouldn't get me climbing up to the top. How tall will the tower be?'

Pep shrugs. 'If they form six or more tiers it could be about ten metres, I suppose.'

'That's about twice the height of our *finca*,' says Ollie in amazement.

'*Si*, you need a head for heights, Ollie,' laughs Pep, 'but remember that the person at the very top is always a child of about your age.'

'Pre-teenager, thank you,' corrects Ollie.

People are whistling and calling out, while others clap and sing. The excitement is palpable.

Three levels have now been formed. The men clamp their arms around one another's shoulders on each level to maintain a strong, unified ring. As each layer establishes itself on top of the previous one, there is a slight wobble as the *castellers* test the stability of the ring with their feet, which rest on the shoulders of those below. Once they feel it is secure, they call for the next team of *castellers* to climb up onto their shoulders to form the next tier. We watch as the fourth layer begins its ascent.

'It's like a gigantic layered wedding cake.' I shout above the din of the crowd.

'More like an enormous jelly,' says Ollie.

'You know, it takes great skill and courage to be a *casteller*. The motto of the *castellers* is "*Força, equilibri, valor i seny.*"'

I repeat the words out loud. 'Strength, balance, courage and reason.'

Pep claps me on the back. '*Molt bé*. I suppose "sense" might be a better translation than "reason". It's said that the *castell* is an analogy for the Catalan people. The building of a perfectly formed castle requires special skills and courage from its people which in turn will offer them a secure and prosperous future.'

'It could apply to the ambitious individual, too,' I muse. 'How to reach the top without coming a cropper.'

'I suppose the whole thing's up for interpretation,' Alan chips in. 'They certainly need courage to climb in this wind.'

He's right. The wind is strong and ripples through the clothing of the climbing *castellers*. We hold our breath as the last of the fifth layer takes his place. Now the sixth group begins its difficult and arduous ascent. Each of the higher layers holds four people. The cheering from the crowd is now deafening and we find it near impossible to converse. Another layer is in place and then from nowhere a thin child carefully crawls from shoulder to shoulder, higher and higher towards the far-off tip of the *castell*.

'Once the *anxeneta*, the child at the top, is in place, he must raise one hand in the air and show four fingers. This symbolises the stripes on the Catalan flag.'

'And there I was thinking this was just a fun event. I didn't realise it was quite so symbolic.'

'We Catalans are very profound people,' says Pep with a wink.

A cheer rises as the little boy triumphantly stands erect, the eighth layer of the tower, and pushes his right hand in the air. Seconds later he carefully begins his descent to hysterical clapping, wolf whistling and music.

'That was incredible,' I say.

'Fantastic,' say Ollie and Angel in unison.

We stand transfixed as the *castellers* descend rapidly and are soon on ground level.

'Now you understand why it is such a special event,' says Pep.

We have little time to catch our breath before another pipe sounds and the poetry competition is announced.

'Venga!' shrieks Pep. 'I must make myself known to the organisers.'

We follow in his wake as he squeezes through the multitude, finally arriving at the foot of the stage. An official bends down from the wooden platform to speak with Pep and he is cordially invited up to join the Mallorcan *glosadors* team.

'A bit of luck,' he chuckles. 'I should have registered but as it happens they are one man down so are happy for me to step in.'

'The hero of the hour,' whispers Alan, giving me a surreptitious tap on the arm. I grin.

'Best of luck!' we all cry.

Pep stands on the stage side by side with another seven Mallorcan poets. The Menorcan team make their way onto the other side of the stage. And so the battle of wit begins.

Pep is sitting by the hearth with his legs outstretched, a glass of cava in his hand. By his side is a modestly sized gold trophy. He reaches down and scoops it up with his free hand.

'This is a testament to strength, balance, courage and reason,' he announces with a glint in his eye.

Juana is tutting away in her chair by the fire. 'Only the *castellers* can use that motto. It doesn't apply to an amateur poet like you. I still don't know how the Mallorcan team won last night with you on their side.'

Pep tells her to be quiet.

She persists. 'And it's very egotistic to be carrying that trophy about with you the day after the event.'

The Scotsman laughs. 'Juana, you should have been there. Pep was an inspiration. His verses flowed and the crowd roared with laughter.'

'Of that I have no doubt,' she snipes. 'They probably all realised he was a fraud and no more a *glosador* than Gaspar the delivery man.'

I interrupt. 'The point is that the Mallorcan team won with its wit and humour. Admittedly, I couldn't understand everything spoken but when it came to Pep's turn the crowd genuinely whooped.'

Juana shakes her head. 'Of course they did. They hadn't expected a clown to pitch up to keep them amused.'

Alan waggles a finger at her. 'You're being very unfair. Pep deserves our congratulations. His performance was a triumph.'

'You know, I think it was my *glose* about the priest chasing the widow into the closet that brought the house down,' says Pep with misty eyes.

Juana winces. 'Oh please, don't say any more. I can't bear it!'

'But I was going to recite it to you. The punchline is disgusting.'

Alan pats Pep on the shoulder. 'Perhaps best saved for another day, *mi amic*. I think Juana might self-combust otherwise.'

'I thought the Menorcan team was funny too. They even did one *glose* altogether about fat, gossiping women,' says Ollie.

'Yes, I wasn't too happy with that poem,' I say.

Alan smiles. 'It definitely was a close-run contest but in the end Mallorca had the edge on Menorca. Each of you deserved those trophies.'

'Well, it was the highlight of my year,' sighs Pep. 'An unforgettable night, whatever you think,' he says pointedly to his wife.

Alan replenishes his glass.

'Dinner will be served any minute,' I say, getting up from my seat.

Pep raises a hand. 'Wait a minute. I have a little something for you. You could say it's for the excellent moral support you gave me at the poetry competition yesterday. It's something I ordered a while ago.'

Juana pulls a heavy packet from her bag and passes it to me. She and Pep wink at one another. Ollie slides down the banister from his room, his radar always alert to gifts being handed out.

'Why don't you unwrap it?' I say, passing it to him.

He carefully tears off the wrappers and finally uncovers a large terracotta square. With a puzzled look, he turns it over to reveal in glazed, white letters, the names Minny and Della and beneath, the image of two donkeys' heads.

'It's beautiful!' I yell, giving Pep and Juana a big hug.

Ollie turns to his father. 'So now you've got to let us have the donkeys.'

Alan hangs his head. 'I suppose there's no way out. You're a real pal, Pep.'

'Take it like a man,' Juana goads. 'Think how lovely it will look hanging on the donkeys' gate.'

Pep gives him a slap on the back and waggles two huge Cuban cigars in front of him. 'A little something for us to share after dinner.'

Alan's eyes light up.

Feigning sobriety, Pep places a hand on his heart. 'After all, it's the very least I can offer a condemned man.'

NINE

A GOOD FERRET

The sweet tang of spring is in the air as I stroll across Sóller *plaça*, stopping briefly to contemplate the towering plane trees, which are just beginning to shoot soft green leaves. For months they have stood frozen and naked in the square with nothing to hide their modesty and now at last can look forward to a full dress of leaves. The clock face on the facade of the town hall tells me it is ten, time for coffee, but first I must pay a visit to the bank. I pull open the door of Banca March to find it deserted. Various members of staff look up and, seeing I'm one of their regulars, mutter a cheery '*Hola!*' and carry on with their work.

'Where is everyone?' I ask them.

'Enjoying the sun or having a coffee, perhaps?' muses Miguel, one of the clerks.

Tolo, the deputy manager, beckons me over. 'Are you free next Saturday evening? We're having a few friends round for supper. Bring Ollie.'

In London I'd never have dreamed of becoming chummy with my local bank manager but Tolo and his wife have indeed become good friends over the years and we all enjoy getting together for informal suppers when time allows. He pulls out a chair by his desk. I sit down and quickly check my diary. 'Looks fine. We'd love to come over.'

Sitting back in his leather chair, he gives me a radiant smile. 'What can I do for you today?'

'I just wanted to pay in a cheque.'

'Someone's giving you money? What's happening?'

He scrutinises the written amount and gives me the thumbs up.

'It was for an article I wrote for a newspaper back in the UK but if you take into account all the research time it works out at about five euros an hour.'

He laughs. 'Well, I suppose every little helps. So what's new?'

'Nothing much. I'm still trying to sort out a new building for the cattery and I'm hugely busy with the company back in London.'

He raises his eyebrows. 'Aren't you supposed to be merging?'

'That's the plan, but most of the companies I've heard from want to tie me in to a long-term contract, which means commuting weekly for years to come. I've had enough of that.'

'I don't blame you. Life's for living. Well, at least you've got your running to keep your mind off work. I've seen you jogging along with Tina in the port. I wish my back wasn't so bad or I'd join you.'

Tolo has been a keen runner for some years but of late has sustained a bad back injury, which has put paid to his fitness regime for some months.

'You should try Jaume's new Tot Pilates studio. It's the talk of the town.'

'Pilates? I'm not sure if it's for me. Do you go?'

I laugh. 'Are you joking? I'm a pilates junkie. I train there twice a week with Joana, Jaume's partner.'

'Of course, I remember now, you've been doing pilates classes for some time up in Deià with Marilyn, the Australian former ballet dancer.'

'Exactly. So this is an extra boost.'

He looks at me doubtfully. 'Alan isn't going too?'

I tap his desk. 'Touch wood, he'll be starting this week. As it happens he's just won a part in a French TV commercial, playing a butler, so he's begun to take an interest in his appearance.'

Tolo roars with laughter, startling the other staff.

'A butler? You're joking? Mind you, he is tall and has bearing.'

'The director told him he was a cross between Sean Connery and Roger Moore, so you can imagine how that pleased him.'

Tolo shakes his head. '*Madre mia*! Maybe Hollywood beckons. The next thing, he'll be charging me for his signature on cheques.'

A few minutes later, I walk out into the gentle sun. Soft, wispy clouds like whisked cream daub the vivid canvas of the sky and a skein of geese race by, their perfectly aligned forms glinting in the sun. Mateo, one of the waiters at Café Paris, is looking up into the sky.

'Spring has arrived.'

'You think?'

He holds a finger to his lips while balancing a silver tray with his other hand. 'If you listen carefully, you can hear the singing of the sun. It sounds like bees.'

I concentrate hard. Is it my imagination or can I hear the sun talking to me?

He grins. 'I think you need a coffee.'

Throwing myself into a comfortable wicker chair in the sun, I watch as he potters off inside. I've only been there a matter of seconds when Senyor Bisbal appears with his quivering *ca rater*, Tío. With some concern, I study the little dog as it shakes uncontrollably at the side of his master.

'I worry about Tío. He seems to feel the cold terribly.'

Senyor Bisbal gives an impatient rasp of the throat. 'He's just excited. As soon as I open the front door, he begins quivering.'

I laugh.

'Any news on your cat hotel?'

'Yes, I have a man coming from England who's created a new design.'

He gives a little snort. 'One day, when it's up and running, you must invite me for a viewing.'

'Of course. You may even want to stay in it.'

He blows his nose amid gales of laughter and taps me lightly on the shoulder.

'Sometimes I think you came here just to keep me amused.'

'Well, that at least gives a purpose to my life.'

I watch his face crumple with mirth as he takes his leave with Tío at his heels and heads for his favourite table at the back of the cafe. Mateo arrives with a coffee and croissant as well as a copy of the *Diario de Mallorca*. The front page concerns a drug raid in a down-at-heel part of Palma. A ring of gypsies has apparently been apprehended in a police sting operation known as *chinche*. I call over to Mateo to help translate as I often do when a word stumps me. I giggle.

'Really? A sting operation called Creepy Crawly?'

He puffs out his bottom lip. '*Sí*, it's a kind of *bicho*.'

'It's hard to take it too seriously when it's called creepy crawly or bug.'

He smirks. 'You're right. It's an interesting choice of word, but maybe that's not such a bad word for drug pushers.'

I look round and see Gaspar walking furtively across the square. I imagine he must have just finished his paper round and expect him to come and join me but instead he gives a cursory nod and, with his hand inserted protectively inside his jacket, sets off towards his *moto*, which is parked by the chemist.

'What's up with him?' I ask Mateo.

He frowns. 'Maybe he's hurt his hand or he's hiding a package.'

We watch as he carefully mounts his bike and, with a gentle pat to his jacket, starts the engine and pulls slowly away from the kerb. I drain my coffee and hand some coins to Mateo. What on earth can be the matter with Gaspar? A growing curiosity takes hold of me as I puzzle over what he might have been concealing inside his jacket. Whatever the weather, I shall make it my business to find out.

The Scotsman is standing in the *entrada* sporting a black suit and wing-collared shirt.

'Off for a spot of gardening?' I ask.

He eyes me impatiently. 'Very droll. As it happens I'm just trying to find a shirt and jacket that might work for my butler role.'

I feign shock. 'But surely they'll be making you a tailor-made outfit as befits a leading screen star?'

'You may laugh, but the nice wardrobe mistress has said she'll organise a suit if my own clothes aren't appropriate.'

I give him the once over. 'Actually, I think you'd be better using one of their suits. I mean, the jacket is ancient and the trousers are too short.'

He sighs heavily. 'That's what I thought. The trouble is that I rarely wear suits these days.'

'When are you leaving?'

'I've got my first pilates class at Jaume's studio and then I'm off to meet the casting director at Focus Films. It's a frantic day.'

I hide a smile and retreat to my office where a screen full of emails is awaiting my urgent attention. I wish I had the courage to walk away but viewing incoming emails is an addiction, some might say an affliction. Rachel has sent a long message with details for the first of April public open day at Frithington Manor.

It seems unbelievable that it's only a month away and I can't say I'm looking forward to it at all. Not only will I have to stay in the creepy manor with the possibility of the ghost hound sniffing at my bedroom door again, but I'll also have to contend with Dannie and Greedy George as fellow house guests. Rachel has organised some professional models and actors to dress up as spooks that will waft across corridors and appear from wardrobes to strike mild terror in the public and journalists attending the event. Much as I can see the media potential, I worry that we may be unleashing more than we bargained for. Still, the Claverton-Michaels' are full of anticipation and firmly believe their efforts will greatly undermine those of the Rolling Meadows attraction nearby. Time will tell.

Alan pops his head around the door.

'Cheerio. I'll see you later.'

'Good luck!' I call after him.

I hear the door slam and the engine of the Mini whirring into action and then silence. I work away at the computer until I hear a ring at the front gate. Peering out of the window, I am puzzled to see Gaspar astride his *moto*. I rush downstairs and out into the courtyard. He kills the engine and removes his helmet.

'Well, this is a surprise. I thought you weren't speaking to me this morning,' I say teasingly.

He gives me a peck on both cheeks and touches his chest. 'There was a reason for that. Look, I have a favour to ask.'

'Is something wrong, Gaspar? You seem rather stressed.'

He rubs his eyes wearily. 'I haven't had much sleep and it's all because of this.'

He opens up his jacket and a small, whiskery face peeps out. I give a start.

'My gosh. What is it? A weasel?'

He looks around him as if under surveillance and says in hushed tones, 'It's a *furó*.'

'A ferret? Where on earth did you get it?'

He indicates that we should talk under the porch. He follows me across the gravel and takes a seat on the stone bench. 'I've stolen it.'

'Who from?' I say in alarm.

'*Pues*, my father lives in Sineu, next door to a farmer who is not a very nice man. He recently bought this ferret to get rid of the rabbits on his land but he treats it terribly.'

'I see.'

'Whenever I visited my father, I couldn't bear to see this creature stuck outside in all weathers in a tiny cage. It was hardly fed and it cried out all day. He'd shout at it and rattle the cage to frighten it.'

I already want to throttle the farmer. 'So what did you do?'

'The other night I told my father I was going to free the ferret. He is quite an old man and he told me that if I got caught it would make life hard for him. I waited until two in the morning and then I crept over to the farm. There was a full moon and I had good visibility, so I didn't need my torch. Very carefully I swung myself over his gate, threw some old meat bones to his two dogs and ran across the yard to the ferret's cage. He had a padlock on the bolt but I'd already anticipated that, so I took out my heavy pliers and snapped it.'

'This is like something out of James Bond, Gaspar.'

He doesn't disagree. 'There was a moment when I thought the *furó* wouldn't come with me but I managed to get him into a sack, although he bit my finger badly, and I made off back to my father's home.'

'Quite an adventurous evening. What then?'

'I took the ferret out of the sack and then he escaped for an hour around the house. Finally I caught him and drove back to my flat in Sóller. I had to let him loose so I've hardly had a wink of sleep. Trying to catch him this morning wasn't easy.'

'Has he been fed?'

He fretfully brushes his lips with his hand. 'I gave him some chopped up steak this morning but he didn't seem to like it.'

'Poor little chap probably prefers to hunt his prey. What about cat food? I remember reading somewhere that ferrets like kibble.'

I lead him into the house, first making sure that our cats aren't lurking in the kitchen or *entrada,* and close the door.

'Now, whatever happens, Gaspar, do NOT let the ferret escape.'

I fetch two bowls and fill one with cat kibble and another with water. Very slowly, Gaspar undoes his jacket and lets the ferret loose. I'm relieved to see he has a small collar on it tied to a piece of rope. The ferret sniffs around the bowl and finally settles itself down and begins to feed. I marvel at the perfect, diamond-shaped, nut-brown patches around each eye and the inquisitive pink nose, which twitches as it eats. Its long, dark whiskers skim the bowl as it tucks into the food.

'It's very sweet. Is it a male?'

Gaspar raises his eyebrows. 'To be honest, I've no idea. I'm calling him Feno *el furó.* You know, a *sobrenom* for *fenomen.*'

'Feno the ferret. That's a rather nice nickname and I suppose he is a phenomenon of a kind. What are you going to do with him?'

He taps his chin. 'That's what I wanted your help with.'

'What do you mean exactly?'

'Well, I wanted him to have somewhere to lie low until I sort out a place for him to go.'

I'm not sure this is such a good idea. 'Gaspar, much as I love the idea of having a ferret, I can't possibly keep him. I've got three cats, an army of strays and a coop of hens.'

He nods slowly. '*Sí,* but you have got that little shed down in the orchard.'

'I can't keep it in there. That's where Alan puts his gardening tools. Besides, what if it escapes?'

He gives Feno a little pat. 'See how happy he is? It'll only be for a few days. Can't you just hide him in there until I sort out a new home for him? It's impossible for him to stay in my flat while I'm at work.'

Weakly I give in and, with some trepidation, take the rope. Feno's big dark eyes watch me carefully and then without any resistance he trots meekly along beside me towards the front door. Gaspar and I walk down the steps from the back patio into the orchard and examine the shed. It's dry and musty inside and full of rakes, spades and gardening paraphernalia.

'We'll need to remove some of this clobber. Perhaps we can put it in Alan's *abajo*?' suggests Gaspar.

I don't like the idea of this. The Scotsman's *abajo*, in other words his lair and secret *puro* supply room in the field, is out of bounds to Ollie and me, and I'd rather keep it that way. I hate to think of the kind of items of memorabilia he stores down there. When once or twice he has unwisely unearthed some of these treasures, such as a branch of a petrified tree and brought them up to the house, I've usually ordered them straight back down again. The ancient Dunlop golf bag in tones of lobster bisque was the scariest object exhumed from the *abajo* and a three-foot-high whisky bottle full of pennies – a gift from a remote Scottish distillery.

'I've been thinking,' muses Gaspar. 'What about the little shed next to the guest room in the basement?'

'It's a bit close to the house but it might be better I suppose.'

We set off to the little-used shed, which is full of dust and cobwebs. I return Feno to Gaspar while I fetch a broom and an old cloth. Half an hour later, it is clean and aired and I have installed a water and food dish and an ancient cat basket with a blanket.

'My father says ferrets sleep a lot during the day, so you should be OK. Just keep the door locked and perhaps don't mention all this to Alan.'

I accompany him to the gate. 'Remember, much as I think he's a charming little fellow, he can't stay. I'll be in terrible trouble if Alan finds out. He already feels we're under siege from the cats.'

He jumps on his bike, which sags heavily under his enormous bulk. 'Relax. I'll sort out a new home for him as soon as possible. *Moltes gràcies*!'

When he's gone, I pop down the steps to the field and carefully open the shed door. Feno is curled up in the cat basket, looking sublimely comfortable. Very gently I reach across and stroke his soft caramel fur. He sniffs my hand and then in some boredom blinks and nestles back down into the basket. I close the door securely behind me and pop the key in the pocket of my jeans.

The Scotsman hobbles into the kitchen.

'That pilates has wrecked me. Every muscle aches. My trainer, Joana, doesn't take any prisoners.'

'Oh, don't be a baby.'

Ollie observes us with a wry smile. 'If you weren't so overweight, it wouldn't hurt.'

'Nonsense!' cries the Scotsman. 'I'll have you know that at my fitting yesterday, the wardrobe mistress thought I was very svelte.'

Ollie and I exchange incredulous glances.

'Maybe something got lost in the translation,' sniggers Ollie.

'She was speaking in English, Mr Clever Dick.'

Ollie yawns. 'Oh well, another dreadful day of torture and agony.'

'It's reassuring to know that you enjoy school so much,' I say.

He pulls on his green school jumper. 'I've never seen the point of school. I'd learn much more by myself at home.'

'I think you'd be bored stiff.'

He shakes his head vehemently. 'No I wouldn't. I'd have a nice long lie in, watch some TV, read a book, have a little snack, maybe play a computer game and then go for a game of tennis in Deià.'

'How would you learn anything?' I counter.

'Well, many of the world's most successful entrepreneurs were self-taught. I've found a website all about them.'

Alan groans. 'Don't get him started on that topic whatever you do. Come on, time to hit the road.'

Ollie picks up his bulky school rucksack, begrudgingly accepts a motherly hug and slopes off to the car with Alan following behind.

Alan calls to me. 'I'll pop into the post office on the way back and then I've got to visit the *ferreteria*.'

'What?' I say, panicking. 'Did you say ferret?'

'The *ferreteria*. I've got to pick up some sandpaper.'

Ah, the ironmonger. For a ghastly moment, I thought he was on to me.

I wave as they set off and stop in my tracks when I hear a familiar quacking-cum-croaking. In great excitement I rush over to the pond to find that several diminutive and lithe green bodies are lining up by the slimy, moss-coated internal wall. I search out the rocks by the pond until I finally set eyes on Johnny.

'You're back!'

He puffs out his cheeks. 'Yeah, me and the boys had a nice break but there's no place like home.'

'That's touching.'

He observes me coolly. 'That's not necessarily got anything to do with you. All you do is fill this place with savage animals. I'd be safer living in a wildfowl sanctuary.'

I giggle. 'Well, I'm glad you're home but I can't chat now. I have to deal with something.'

'Such as?'

I hesitate. 'Actually, I'm temporarily looking after a ferret.'

His eyes bulge. 'Did I just hear you right? FERRET? Have you completely lost the plot?!'

'He's locked up, don't worry.'

'Oh sure, don't worry. Don't tell me, the adrenalin will do me good?'

'Something like that. Cheerio, Johnny.'

I jog into the house, fill a bowl with fresh food and rush down to the shed to feed Feno. As I turn the key in the lock, he patters over to the door and so I have to manoeuvre carefully around him. Setting the food bowl down, I allow him to come over and sniff my finger which is foolish because, without ado, he gives me a little nip. I jump back.

'That's not very kind, Feno. Remember you're a fugitive and very lucky to have a roof over your head.'

He pays me no heed and takes a few half-hearted bites at the kibble. I imagine he might want a little stroll in the fresh air so decide to take him out on his lead. This is easier said than done and it takes me some time to thread the rope through the collar without incurring his wrath. Finally we set off across the field and immediately he becomes animated. His tail sways slightly and he makes little snuffling sounds as he scurries through the long grass, excitedly exploring the terrain. I walk him around the orchard and past the chickens where he pulls hard on the rope. I give him a little yank and we continue up through the strip of land, which we recently acquired, and along to the stream at its tip. He patters along in front of me like a small dog, occasionally emitting a strange grunt and at times a high-pitched cry. We walk back towards the house and it is then that I see Michel at the lower garden gate. I falter, wondering whether I have time to deposit Feno back into the shed before he's spotted, but it's too late. With some effort Michel pulls open the heavy iron gate and strides into the orchard. He stops for a second and smiles when he sees Feno.

'I didn't know you kept a ferret.'

'I don't. It's a fugitive under my roof. A friend is trying to find it a new home.'

'Oh, I see,' he says quietly. 'Can I join you?'

He takes my free arm and slowly we begin another turn of the orchard and the field.

'I used to have two ferrets when I lived in France. They make fantastic pets.'

He is silent for a while and then stops to catch his breath.

'I owe you an apology.'

'You do?'

'Yes. You must think me strange to have refused all this time to acknowledge my true name.'

I shrug and bend down to give Feno a stroke.

'The point is that Sofia loved the poetry of José Zorrilla from the time she was a teenager. He was a lyrical poet of the nineteenth century. It was a sort of joke that she called me José, a compliment and also a shared secret. She never called me Michel.'

'But then why did you write your poetry under the name Michel?'

He leans heavily on his stick and looks across at the mountains. 'When Sofia died, I decided I should become José, the name she chose. When I returned from my self-imposed exile in France long after the civil war and World War Two had ended, I felt I was returning as a stranger, as José. I decided only to use my real name, Michel, for writing my poetry, a kind of objective voice that would enable me to view events from the past more remotely.'

'But were your family happy to call you by a new name?'

He gives a bitter little laugh. 'By the time I returned, my immediate family were all gone except Rosa, the wife of my brother Joaquin, whom I'd never met, and their young son, Ignacio. They quietly accepted me and my new persona.'

'Is it Ignacio that you live with now?'

'Yes, he is my only nephew. When I returned from Paris, I used the money I'd amassed from my writing to build a sizeable house in Sóller and that is where I live with Ignacio and his wife, Marina. He has learned to forgive my past.'

'What happened to Rosa?'

'She also lived with us but died some years ago.'

The ferret is pulling at the rope. We resume our slow pace through the grass.

'Last time we met you told me that, after being trained with the Republicans, you ended up in Madrid and were able to meet with Sofia but suddenly had to leave for Valencia.'

'You listen well. Can we have a coffee?'

I smile. 'I worry that you're becoming addicted to my coffee machine.'

He nods. 'Funnily enough, I have suggested to my nephew to invest in the same one.'

Laughing, we walk to the shed where I deposit Feno back in his cat basket. In the kitchen, I make us both strong coffees.

'I was telling you that I was sent to Valencia. It was complicated. Basically, the Republicans feared that Franco's troops might take control of Madrid and so the Republican leaders fled the city. I went with a large contingent of men in advance of their departure. I was angry because I wanted to remain in Madrid.'

I sit at the table and pass him some biscuits.

'And what about Elena?'

'During October and November of 1936 Franco's troops made huge headway in penetrating Madrid. In early November there was fierce fighting in Carabanchel, a suburb of the city, and the situation was becoming grave for the Republicans. In some desperation, the Republican government, now based in Valencia, asked Buenaventura Durruti, leader of the Anarchists, to leave Aragón and head to Madrid to save the Republicans from defeat.'

'Why him?'

'I only know that he was a charismatic and valiant leader and he brought with him about 3,000 men. In the meantime, the Nationalists had begun bombing Madrid. They even struck schools and the Prado. Philistines!'

I take a sip of coffee. 'The Republicans did their share of damage to churches and historic properties too, didn't they?'

He wags a finger. 'True, but that was anger against the Catholic Church, not against the artisans who created the churches.'

'A weak argument,' I laugh.

'Anyway, the university quarter was under siege. Durruti's army was reduced to about 400 men. On 19 November in heavy fighting between Nationalist and Republican troops, Durruti was fatally wounded. He died in the Ritz Hotel. It had been used as a canteen and makeshift hospital.'

He spreads his fingers out on the table. 'One by one, these young men were butchered. As for Elena, she was a wild card. She was on nursing duty for the Republicans at the Ritz building during those harrowing days but for some reason she joined the fight and was fatally shot the day after Durruti was killed.'

Water pricks Michel's eyes. He bangs the table. 'If I hadn't been sent to Valencia, doing nothing but sitting around in training camps, I might have saved her life.'

'How? Most likely you would have been killed yourself.'

He sniffs heavily. 'She was only twenty-three years old. Sofia managed to write to me, through intermediaries in the Republican forces, and told me of her death. I felt so impotent. All I could do was write to her from Valencia.'

'What of Sofia and Elena's parents?'

'Ah, that was the best part,' he says with bitterness. 'Their father refused to bury the body on consecrated ground. Elena was thrown with her comrades into a communal pit. It broke Sofia and her mother's heart.'

He gets up slowly and wanders over to the *entrada*. 'For months I stayed in Valencia and then there was a series of bitter splits on the Republican side. It was a long time coming. I was persuaded to leave the POUM and I joined the Communists.'

'Why?'

He sighs. 'The POUM had lost its way. A year later, in 1937, its leader, Andreu Nin, was assassinated by Soviet agents so maybe it's just as well I defected. The Russians had become involved, supposedly as allies of the Republicans, but they were just after power.'

'So the Germans and Italians supported Franco and the Nationalists, and the Russians supported the Republicans?'

'Yes, but they all had their own agendas. They were hungry to establish a power base and to take sides before the next stage. Remember, the Spanish Civil War was just a preamble to a far uglier event in world history – World War Two.'

'Did you start writing poetry during the civil war?'

He gives me a surprised look. 'Ah poetry. In all the horror, that was the one thing that kept me alive. That and the belief that I would see Sofia again.'

'Some of the poems in the book you left me, or rather should I say your alter ego Michel left me, are so brutal, so hopeless.'

'I wrote that book while I was living in Paris after World War Two. Thankfully, old family friends helped get me back on my feet while I established myself as a poet. I called it *Ode to War*, a deliberately ironic title.'

'Some of the poems are beautiful. I just wish my Catalan was better.'

He smiles. 'Your Catalan is better than my English, although I was fluent during the war. I often fought alongside the International Brigade for the Republicans. They were a mixed bunch of nationalities. They were from Germany, America, Switzerland, Italy, and many came from England. They were young would-be Communists with a new cause.'

He hovers between the kitchen and the *entrada*, his stick gripped between both hands. 'I remember a young Spaniard named Miguel Hernandez. He was just an ordinary *tío*, a young uneducated chap who wrote a poem in memory of members of the International Brigade killed in action. It went something like this: "Around your bones, olive groves will grow, stretching their roots in the soil, to reach and embrace all men, universally and honourably.'"

I stand beside him. 'What happened to him?'

He gives a heavy sigh. 'He was sentenced to death and died when he was thirty-one. Now, before I depress you further with my hellish tales, I must go.'

'Why don't you wait until Alan returns? He's so keen to meet you.'

He pulls open the front door. 'I would love to stay but I have an appointment at the lawyer's office with my nephew that I must keep. Another time, I promise.'

He kisses my hand with cool, trembling lips and ambles across the courtyard to the gate. I watch him go, angry with myself that I had never thought to take his coat and hat.

Alan arrives home and begins unloading the boot.

'I've got some great news.'

He pauses. 'What's that then?'

'Johnny and the frogs are back.'

He laughs. 'Ah, good, a sure sign that spring has arrived.'

He carries two trays of seedlings into the house and sets them on the table.

'What are those?' I ask.

'Just some strawberry plants I picked up. Now, I was at the *ferreteria* getting the sandpaper and I got talking with old Tofol about tree rats. He's such a fount of knowledge, that man. I told him I'd noticed that some creature has been up in the lemon and orange trees, scavenging. He said it would be tree rats.'

'I don't think they do any real harm, though.'

He puffs out his cheeks. 'I'm not so sure. And another thing. I heard some heavy scratching noises coming from the small shed last night. I would have taken a look with a torch but the door seemed to be locked and the key's vanished.'

I rush over to the coffee machine and begin fiddling with the water jug. 'Fancy a coffee?'

He rubs his hands together. 'Thanks, that would be great. I'll just bring in the other stuff.'

He disappears to the car while I double check that the key to the shed is still firmly in my pocket. He returns and dumps a rake and a bag of compost on the kitchen floor.

'I decided to treat myself to a new rake. The old one's very rusty. Now that spring has sprung, I need to get cracking in the garden.'

I bring him a coffee, pleased that we have moved on from the tree rat conversation. He sits down heavily and gives a big yawn.

'Anyway, apart from the tree rats, Tofol told me to watch out for pine martens, especially with our hens. I told him that we'd seen a whole colony opposite Es Turo in Fornalutx last week.'

'Yes, but weren't they gorgeous?'

'Gorgeous? You wouldn't say that if they carried off Salvador in the night. Actually, you'll laugh but Tofol's got a whole range of accessories in his shop for guess what?'

'I've no idea.'

'Ferrets! Isn't that priceless, a *ferreteria* selling ferret accessories?'

I study his face to see if the game is up and this is just a sadistic preamble to his yelling 'Gotcha!' but no, he genuinely seems to have no clue that a ferret is practically living under his roof.

'I doubt your average ironmonger back in the UK would carry such things. According to Tofol, keeping ferrets as pets has become quite a trend on the island. He's got a range of diminutive hammocks and sleeping baskets and the oddest-looking carrying cases. It's all quite absurd.'

I laugh nervously. 'Oh well, each to his own. I've heard that they make very loyal and tranquil pets.'

'I have my doubts. The joke about ferrets up trouser legs must have started from somewhere.'

He takes a sip of coffee and laughs. 'There are some daft people around. They'll be making pets of tree rats and pine martens next.'

'I'm sorry to say that while you were out Michel the poet popped by.'

He taps the table with his car key. 'That's a shame. I'd love to meet the old boy. When might he be back?'

I laugh. 'I'd need a crystal ball to tell you that. He just turns up like Mary Poppins used to when the wind changed. He told me today that he only likes to be called Michel when he's in poet mode and José the rest of the time.'

Alan narrows his eyes. 'Who's José when he's at home?'

'José Zorrilla was a Spanish poet whom Michel's girlfriend, Sofia, admired.'

'What, she had two poet boyfriends on the go?'

'No, you dope. José Zorrilla lived in the 1800s. She just liked his poetry and for some bizarre reason preferred to call Michel by the name José.'

The Scotsman mulls quietly. 'Is he quite sane, this poet of yours? I know he's in his nineties but he seems to have some very odd notions.'

I see Minky scratching at the pane of the back door and let him in.

'Oh Michel's got all his marbles all right. He's just constantly reliving a nightmare. The lighter moments are all too infrequent.'

He gets up and takes his cup to the sink. 'It's almost impossible to imagine how grim it must have been living during the Spanish Civil War. In fact, how does one ever really recover from war?'

There's a *pop pop pop* and the angry hornet sound of a *moto*. The gate bell sounds loudly.

'No peace for the wicked,' grumbles the Scotsman. 'Now who is it?'

We hurry over to the front door and out into the courtyard. To my horror I see Gaspar grinning cheerfully from his bike as he swerves onto the gravel. He gives me the thumbs up as he kills the engine.

'Good news! I've got him a nice home. A whole family of ferrets!'

Alan observes him with complete puzzlement. 'Did you say ferrets? What are you talking about, Gaspar?'

I try to give him a zip-lip sign but it's too late for that. Like a child who's forgotten his line in the school play, Gaspar momentarily claps a big hand over his face and then mouths 'Lo siento' at me. Sorry? It's a bit late for that.

Alan looks first at Gaspar and then at me, a seed of suspicion firmly planted in his mind.

He places his hands on his hips. 'Now what on earth have you two been up to?'

I give my lumbering, former running companion a radiant smile. 'Over to you, Gaspar. I'll just go and put on the coffee.'

TEN

HAUNTED HOUSE

8.20 a.m., the club, Mayfair

A trickle of laughter and the sound of swift feet echo from the circular stairwell. I chug behind, gripping the broad mahogany rail and wondering why I'm even bothering to try to keep pace. One flight later, I reach the grand and fusty first-floor landing just in time to note a faint tremor from one of the doors of the library. Someone must have shaken it from its slumber, and probably just in the last few seconds. Controlling my breath, I push back the doors and enter the wide, dimly lit room. With the pungent aroma of polished mahogany hitting the chance visitor like a wall, I'm not surprised to find it devoid of life. On all sides the walls are lined with books from floor to ceiling, and random items of furniture – coffee tables, antique escritoires, sunken sofas and armchairs – have been strewn around. But where is Ollie? I peer under tables, behind the elaborate swag curtains that hide the unremitting greyness of South Audley Street, but he is nowhere to be found. I stand in the centre of the library, contemplating my next move, when one of the bookcases emits an eerie groan and swings back violently to reveal my prankster son on the other side.

'Ha ha, that fooled you! It's the secret panel. Come here.'

He beckons me over to the faux book panel beyond, which is a small snug room with a window overlooking the street.

'I wish we had a secret room like this at home.'

I laugh. 'We did once. Next to our *entrada* was a dark little room used for Catholic priests to hide during Moorish invasions.'

'Why did you get rid of it?'

'Because it served no purpose. It was just a dark hole. Not very inviting.'

I usher him out of the hidey-hole and together we jog down the stairs and hail a taxi in the street. As an Easter holiday treat, Ollie has accompanied me to London. While I attend meetings, he will spend time with Hilda, his former Mary Poppins, lovingly known in the family as Dooda, a throwback to one of Ollie's mispronunciations as a toddler. As an erstwhile maternity nurse at St Thomas's Hospital, she can truthfully claim to be one of the very first beings to have welcomed Ollie into the world. Of course Dooda isn't a normal nanny in any sense of the word. As a dyed-in-the-wool cockney and proud of it, ta very much, she introduced Ollie from his toddler years to experiences he would never have had with a conventional nanny from one of the straight-backed nanny school establishments. He spent his formative years on and off the city's buses, visiting South London fruit and veg markets, and hanging out with Dooda's family and neighbours and visiting her local community haunts. He was soon a willing apprentice in cockney vernacular, yelling out, 'That's torn it!' at his chi-chi nursery school in Pimlico to the deep distress of his terminally affected headmistress.

We arrive at the agreed rendezvous, Victoria Station, and Dooda is waiting outside the station's grubby and crowded Starbucks. She grabs Ollie and they exchange shrieks of delight and hugs, while I stand about like a spare part. Graciously they concede to give me a cursory *adios* and a wave, and skip off towards a red bus. I hail a cab and set off to RTB Communications where I am once again to meet Paul Fortescue together with some senior colleagues.

10.30 a.m., Mansion House, London

Paul Fortescue and his fellow directors, Amanda Rawlings and Tony Richards, are sitting across from me on a fat leather sofa. Paul flops back against the sofa, his hands welded behind his head.

'So, what do you say?'

Amanda smiles, winningly. 'Think about the board position, generous financial package and…'

'… bloody hot car,' rejoins Tony.

They sit chuckling at their own skilled sales pitch.

'This is the real deal. A six-figure salary, working for one of the world's most profitable PR businesses and running your own show.'

'It's a very generous and tempting offer.' I say.

Paul laughs. 'We like to think so.'

'But something's troubling you,' says Amanda with concern.

I feel like a contestant on some grim talent show being offered the top prize yet knowing there's an ominous catch.

'It's the idea of being tied in to a long-term contract that puts me off.'

Tony nods reassuringly. 'Of course, it's normal to feel that way – but just think. It's only three years.

I see Mammon reaching out to me. A box of treasure, trinkets, a pile of cash, a car, maybe even a cuddly toy, but no. It's. Just. Not. Right.

I gather up the papers and pop them in my briefcase. 'It's been a great meeting and I hugely appreciate the offer,' I say. 'Let me sleep on it and I'll come back to you tomorrow.'

Paul gets to his feet. 'No rush. Take your time. Some deals are just too good to believe!'

More self-congratulatory laughter. We stand smiling beatifically at one another until I take the initiative and head for the door.

Before I disappear back to the Mowgli jungle foyer, Paul grips my arm.

'Word to the wise – these opportunities don't come often. We're going through expansion in the States and there's a lot of dosh swilling around.'

The lift gives a little shudder and a few moments later I'm back on the street, contemplating the vagaries of life.

1 p.m., sandwich bar, Mayfair
Rachel is chomping away on a plate of salad while occasionally glancing at her notes.

'I hate diets but if I don't start a regime now I'll never get near a bikini this summer.'

I finish my large bowl of soup and graze on a bread roll. 'Well, I'd rather exercise and eat pretty much what I like. I can't be bothered with diets.'

'So I can see,' she laughs. 'Anyway, you're lucky because they like the fuller figure in Spain. So I've heard.'

'It's true. Most Spanish machos don't go for stick insects.'

'I was talking to Liu at China Dreams yesterday and he's going to give me a super-slimming Chinese diet.'

'How come? I've never met an overweight Chinese person,' I protest.

'Exactly, so it shows it must work!' she chirrups.

Rachel pushes her plate away and dabs her lips with a paper napkin. 'It looks like everything's under control for the big event at Frithington Manor on the first of April.' 'What about Dannie and Greedy George?'

'Oh they're driving down on Saturday morning and will stay over that night.'

'Who are these actors you're bringing along?'

She grins. 'It's going to be quite a laugh. I've got a woman dressing as a Victorian lady in a scarlet shift and wild hair, and we've got some great costumes for the others. I've got them from a local agency.'

'Sounds like fun. I'm glad Ollie's coming with me. He's really looking forward to the visit and seems keen to run in to a spook.'

She looks at her watch. 'We'd better get going. Hey, how did the meeting go with RTB?'

I stiffen. 'OK, but I'm still not convinced. They're throwing a lot of money at the deal but I'd be tied in for three years.'

She cups her face with her hands. 'Is that really so bad?'

'I'd have to commute every week for another three years. Could you do that?'

She gives a sigh. 'Yes, I probably could but that's because I haven't got a family and am at a different stage in my life. It's a tough call.'

She rises to her feet. 'Anyway, we'd better get going. Remember we've got our date with Bruno later.'

'I can't wait,' I say with a wink. 'So, where are we going to meet our drag hatter friend?'

'It's a club called Drag Haven, off Wardour Street. Let's meet outside at 7 p.m.'

I pull on my jacket, acknowledging that it's still raining outside. 'How do you put up with this weather?'

Rachel shrugs. 'You forget it after a while. Are you off to see Alicia Romstead now?'

I feel rather disingenuous. I am indeed off to visit Alicia but not for the reason I offer to Rachel. 'Yes, she wants to show me some of Charlie's new works. Apparently, I can't meet him because he's locked in the basement again.'

Rachel giggles. 'He has a tough life but she's a formidable promoter. I mean, think how many paintings they shifted at the Chink of Light exhibition.'

'True. That's what I rather like about her. She's a no-nonsense woman.'

We stand on the pavement in the driving rain, battling to keep our umbrellas up.

'I hope you have a productive meeting,' she bawls above the wind.

'I've a funny feeling we will,' I say with a wry smile.

4 p.m., Fitzroy Square

Alicia Romstead is pacing around the drawing room, sipping at her Assam tea.

'So, let me get this straight. Your client George Myers is trying to set up a range of rare donkey hide products from China?'

'As I said on the email, it's a special black breed of donkey.'

She sets her fine porcelain cup back down on the table and flicks back her lustrous blonde hair. 'I have done a little homework on this. As you know, donkeys are a domestic breed and are therefore not an endangered species. But having said that, DDT, the Donkey Defence Trust, with whom I work, won't tolerate cruelty or abuse of donkeys.'

'So what do you suggest?'

She gives me a sardonic smile. 'Oh, we have ways and means. For example, it would be simple to set up a few protesters to heckle outside the store.'

I shake my head. 'I don't want the business to suffer. Maybe a stern letter from the chairman of your donkey trust would suffice?'

She nods. 'That's easy enough.'

'Great. All I want is for him to get bored by the whole idea.'

She rises to her feet. 'I'm happy to be of help. Now, shall we take a peek at some of Charlie's new work? It's all in the attic studio.'

'Sure. What's the new concept he's working on?'

She raises her hands in the air. 'He just creates a whole lot of abstract stuff and waits for me to give it a label. I usually pluck a title from the air that sounds fairly ridiculous, knowing that the moneyed art crowd will lap it up.'

'What about "Title From the Air"? That sounds faintly silly.'

'Yes, they'd like that. I'll add it to the list.'

'Is Charlie joining us?'

She looks indignant. 'Certainly not! He's not leaving the basement until he's finished another canvas.'

'You're a bit of a taskmaster,' I say.

'Yes, but we're a good team. He paints, I sell and the school fees get paid.'

'Isn't that a bit cynical? Where's the creative nerve, the suffering for one's art?'

She gives a little grunt. 'When Charlie produced his best, non-commercial work he got nowhere and we were practically out on the street. That's not funny when you have kids.'

She softens slightly. 'Sometimes I feel sad that he's churning out stuff that is meaningless to him but needs must.'

As we cross the kitchen, I notice children's drawings stuck on the fridge and on the walls and feel a tinge of pity for Charlie. The bittersweet meaning of suffering for one's art must forever haunt him.

8 p.m., Drag Haven, Soho

The applause is thunderous. Kitted head to toe in gold glitter and silver sequins, Miss Taken, otherwise known as Bruno, the Mad Hatter's window dresser, is an obvious hit with the crowd. Rachel and I have been awarded VIP status and are seated at a lacquered wooden table close to the elevated stage. It amazes me that this ostensibly modest venue down in a dubious basement in Soho is so capacious. Aside from the ample stage, an unashamedly kitsch bar decked out in black and white zebra print runs the length of one side of the room and high above a myriad of tiny strobe lights glare down from a midnight blue ceiling. Most of the guests are wearing outrageous outfits and so I feel relieved that Rachel insisted I at least don black evening gear and some heels. A drag hostess with the name badge 'Diana Desesperada' approaches us with a second glass of champagne. She is breathtakingly tall and slim and wears a minute Lycra red miniskirt and plunging black top. The platinum hair is wild and long and her dark eyes are framed by the most extraordinary silver- and purple-tipped eyelashes.

'Compliments of Miss Taken,' she says with a strong Liverpudlian accent. 'She'd like you to join her backstage after the show.'

'Great,' shouts Rachel above the din.

The hostess bends to whisper in my ear. 'Is that hair natural?'

I'm not sure whether to take this as a compliment or not. 'I'm afraid so.'

She gives me a flash of the spangly lashes. 'You're lucky. I'd love some curls.'

I watch as she saunters off on red, towering, wedged heels.

'You'd be at home here,' I say to Rachel.

'I beg your pardon!' she yells.

'I mean because of the heels. They're all giraffes like you.'

She pokes my arm. 'Maybe I should consider a career change?'

We chink glasses. Despite my initial reservations, I'm enjoying the show. We've had an impersonation of Lara Croft, two group dance routines, a skit based on Posh and Becks with both drag artists dressed as their lookalikes and now Bruno, king of the show, is performing a string of West End musical hits.

'He's got a good voice,' I comment.

Rachel sniggers. 'It's not him singing. He's lip-synching.'

'That sounds rather rude.'

She takes a gulp of champagne. 'You know, it's like miming.'

'Ah,' I say with some disappointment.

The show carries on and I am suddenly acutely aware of someone watching me from the bar. I turn my head and to my shock see Serge de Camp, Manuel Ramirez's chef from H Hotel Soho, sipping on a glass of champagne and observing me with similar surprise. I decide to raise my glass, which he reciprocates. A few seconds later he quits his stool and heads towards us. I give Rachel a warning kick.

'Well, Serge, what a surprise!' I simper.

He gives a nervous tinkly laugh. 'For me too! Do you come here often?'

Rachel sniggers. 'We're guests of Bruno. He works for one of our clients.'

He gives a broad smile. 'But that is why I am here too. Bruno is an old friend from Paris. I come here after work for a little drink and entertainment sometimes.'

We intimate for him to join us.

'I was just talking with Manuel Ramirez the other day,' I say carefully. 'Perhaps we could have an off-the-record chat sometime about things at the hotel?'

He nods vigorously. 'I would welcome that. Manuel is at times a very uncompromising man and also very macho.'

'He's Panamanian, what do you expect?' says Rachel with a chuckle.

'I suppose,' he shrugs, 'But I am finding it hard to work with him.'

He drains his glass and gets to his feet. 'I must get back to the hotel now. Ring me.'

He leans down and pecks us both on the cheeks and makes his way to the exit.

'The night gets curiouser and curiouser,' I say.

'It most certainly does,' replies Rachel. 'Do you think he's a cross dresser too?'

'Perhaps, but the important thing is that we may well have killed two birds with one stone. I had been wondering how to approach him about Manuel's concerns.'

'The stars were right. We were meant to come tonight,' says Rachel inanely.

After a wild dance routine performed by a flurry of drag artists dressed as swans, the show is over. Our hostess returns.

'Miss Taken is expecting you backstage. Please follow me.'

We scurry behind the long legs and find ourselves peering through vermillion drapes at a barren area beyond the stage. We follow her up a narrow flight of stairs and there in a cramped dressing room, surrounded by mirrors is, we assume, Bruno. He is dabbing his heavily made-up face with baby lotion and peering into an under-lit mirror. He jumps up to greet us.

'I won't kiss you, girls, with all this mess on me. Did you enjoy the show?'

'It was fantastic,' I say without irony.

'That's a relief. Well, let me get this clobber off and we can go and have a drink and a fag.'

Rachel politely walks towards the exit. 'We'll wait in the corridor.'

He laughs. 'Don't be silly! Just take a pew and avert your eyes. I won't be long.'

He swings the ornate gold and brown wig onto the dressing table and begins sponging down his face.

'You know, I loved your idea for a drag hatter show at The Dorchester. All the girls are so excited!'

I grin and give Rachel a prod with my arm.

'Really?' she says limply.

'I've got some amazing ideas we can incorporate into it,' he continues.

Rachel passes me an inscrutable look. 'Well, let's have a brief chat about them now over a drink.'

Bruno is on his feet. 'All done. Come on girls, let's get planning.'

Saturday 1 April, 8 a.m., Starbucks, Oxford Street

My ever-anxious friend Ed is nursing a large cappuccino in his hands and shaking his head.

'Sorry to bang on about this but I don't think holding a ghost fun day at Frithington Manor is wise. You may unleash dangerous spirits that previously lay dormant at the house.'

I giggle and kick his leg under the table. He tuts crossly.

'Lighten up, Ed! Look, it's just a bit of fun. There are no ghosts at the manor. All we want to do is create a bit of a stir.'

He gives a little grunt. 'You might well do that but not in the way you'd expected.'

I drain my cup, secretly a little unsettled. 'Anyway, tell me how things are going with Irina.'

He picks forlornly at some residue crumbs on his plate and sighs deeply. 'I feel it's not to be. Irina has a vile temper and seems to want to shop constantly. The other night she demanded that I show my devotion by buying her a Gucci handbag.'

'That's ridiculous!' I say.

'On a BBC salary it is,' he grumbles. 'Anyway, did you like my poem?'

I frown trying to recall its theme. 'Ah yes, it was very intriguing. Quite thought-provoking.'

He eyes me intently. 'I'm glad you thought so. And what about your poet, José?'

'He's a fascinating man, as I mentioned before. He's told me so much about the Spanish Civil War. Things I never would have known or believed possible.'

Before he can respond, the door swings open and Rachel comes striding towards us.

'Time up you two. We've got to go.'

We rise from our seats.

'You did say it was going to be a quick coffee,' says Ed dryly, giving Rachel a peck on the cheek.

'Yep, well I'd like us to arrive at the manor on time. I've got a taxi to take us to the station waiting outside.'

We walk out into the early morning crisp air.

'Remember what I said about waking the dead,' Ed warns. 'Sometimes it's better to let sleeping dogs lie.'

12 noon, Frithington Manor

Rachel and I stand in the middle of the expansive lawn that runs from the back of Frithington Manor, all the way down to a rather picturesque stream. Local media has arrived in force and, to our delight, also a rather handsome young steed from the *Daily Telegraph* who intends to write a full feature on the Claverton-Michaels' and their trials and tribulations in maintaining a stately home as a paying attraction for visitors. For the last half an hour people have been streaming through the front gates, noticeably excited at the prospect of attending an open day at a haunted house. Rachel eyes them keenly and fidgets with the walkie-talkie in her hand.

'I think we'll kick off the spook action once the punters start walking through the house. The actors are all in place.'

I laugh. 'You don't think anyone will be fooled, do you?'

'Are you kidding? Of course they will be.'

'OK, well let's just mill around and chat up visitors until the house is buzzing.'

She yawns. 'By the way, where's Ollie?'

'The gardener took him off to help clean out the horses. Hopefully he's having fun.'

'No doubt he'll be exchanging racing tips, if I know Ollie.'

We potter over to the front garden and courtyard and welcome the cheerful throng through the gates.

'Is the manor really haunted?' asks one excited elderly lady.

'So they say,' I reply. 'There was a grisly murder here during Victorian times and the ghost of the murdered mistress of the house is supposed to wander the grounds.'

'Ohhh! How creepy,' she says, with a shiver. 'I shan't go wandering off on my own, that's for sure.'

Rachel watches as she and her grandchildren quickly walk off towards the refreshments tent in a nearby field.

'Isn't this haunted house theme just a bit of fun to celebrate April Fools Day?' asks a ruddy-faced gentleman in a raincoat. His wife looks at me expectantly.

'I suppose that depends on how you define fun. All I know is that when I stayed here, some supernatural presence was at my bedroom door and the house was the scene of a horrible murder many years ago.'

'Oh, ugh!' the wife says. 'That sounds horrid.'

'It sure was.'

'Thanks for the warning,' her husband replies and off they head towards the house with a look of deep concern etched on their faces.

'Is that really true about the murder?' asks Rachel.

'I sincerely hope not. I just made it up on the spot to add a bit of atmosphere.'

'You fool!' she cries.

I look up at the bunches of balloons and brightly coloured bunting running along the stone walls of the house and think how much it cheers up the dull old facade. On the lawn there are all manner of stalls selling gift items, potted jam, home-made cakes and biscuits, and the guests are lapping it all up. A soothsayer has also been installed in a caravan to read people's fortunes. There's a sudden crackle from Rachel's walkie-talkie. It's time for action. Quickly we make our way into the house and mingle with the excited throng of guests. Rupert is standing halfway up the elegant mahogany staircase.

'Do enjoy your visit but be warned, the house is unpredictable and the spirits...,' he pauses for effect, '... are mischievous!'

There's a trickle of laughter from the assembled crowd but a few faces show unease. The guide beckons us all to follow him into the large library. There's a general hush as he begins recounting some historical anecdote. Suddenly there's a creak from one of the towering bookcases lining the walls and two shelf-loads of books tumble to the ground. A woman shrieks and people jump back. The guide affects surprise and hastily cuts short his words, ushering the group through to the kitchen and casting a few anxious glances backwards at the offending room. The kitchen is warm and cosy and the long oak table has been set up with an old tea set and teapot. The visitors wander around, keeping back from the cordoned-off areas.

'What a gorgeous tea set,' remarks an elderly lady.

'Yes, reminds me of Aunt Jessica's mum.' She bends forward and flies back in shock when a teaspoon flips in the air and whizzes across the room.

'Oh. My. God!' yells the woman, clasping her chest. 'What was that??'

There's a deathly hush as people exchange nervous looks. Rachel kicks me hard on the ankle, an evil smile playing on her lips. The ghostly plan is going like clockwork.

In the master bedroom there is mass hysteria when a wardrobe flies open and an emaciated white hand shoots out. Even on the stairs as we cross the landing there is the sound of pattering feet and yet no ghostly form is in evidence. But the *pièce de résistance* is in the grand ballroom. As we gather at the end of the room, which is gloomy and half-lit due to the heavy curtains covering the enormous windows, a narrow, hidden door pings open from the far end and a ghostly woman in Victorian garb emerges soundlessly and glides across the room to the other side and seemingly disappears through a wall. In the panic that follows, several visitors make for the stairs.

'Ooh, I've had quite enough!' shivers one middle-aged woman. 'I never believed in ghosts until today. This place is cursed.'

There's a low murmur as people huddle closer, peering around them as if terrified to move.

At the end of a harrowing hour, the guests tumble out into the sun, relief etched on their pale faces. I approach one of the ashen women.

'That was scary, wasn't it?' I say.

'Terrifying. Absolutely fantastic!'

'You honestly enjoyed it?' says Rachel, feigning horror in her voice.

'Are you kidding? I'd do it all again tomorrow!'

I catch Rachel's expression. She's like a cat that's got the cream.

6 p.m., the drawing room

Clarissa and Rupert are sitting by the fire knocking back strong G&Ts. Animatedly, they chatter away like long-lost friends with Dannie and George. I watch as Dannie swivels her cocktail stick, loaded with three fat green olives, in her glass of iced vodka.

'Oh, it sounds like a magical day!' she gushes. 'I mean did the actors genuinely frighten the visitors?'

Clarissa is chuckling into her drink. 'Yes indeed. When one of the wardrobes upstairs creaked wide open, apparently there was a stampede down the main staircase. Then one of the actors let out a chilling howl from the attic and began stamping heavily across the floorboards, which caused major hysteria. They all frightened themselves silly!'

'The ghost in the ballroom was the cracker,' I say. 'You should have seen the expressions of utter terror.'

'Wish I'd been there,' puffs George. 'Had to deal with a few urgent matters back at the shop unfortunately or we would have got here sooner.'

Rachel strides into the room in a dazzling red evening dress and teetering heels.

'You look fab!' cries George. 'We hear your little stunt was a great success.'

'Well, I think it's put the manor on the map. The press loved it.'

'Were they in on the joke?' asks George.

'Not really. We kept them guessing. When the local radio chap saw a spoon clatter across the floor in the kitchen with no evidence of human intervention, he went a bit pale,' giggles Rachel. 'It's the best April Fool's spoof I've ever known.'

I take a sip of champagne and, rising to my feet, peer out at the darkening sky. 'I'd better get Ollie to come in now. He's been devoted to your gardener all day.'

Rupert nods enthusiastically. 'Yes, I noticed they were getting on famously. Old Adams the gardener tells me your son is a great coin collector so I must look out for some of my old pennies for him. I might even have the odd antique coin.'

'Steady on,' cries George. 'Don't spoil the lad. He's a sharp little bugger. He'll have half your silver while he's at it.'

Rupert erupts with laughter. 'Good for him. I like to see a bit of initiative and drive.'

Excusing myself, I step out into the stone corridor and pull open the heavy front door. It groans as I heave it against the internal wall with a dull thud. A sharp wind blows and a streak of crimson light scores the slate sky. Pulling my shawl up around my shoulders, I walk along the gravel path and head for the lawn at the rear of the house. Beyond it lies a small clump of dark trees and the paddock where I am relieved to see a soft amber glow escaping under the door of one of the outhouses. Silhouetted against the sky I can just about distinguish the forms of three docile horses grazing in the field. The grass ripples in the breeze as I head quickly across the lawn towards the light and a plaintive bird lets out a wild cry in the encroaching dusk. Just as I reach the paddock's gate, my eye catches some movement near the rear of the mansion. I turn around quickly and see a young woman in Victorian garb with a large-brimmed hat and veil walking purposefully up the back steps of the terrace towards the French doors. She appears to be carrying a parasol of some kind. I observe her for a few moments and then, as quickly as she appeared, she is gone. I unlatch the gate, wondering why this young actress hasn't already returned to the nearby town with her colleagues. She must be freezing, wandering around in such flimsy gear at this hour. As I approach the outhouse, the door swings open and Adams, the gardener, appears.

'Hello there, I suppose you wonder what we've been up to all day. I was just going to escort your young man back to the house.'

Ollie, rosy cheeked and grinning from ear to ear, is perched on a rug by a small electric fire, drinking what appears to be cocoa.

'Do I have to go?' he wails.

'I'm afraid so. It's getting dark and George and Dannie are dying to see you.'

He rolls his eyes. 'I'm sure. Not.'

The gardener laughs. 'I taught him to ride bareback today – tell your mother what you did.'

Ollie weighs his words carefully. 'Don't have a fit but I stood on top of a horse.'

I try not to express shock. 'You stood on top of a horse unaided?'

The old man chuckles. 'My dad taught me that trick when I was about his age. You've got to gain the horse's trust or you fall off in a jiffy.'

'We built a trench by the river as well.'

'Excellent,' I say a tad nervously.

'Then we went for a little shoot,' smiles Adams.

'A shoot?' I gasp.

'Only rabbits,' says Adams. 'Didn't catch any of the little devils.'

Ollie sighs. 'I wouldn't have been happy if we had. I love rabbits.'

'You've got to be less soppy about animals, my lad, or you'll never be a true countryman.'

Ollie drains his cup and jumps off his seat. 'I'll think about it. Thank you for a fab day.'

'My pleasure,' says Adams. 'Come and stay again any time.'

Ollie and I set off in the cold wind.

'I just saw one of the actresses running into the house. I thought they'd all left earlier.'

He turns to me with a yawn. 'Maybe she got lost. It's a big house.'

I frown. 'Very odd, all the same.'

The drawing room is wonderfully warm when we enter. Ollie receives a bear hug from George, while Fenton strides around the room refilling glasses. He hands me a flute of champagne.

Dannie gives Ollie a peck on both cheeks. 'How handsome you are, Ollie! You could star in a movie.'

'Maybe one about vampires,' giggles George.

'Did that actress find her way in by the back door?' I ask Fenton.

He eyes me in some puzzlement. 'Actress, ma'am?'

'Yes, I just saw a young woman in what looked like Victorian costume and carrying something, running up the back steps of the house.'

He studies the floor. 'I fear you are mistaken. All the actors and models left some hours ago.'

I watch as he studies his white gloves for a moment and then turns to me. 'You say she was in white Victorian wear and carrying a parasol?'

Never having mentioned the parasol or the colour of her clothes, I now feel sure that I am not alone in having set eyes on this vision. 'So, Fenton, have you seen her too?'

He gives a terse laugh. 'Absolutely not, ma'am.'

George bursts into hysterical laughter. 'Maybe you're just going barmy, guv?!'

Rachel stares at me and, with a controlled edge to her voice, asks what the woman was wearing. I describe her as best I can.

'How odd,' she says faintly. 'It doesn't match any of the costumes of the actors I hired.'

Fenton gives me a sharp look. 'Sometimes, ma'am, it's best not to dwell on such things.'

The Claverton-Michaels' don't appear remotely concerned.

'Must have been one of the staff playing a prank, although why they should choose to do it now when the press have all left, heaven knows,' says Rupert, rising to his feet. 'We'll go and see what they're up to.'

'Yes, if you'll excuse us, we'll go and check on developments in the kitchen.'

When they've gone, Dannie turns to George with an impish smile. 'Perhaps we've hit supernatural gold, George.'

He slaps down his glass. 'I don't believe in any of that ghost rubbish. Guv was probably hallucinating. She's got a highly developed imagination, haven't you?'

'I need it to cope with you.'

Dannie turns to Ollie. 'Don't worry about all this silly ghost talk. Now tell us about your school in Mallorca.'

He groans. 'Do I have to?' I'd rather talk about cars.'

'So what's your favourite?' asks George.

'A Lamborghini Murciélago with a personalised number plate'.

George sucks his teeth. 'Risky. You should never have anything with your initials. My old man taught me that it's the quickest way the Old Bill can arrest you.'

Ollie frowns. 'Why would the police be after me?'

He taps Ollie's head. 'You never know. We live in a police state. Best to be prepared. Anyway, tell us about your school.'

'It's called Llaüt.'

'Lout? What kind of name is that?'

'It means "fishing boat" in Catalan. Why, what was yours called?' says Ollie defensively

'Borstal.'

Ollie frowns. 'Odd name. Was it a private boarding school?'

'Of a kind, Ollie. A very strict place in Kent.'

I regard George with some impatience. 'I wish you wouldn't talk such nonsense. He'll believe you.'

'But it's all true,' he protests. 'Best education for a boy.'

The butler returns with a sanctimonious smile.

'If you would all like to adjourn to the dining room, dinner is served.'

Sunday 3 p.m., Frithington Manor

We stand on the front step saying our goodbyes.

'Thanks for a thoroughly relaxing weekend,' shouts George, full of bonhomie. 'Shame we didn't see any ghosts, but I didn't have high hopes.'

Dannie gives an ingratiating smile. 'Yes, it was a complete delight for me to stay in such a beautiful English historical house. And your staff were so charming and helpful.'

'It was our pleasure,' beams Rupert, hobbling down the front steps to where the butler has stationed himself by the cars.

'You must all come again,' trills Clarissa.

Rachel gives me a nudge and we share complicit smiles.

Rupert taps Ollie on the shoulder. 'Oh before I forget, young man, here's a little bag of old coins for you.'

Ollie gives a whoop for joy. 'Wow! Thanks a lot.'

'My pleasure,' beams Rupert. 'Come and see us again and I'll find you a few more.'

The luggage is stowed in the boots of the two cars. Rachel, Ollie and I watch as George jumps into the driving seat of his high-spec Range Rover with Dannie wrapped in a cashmere throw beside him. They wave as they head off slowly along the drive. Rupert's chauffeur is driving us to London in the Daimler, a treat that we couldn't possibly refuse. He pops his head through the open car window.

'By the way, none of the staff knew anything about that woman you saw on the lawn the other night.'

'Yes, bizarre,' says Clarissa breezily. 'Perhaps it really was a ghost.'

Rupert and Clarissa laugh cheerfully as they wave us off, I turn and smile. The tall, erect figure of Fenton stands behind them, his black-suited frame forming a dark stain on the soft grey sky. As our eyes meet, he lifts his right finger to his nose and gives it the subtlest of taps. I give him a cursory nod and turn back in my seat relieved that Rachel and Ollie are chattering away, oblivious to the exchange. I contemplate my woman in white, certain that Fenton and perhaps other members of the staff have been party to the strange goings-on at the house. All I can hope for is that one of these days Fenton will finally spill the beans. Until then, it must remain his and my little secret because I'm pretty certain that what I saw is exactly what the butler saw too.

ELEVEN

PLUM IN THE MIDDLE

For three whole days a single queue like a giant, writhing basilisk has practically gobbled up Calle sa Lluna. Three or four people deep, it curls its way around the sharp curves and bends in the long cobbled street, reaching almost as far as my favourite deli, Colmado sa Lluna. The air is soft and warm as Ollie and I wend our way across Sóller's leafy *plaça* in the hope of finally gaining entry to this newest of attractions in town, Can Prunera, the house of the plum tree. It would be hard to imagine a more dedicated, excited and loyal response from Sóllerics to any event unfolding in the town's centre. I doubt if Madonna offered an exclusive appearance at Sóller's town hall she would be able to rival the wild enthusiasm generated by the opening of this modern art museum.

As we set off up Calle sa Lluna, I voice my thoughts to Ollie. He gives an impatient sigh.

'It's nothing to do with loyalty, mother. If you visit Can Prunera during the first three days, entry is free. Mallorcans like a good deal, simple as that.'

I'm disappointed that he should be turning into such a little cynic.

'Well, I shall ask people in the queue their opinion on the matter just to prove you wrong.'

He doesn't bother to reply and instead mutters *'Mother, mother, mother!'* pityingly under his breath. We never reach the facade of Can Prunera, which lies a good three-quarters of the way along the street, because the queue is already stretching towards us like an impatient wave. We look at each other resignedly.

'Perhaps we'd better forget about visiting it until the excitement's died down,' says Ollie matter-of-factly. 'I mean, it's just an old house with a few paintings. What's so brilliant about that anyway?'

I remonstrate. 'The brilliant thing about Can Prunera is that it's a beautifully restored example of what a wealthy merchant's house would have been like at the turn of the last century.'

'Fascinating,' he yawns.

'It also happens to be stuffed full of modernist paintings and sculptures. You might learn something.'

'Goody. Just what I need on a Saturday morning.'

I walk past the end of the queue, a noisy, throbbing mass of humanity. Babies wail from prams, toddlers run in the street and all the while their good-natured mothers chat away happily, unfazed by the long wait. Searching the faces, I suddenly see two of the mothers whose children attend my weekly English class. We exchange hugs.

'Do you want to join us?' they ask, kindly ushering us towards their pitch in the queue.

I shake my head. 'That wouldn't be fair, but thank you. Have you been here long?'

'About forty minutes,' chirrups one of the mothers.

'I don't think I've got the patience,' I admit.

They look disapproving. 'But it's free! If you don't get in today, you'll have to pay an entrance fee.'

Ollie nudges my arm and gives me a smug little smile. Wishing them luck, we set off back along the street.

I glance at Ollie.

'OK, you've made your point. Let's live wildly and visit as paying customers in the next few days. In the meantime there's nothing for it but to have a cup of coffee.'

'Chocolate cake and Bitter Kas?'

'If you must.'

I still find it odd that Ollie combines sweet cake with Bitter Kas, a violently hued red fizzy brew reminiscent of Campari but without the alcohol. As we approach Café Paris, I'm surprised to see Jorge, the postman, languishing by the doorway. He gives us a dazzling smile. 'Given up on the queue?'

'How did you guess?'

He laughs. 'Everyone's in town to visit the museum so I guessed you must be too. Beatriz is still queuing but I got bored and came here for a beer. I'm on my way back.'

'Before you go, can we agree a time for you to pop by for a drink? The wedding's not far off.'

He slaps his chest in a gesture of mock anguish. 'Don't remind me! We've still got so much to organise and Beatriz's mother is driving me mad.'

'That's what mothers do,' grunts Ollie.

Jorge laughs. 'Too right, *chico*!'

'It'll be fine on the day,' I say cheerfully.

He grimaces. 'I hope so. My whole family is flying over from Buenos Aires. Can you imagine? It'll be a riot.'

'I look forward to meeting them all. Is your brother the footballer coming?'

'Of course. He wouldn't miss it.'

Ollie is intrigued. 'Is he a good footballer then?'

He shrugs. 'He plays for my country so I imagine so.'

'Cool,' enthuses my son. 'Will he give me his autograph?'

'He's a footballer so I'm not sure he knows how to write.'

Ollie opens his mouth in some surprise. 'Are you being funny?'

Jorge laughs. 'It's a joke in my family. We like to pull his leg about only knowing how to kick a ball. The truth is he has a university degree and is cleverer than all of us put together!'

He rubs his hands together, gives us both a hug and ambles off.

Ollie watches him go. 'Imagine having a footballer in the family? Wouldn't that be amazing?'

'Yes, because they earn more than most and you could care for your poor father and me in our dotage.'

'Huh! Dream on.'

We walk into Café Paris' warm interior. José is cleaning glasses behind the bar and manages to yell a *'Hola!'* in our direction above the hissing sound of the coffee machine. As usual, he prepares our order without a word being exchanged. Ollie takes a seat near the bar.

'Just think we could be out there now queuing instead of having a nice relaxing time as we are, at Café Paris. I know which I prefer.'

I sit back in my chair and have to admit that as usual he's made a very good point.

Neus is standing in the front garden, bossily telling the Scotsman how to tend his *cirerers*, his beloved sapling cherry trees. He listens patiently, occasionally trying to interrupt with some of his own horticultural musings but she's none too interested. It is when he makes the foolish mistake of mentioning the purchase of a *figuera*, a fig tree, that Neus clutches her head in horror.

'*Madre de dios*! Where have you planted it? Have you any idea how strong the roots of a fig tree are?'

'Yes, Neus, but the point is…'

'The point is that the roots will tear through the soil in search of moisture, ruin your *cisterna* and, God forbid, even break through your garden walls!'

A fig tree with the strength of the Incredible Hulk, I just have to see. She calls to me.

'Don't let him ruin your walls!'

I try to hide my mirth as I unpack the shopping bags from the boot of the car.

'I'll keep an eye on him, don't worry, Neus.'

Alan sighs. 'What I was going to say is that I've planted the tree in the field, away from anything else.'

She digests this news with some disappointment. 'Ah, that's not so bad then. What about your *pruneras*?'

He is pensive, perhaps wondering if this is some kind of trick question. 'The plum trees? I've planted the new ones on the edge of the field and our lovely old war horse, the ancient plum tree we inherited that yields so much fruit, is situated in the middle of the orchard.'

She claps her hands together. '*Molt bé.* That's OK. You are learning.'

Alan bites his lip.

'You know a funny thing about oranges?' she says with a sly grin.

'Surprise me?' he mutters.

'Strange though it sounds, if you don't water them very much the oranges actually get sweeter.'

He looks confused. 'But surely that can't be good for the tree?'

'Not particularly, but it's a fact.'

Neus crosses the front porch and, shielding her eyes, peers down into the field.

'What are those flowers?'

'Ah, Neus, they are my prized cardoons, and over the other side you'll see the flowering plumbago.'

'They look fairly healthy. Now what sort of fertiliser are you using?'

'I have the magical soil from my wormery. Nothing can beat it.'

'Yes, but my own compost is fantastic too. You should see my artichokes!'

I listen to this horticultural exchange of one-upmanship with growing amusement. It's rare for the Scotsman to be trumped by anyone when it comes to gardening matters but Neus was brought up on a small farm and has an impressive knowledge of trees, plants and harvesting matters. A complete novice, I can only stand back and marvel at her and the Scotsman's knowledge.

I decide a truce must be drawn. 'Anyone for a coffee?'

'That would be very nice,' says Neus, walking slowly behind me. I notice she winces when her right foot touches the floor.

'Is that leg bothering you?'

She flicks a hand at me. 'Oh it's just my hip. There's nothing that can be done. Doctor Bisbal offered some pills but told me it was better to try to do without them and exercise more.'

'Good advice but if the pain becomes too much you must let him know.'

She nods and, following me into the house, sits down at the kitchen table.

'Anyway, Alan told me you were visiting Can Prunera today. What did you think of it?'

Ollie wanders into the kitchen. 'The queue was too long so we gave up.'

'You know us Mallorcans. When something's free, we're there like a shot!'

'Fancy that?' Ollie says with a pointed look in my direction. 'I think my father's got a lot in common with the Mallorcans.'

Neus gives him a pat on the arm. 'They do say that the Scottish are frugal. Is that true?'

'Mean, Neus,' says Ollie with a grin. 'Trying to get pocket money out of my father is almost impossible.'

Neus slaps her knee. 'That's funny! Well, let's hope your father's saving his money for your future.'

Ollie raises an eyebrow and turns to face her. 'I'm not sure about that. Anyway, Neus, what do you think of Can Prunera?'

She takes the coffee from me. 'It's special because it was built by a very rich Sólleric in 1911 who made his money abroad and came back to the town wanting to create the most beautiful house he thought money could buy.'

'So is it the most beautiful house in Sóller?' Ollie asks.

'Not in my opinion. The thing is that lots of Sóllerics came back home to retire having spent years away in France and even the Americas, making a good living. They all built themselves huge houses. It was a sort of game to show who had better taste, or rather more money.'

I cut Neus a piece of plum bakewell tart.

'My favourite,' she beams. 'You must show me how to make this one day.'

'Of course. It's a bit fiddly though.'

She takes a bite and closes her eyes. Ollie giggles.

'How can you like it? I'd rather have chocolate cake any day.'

Neus shakes her head. 'No, this is much tastier. Now, where was I? Ah, yes, now these fancy houses that you see in Sóller had a lot of French touches because the rich Sóllerics were all influenced by the art nouveau workmanship in France at that time. It was all a bit fussy, to be honest.'

I wipe my mouth on a paper napkin. 'I'm looking forward to seeing the art. Apparently they have more than a hundred artists' works displayed.'

Neus licks her fingers. 'I don't know about that, but the house is worth seeing at any rate. You'll notice that it's very ornate, just like San Bartomé church and the Bank of Sóller in the *plaça*.'

'They're very Gaudi-esque,' I say.

'*Segur*, it was the style at that time. A bright young disciple of Gaudi called Joan Rubiól designed the facade of the church. It was a period of big change for our town especially after such bad times.'

'What bad times? You mean all the pirate attacks?' asks Ollie.

Neus giggles. 'You're thinking of Moorish attacks far back in our history. No, I'm talking about the economic crisis in the nineteen hundreds. We lost all the *moreras*, which put an end to the silk trade.'

Alan enters the kitchen and nods. 'Ah yes, the mulberry trees. It's odd to think that there used to be a silk trade here.'

'More than that,' says Neus animatedly. 'We had the finest cotton textiles, with thriving factories in Sóller.'

'It's hard to imagine,' I say.

'Well, competition from overseas ended the cotton industry. We still have a few places in Pollença and elsewhere making the traditional *roba de llenguas*, the coloured fabric that has a sort of water-stain pattern, but not many. It was a sad day in Sóller's history.'

'But everyone grew oranges anyway so they probably didn't need money,' argues Ollie.

'Pah! The oranges were a dead loss when they were hit by a terrible plague. As if that wasn't bad enough, phylloxera, a sort of plant bug, killed off the vines.'

'What about the loss of the Spanish colonies, wasn't that another blow?' asks Alan.

Neus rubs her cheeks with her hands. '*Si*, it was a disastrous period. We lost Cuba and the Philippines in the late nineteenth century and that put an end to shipbuilding here. Is it surprising that everyone wanted to emigrate?'

'Why didn't your family emigrate?' asks Ollie.

'Oh they did! My uncle was more French than Sólleric by the end. He and his wife lived in Marseilles and had a successful fruit business. My father never had the courage to leave Sóller. If he had, we'd have been a lot wealthier by now.'

'Are Sóllerics still emigrating to France?' asks Ollie.

'Good lord, no! That all stopped years ago. No one wants our oranges any more because so many other countries produce them more cheaply. It's hard to even give them away now.'

Ollie excuses himself and slinks off to his bedroom with Inko at his heels.

Neus sighs. 'You know, I don't have any regrets. Riches aren't everything in this life. I've got my health and good friends so I should thank God every day.'

I give her a smile. 'Talking of good friends, how is your chum, Bernat?'

She is very coy. 'Oh, he's fine. We're off to dinner tonight.'

'Where's he taking you?'

'Sa Teulera. They do the best grilled meat.'

'They certainly do. It's great that you're seeing so much of each other.'

'Not that much! Don't exaggerate. We're just old friends.'

She taps the table and with tremendous effort gets to her feet.

'I've got to get home to feed El Gordo. I've neglected the poor dog of late.'

Similarly to many Sóllerics, Neus, has a quivering *ca rater*, the fine-boned, little black and brown Mallorcan dog that has such spindly limbs that I often worry that they might snap at any given moment. Why Neus calls hers 'the fat one' is beyond me. It may of course be a reference to *El Gordo lotería*, the famous Spanish lottery which is seen as the luckiest thing that can befall anyone, but I've never broached the subject with her. El Gordo certainly is a 'lucky' little dog having survived being run over three times albeit that he now walks with a slight limp.

I take her arm and together we make our way to the front door while Alan walks a few steps behind. Neus suddenly stops and gives him a prod with her stick.

'That's what I like to see. A man walking several paces behind.'

The Scotsman gives a frustrated little cough, but magnanimously bends forward to give her a peck on the cheek. Before she heads off, she waggles her stick at him. 'Take care of that *prunera* tree. You know they have magical powers.'

We watch as she disappears along the track.

'She's a feisty old bird,' he sighs. 'She always gives me such a hard time.'

'It's only because she's fond of you.'

'Then I dread to think how she'd behave if she didn't like me.'

I slap him on the back. 'Let's hope you never have to find out!'

Rachel catches me on the mobile as I wave goodbye to Jorge and his lovely fiancée, Beatriz. I watch as they make their way to the gate, feeling happy that he has evidently made such a good choice. She is slim and pretty with long lustrous hair, doe eyes and the most wonderful sense of humour and *joie de vivre*. Rachel's voice is calling my name.

'How are things?' she chirrups.

'All fine. We've just had my postman and his girlfriend round for drinks.'

'How hilarious! Imagine that happening in London?'

She's right. I can't recall ever having met my postman in London and besides I'm not even sure that they had one regular person doing the rounds.

'You do realise that it's 8 p.m. over here?' I say.

'I know, but since I'm still at the office I thought I'd make you suffer too.'

'Go home. You shouldn't be working so late.'

'Fat chance of that. Two things you should know about. Greedy George received a letter from some donkey trust demanding that he reconsider the use of Chinese donkey hide for his new product range. He was mystified as to how they'd got hold of the information.'

'That is very strange,' I say disingenuously. 'Still, now he'll hopefully give up on the idea and that'll be the end of it.'

'It's not that simple. We had a bit of a crisis on our hands. George told me he sent them a letter back telling them to – in his words – "bog off", and two days later there was a group of demonstrators and press outside the Havana store.'

My heart misses a beat. What have I started? I had specifically told Alicia Romstead only to get her chairman to send a warning letter, not to stage a demonstration.

'When did this happen?'

'Two days ago. I didn't want to alarm you. Besides, I had the crisis under control.'

'What did you do?'

'I gave the press a statement from Havana, saying that George Myers would never support abuse of animals and had in all good faith believed the Chinese donkey not to be an endangered species. Actually, it isn't.'

'What happened?'

She laughs. 'Oh it was great. George came out with a sanctimonious statement saying that even though he was within his rights to produce a donkey hide range, he wouldn't as a mark of respect to the donkey trust and donkey kind.'

'I don't believe this.'

'It killed the story dead and Havana even got a nice little mention in the *Standard*, applauding his decision. He's already moving on to some specially treated deer hide.' 'He never gives up.'

'In fairness, he is a leather merchant. Anyway, you must be pleased?'

'I certainly am. It's extraordinary how fate plays its hand.'

'Hmm… sometimes with a little help,' she says wryly.

Perhaps she sniffs a rat. I change tactic.

'Anyway, what was the second thing you wanted to ask?'

'This is potentially good news. Now that you've turned down RTB, I've looked though one of Simon Rendall's other proposals for a merger and I think you'll like it.'

I feel guilty for putting a spanner in the works with RTB but knew instinctively it wasn't the right deal.

'Tell me about it.'

'It's called Dynamite Communications, a medium-sized lifestyle agency that wants to expand and liked the look of our client portfolio. The thing you'll like is that they'd only expect you to pop back and forth during the first year and then bow out.'

'Ah, that does interest me.'

'Thought so. Then I shall set up a meeting with them for you.'

'Goodoh.'

'Anyway, I must fly. I've got a proposal to finish and then I'm off out to dinner.'

'Your life's just one big social whirl.'

'Yeah right.'

I finish the call and return to the kitchen where the Scotsman is poring over the local newspaper.

'My Catalan's coming on, you know. I can just about understand this feature about Sa Fira I Es Firó fiesta.'

'I should hope so by now. It's more or less the same information every year.'

'You're wrong, actually. The main battle in the square is starting at a slightly revised time and they're altering the stage arrangements.'

'Oh, big changes then?'

He gives a chortle. 'I love the Moors and Christians battle.'

'They're calling it Peasants and Pirates now.'

'That's very worrying. Even Sóller has been hit by the PC brigade.'

This most famous of mock battles, carried out annually, commemorates the defeat in battle of a group of marauding

Moorish pirates by valiant Sóllerics on 11 May 1561. It's a noisy four-day affair but a fun event and beloved by the locals.

He gets up and pours himself a glass of red wine. 'Ollie's finally decided to go as a Christian having been a Moor for the last few years. He wanted a change.'

'I can't blame him and it means he doesn't have to wear boot polish on his face,' I reply.

'True. I'm glad it's not happening for a few days because I'll be exhausted after the shoot tomorrow.'

I'd forgotten about the Scotsman's acting debut as a butler.

'What time have you got to set off in the morning?'

'The taxi's picking me up at 5 a.m. and we could be filming all day.'

Despite endeavouring to sound blasé, I know that he is hugely excited about the whole venture. It's not every day that one gets to play Jeeves and get paid for your efforts.

'Gosh, that is a bit early. You'd better get an early night. Don't forget that we've got to have everything organised for Chris's visit.'

'The cattery man? When's he flying in?' Alan asks.

'Thursday night, so we'll have him over Friday morning to meet Stefan and view the land and he'll fly back later the same day.'

He looks weary. 'I thought we were moving to Mallorca for less stress!'

'Oh come on. It's not that bad. Once we've got everything sorted we can fix up a time to view the donkeys.'

He takes a big gulp of wine. 'Can we leave the donkeys for another day? Much as I like the sound of Jacinto, I was none too happy about your account of him inviting his Rosa to check out the *entrada*. Had I been here at the time I wouldn't have allowed him past the threshold.'

I giggle. 'All right, one thing at a time.'

Ollie enters the kitchen from the patio gasping and rushes over to Alan. 'You've got to rescue Orlando. He's got stuck in the plum tree in the field.'

'What?'

'He was being chased by Tiger and ran up the tree but he's stuck in the middle.'

Alan rests his head on the table for a moment, then snaps his newspaper shut and somewhat desolately follows Ollie out into the garden for his cat rescue mission.

Chris is standing in the field with a large clipboard, taking notes. He occasionally looks up and explores the terrain with his eyes before scribbling away again. Stefan stands solemnly by with one of his workmen in tow.

'I think we can easily make the new concrete foundation to Chris's spec,' says Stefan confidently.

'What was that?' Chris enquires.

'Stefan was just saying that he thinks making the new cattery base won't be a problem.'

He smiles. 'Good. It's actually quite straightforward and hopefully it won't take too long now we've reduced the size of the building.'

'What sort of timescale are we looking at?' asks the Scotsman.

Stefan gives a shrug. 'We could probably start next week.'

Alan translates this to Chris, who raises his eyebrows. 'That's a bit fast for us. I'll need to make a firm order for the cattery components now I'm happy that the spec is right. I doubt we can ship everything out sooner than next month but that shouldn't stop Stefan getting on with the base.'

'That's fine by us,' I reply. 'We've got more than enough to do and Stefan can get started on securing the donkey area and building the new hen house first.'

'You're getting donkeys? That's fantastic. They're beautiful animals and I imagine this would be a perfectly tranquil setting for them.'

'Everyone seems to think so,' says Alan with heavy irony.

Stefan gets the gist of the comment and grins. 'You thought you were going to have a simple life here in the hills but you were wrong, Alan.'

Catalina, who has jogged down the steps from the back of the house to join us, catches her brother's arm. 'Don't feel sorry for him, Stefan. He wants a Hollywood career so what does he expect?'

Stefan winks at me. 'How did the shoot go?'

'It was very good, thank you. The ad will be shown on French TV next month.'

Catalina lets out a screech of laughter. 'We must have a fiesta and popcorn and invite all the neighbours round! Actually, you can serve us all drinks, Alan, since you're an accomplished butler.'

'Very amusing, Catalina,' mutters the Scotsman.

'I didn't know you were a famous actor,' says Chris with amusement.

'Oh yes,' says Catalina enjoying the moment. 'He charges all the locals for autographs now.'

He laughs. 'Well, I hope we get to see it on YouTube.'

Catalina pats Alan's arm. 'Come on, let me make you a coffee.'

I turn to Chris. 'Do you need to see anything else?'

He shakes his head. 'No, I'm done. I can get cracking with getting the components sorted as soon as I get back to the UK.'

'Good, well let's have a coffee in the kitchen and if you need to discuss anything else with Stefan, Catalina can translate.'

'Excellent.'

We make our way across the field to the stone steps. Chris turns to stare out over the mountains.

'It's so breathtakingly beautiful here. Those mountains really shimmer in the light.'

'We're very lucky to live here and the best part is that we know it.'

'What's that gorgeous tree there?' Chris asks, pointing into the middle of the field.

'It's my old plum tree,' says the Scotsman proudly. 'It's one of my favourites.'

'It looks quite extraordinary in the light. It's almost as if it has a golden halo around it.'

'Well,' says the Scotsman authoritatively. 'They do say plum trees are magical.'

'Is that so?' nods Chris as he follows Stefan across the patio.

Alan winks at me. I never thought the day would come when I'd find him borrowing one of Neus's horticultural myths. Whatever next?

Ollie and I reach the grand exterior of Can Prunera with its ornate wrought iron window grills, pine green shutters and expansive upper verandah. The stonework is ornate and the vast wooden doors elegant and lovingly carved. We peer through the large glass doors only to find the entrance deserted. No one is seated at the ticket desk and there isn't a soul queuing in the street.

'Whoa! Something's up,' says Ollie. 'Maybe it's closed to the public today? I'm beginning to think we should just give up on the whole idea.'

Ignoring him, I push hard on the door and find myself jet propelled into the silent lobby.

No sooner have we set foot in the place than two efficient women appear behind the reception desk with welcoming smiles.

'Hurrah! It's open,' I say to my sceptical son.

Fumbling for a purse in my handbag I'm about to pay when one of the directors appears. He gives me a welcoming hug and explains how happy he is to see the project come to fruition. I explain in laborious detail about the endless queues and with a wink he opens the entry gate and waves us through.

'Now you don't have to queue or pay and you have the whole place to yourselves. How about that?'

'Fantastic! And to think you were waiting just there for the moment when we'd arrive.'

He laughs and wishes us a good tour. It is an extraordinary feeling walking around so stunning and spacious a property that from street-level seems of modest proportions. The painted ceilings are lofty and decorative and the bold, tiled floors a labyrinth of detailed patterns and bright colours. Spectacular works of modernistic art and furniture of the period can be seen in each room, illustrating a wild and eclectic fusion of art nouveau and elaborate Edwardian design. Ollie wanders around in a daze, slightly awed by the splendour of the restoration and scale of the building. He stares up at the spectacular snail-shaped staircase with its wrought iron banisters and stone steps that curl up to the top floor.

'That staircase is so cool,' he whispers.

'Shall we go up?'

A series of bedrooms run along the top floor, all with elegant turn-of-the-century furniture and mahogany, decorative beds that two dwarfs might just about find roomy enough. Mallorcan antique beds have always fascinated me because they seem impossibly small and I can only imagine them leading to divorce for many sleep-deprived newlyweds.

We soon find ourselves in a room full of glass cabinets containing antique dolls. They follow us with their large glassy eyes and waxed and porcelain limbs as we head off down to the basement to see the contemporary art section and installations. It is fascinating to see how the architect has transformed what must have been a grimy, unlit cellar into a funky art den. The sheer opulence of the house and its restoration is an indication of the wealth enjoyed by affluent Sóllerics, returning from a life working overseas to retirement in the Sóller Valley.

After exploring the more modest gardens, designed in modernistic style, a far cry from how they might have been in former days, we return to the entrance. The director is entertaining a news team, evidently there to report on the new museum. They wave goodbye to us as we return to Calle sa Lluna.

'So what did you think of it?' I ask Ollie.

He considers the frontage for a while and then with a sniff replies, 'It was really interesting but they lacked one critical thing.'

I'm puzzled.

'A gift shop,' he says. 'Next time we see one of the directors, I will ask about it.'

'Perhaps they just haven't got round to it yet.'

He eyes me enthusiastically. 'Then perhaps I can tell them what sort of things they should sell in it.'

'They might not appreciate that, Ollie.'

'Why not? On the entrepreneur's website they list the top-selling items for museums and attractions worldwide...'

I stifle a yawn. 'That's scintillating. I'm sure they'll be all ears.'

'Right then.'

Before I can stop him, he's re-entered the building. This time I don't follow. I just hope the director has already made his escape.

We are dining in Pizzeria del Puerto, having spent much of the night celebrating the Moors and Christians grand battle with friends in the *plaça*. All day long guns have sounded, and blunderbusses roared as locals took to the streets of the port and town in celebration of their ancestors' conquest. Ollie is covered in black greasepaint, smeared on him by a gang of rampant Moors as he did mock battle outside Café Paris. It is traditional for those playing Moors to catch and convert their enemies with a daub of black paint. Alan and I didn't manage to escape and discover black fingerprints on our arms and faces.

'You look very silly,' laughs Ollie.

'What about you?' asks the Scotsman.

'Yes, but at least I'm in costume.'

He takes a swig at his Bitter Kas and sits back in his chair. 'I don't think I can eat another thing.'

'What, not even an ice cream?' I taunt.

'On second thoughts, maybe a small chocolate one.'

Jamie, the son of the owners, comes over and removes our plates. 'Not too full for an ice cream, then?' he teases.

A large group of teenagers are dining on the other side of the restaurant and obviously having a lot of fun. I observe their table, noting that not one of them is drinking alcohol. It seems that Fanta and Coke are the order of the day.

'Can you imagine that happening in the UK?' asks Alan dryly.

'No, not really,' I reply.

Ollie accepts his ice cream with gusto and begins hacking into it.

I look out of the window and to my surprise see that rain is falling quite heavily.

'Thank heavens it didn't rain during the battle sequence,' I say.

Alan regards the window with a smile. 'Fantastic! I won't have to do any watering tonight.'

Horticultural matters are never far from his thoughts. Jamie returns to our table to catch up on our plans for the cattery. Despite working in his parents' restaurant, he is trained in zoological work and looks after our cats when we leave the island for a holiday. I'm rather hoping to involve him in the new project.

He agrees to come up to cast an experienced eye over the plans. We settle the bill and slowly make our way to the door. The rain is pounding the promenade outside but fortuitously we have two large golf umbrellas so are well protected in the downpour.

Despite the rain, hundreds of glittering stars are suspended in the dark sky and the sweet smell of ozone rushes up from the wild sea. We walk along the seafront, the wind caressing our hair and teasing our clothes. Making our way, head to the wind, up an unlit side street en route to our car, Ollie suddenly pulls on my arm with a mischievous grin. Several soggy figures clad in rainwear are hovering along the grass verges, scrutinising the soil for unsuspecting *cargols*, snails, which they pounce on and quickly pop into plastic carrier bags. This may be the season to lift the spirits of gardeners across the valley but for poor little snails, it can only mean one thing: the terror of the cooking pot!

TWELVE

BUILDING BRIDGES

It's a gloriously balmy day in June and yet a gentle breeze prevails, ruffling the pink petals of the oleander flowers and carrying the intoxicating perfume of wild lavender far across the valley. Vast clumps of red and purple bougainvillea spill from the roadside in drunken abandonment, while the modest orange trees stand primly in the orchards robed in white blossom like blushing brides. Ollie and I amble towards the bridge that runs like a black gash from one side of the stream to the other. It is due for expansion and large cement blocks, pipes and steel rods lie piled up all the way along one side, ready for action.

A distraught duck is furiously discussing the changes to its habitat with a large attentive group of feathered companions.

'The point is,' he quacks, 'before work began on this new bridge, we used to have complete tranquillity away from traffic and annoying humans. Now it's non-stop noise and chaos and soon we'll have cars thundering overhead. So what do we do? Are we just going to be a bunch of dead ducks or do we fight?'

'Fight!' I say.

Ollie gives me an odd look. 'Are you having one of your imaginary conversations again?'

'Possibly. Don't you wonder what that grey duck is saying to the others?'

He plonks his tennis racquet and sports bag on the ground and glances at the huddle of ducks and fowl strutting along the grass verge.

'Er, no. Sorry to say, mother, I am not quacking mad and I do not wonder what the grey duck is saying. Can we carry on now?'

I give a disapproving grunt and survey the half-finished bridge, once a pretty pedestrian walkway over a large stream right in the centre of Sóller.

'Why did they have to enlarge it for cars? It was so relaxing to stand on the narrow bridge and feed the ducks. No wonder they're fed up.'

He sighs and shakes his head. 'They've communicated with you directly on this point, have they?'

'It's obvious how they're feeling. Anyway, I just hope when it's finished the fumes and noise won't frighten them away from the stream.'

Ollie crouches down on his knees and pulls out some old bread from his bag. He begins throwing small pieces to the throng of birds.

'They don't seem too bothered to me.'

'That's because it's a Sunday and everything is quiet.'

I dump my bag on the grass and make my way carefully down to the stream. Ollie follows behind, guiding himself through large rocks as we slither down the bank. The sun is hot on our backs as we sit by the small trickle of water.

'Have you seen the birds?' Ollie asks, pointing upwards.

I follow his gaze and there in a blue sky streaked with white clouds is a perfectly synchronised fast flying team of swifts.

'Aren't they incredible?'

He nods and lies back against a flat rock, the bright sunlight turning his skin a soft marigold hue.

'If you look at that white trail of cloud directly above, it makes the letter J.'

I sink back against the grass and, true enough, a huge white J scorches the sky.

'Maybe it's a sign that I need to have a long chat with Johnny?'

Ollie groans. 'Yes, you have a nice chat with your little toad and then we can invite the men in white coats round to take you away.'

We sit laughing together until my mobile rings. Reluctantly, I get to my feet and climb up the bank. I pounce on my handbag and catch it on the fifth ring.

'Are you OK?'

It's the Scotsman.

'I thought you'd have picked up Ollie from Pep and Juana's by now. Where are you?'

'I was invited in for a cup of coffee because Ollie hadn't finished his match with Angel. We've just stopped to feed the ducks.'

'Fine. Well, I'm off in a minute to see Paco about the tomato plants and the oranges. We'll probably have a bite up in Fornalutx.'

An all-round horticultural guru, Paco, Catalina's father, is an expert when it comes to growing tomatoes and is experienced at pruning orange and lemon trees.

I click the mobile shut and gather up Ollie's belongings. 'Come on, let's get home.'

'Can we go to the port this afternoon?'

This has become a Sunday afternoon ritual, strolling along the seafront, a mere twenty minutes walk from our *finca*, and browsing some of his favourite haunts such as the main sports shop.

We arrive home to find that Alan has already departed.

'Fancy a quick swim?' asks Ollie.

'Are you sure it's warm enough?'

He rolls his eyes. 'Don't be boring. Come on!'

I watch as he hurtles off to his room to get changed. A loud incessant croaking comes from the pond. I wander over and spy six little figures sitting on the sunny back wall.

'Any sign of Johnny?'

They puff out their cheeks and, like sullen teenagers, regard me with ennui. One of them plops in the water, his glistening, iridescent green legs stretching out behind him. I watch as air bubbles rise to the surface and a serene goldfish streams past seemingly unperturbed by my presence.

'Been out?' a voice calls to me.

Johnny is sitting like a fat brown Buddha in one of his favourite hideouts.

'We've just been for a stroll. They're building a new bridge in Sóller and the poor ducks in the stream below are in a fluster.'

He blinks at the sun. 'Ducks are the enemy of pond life so don't think up some screwball idea like opening a duck sanctuary.'

'I've got quite enough on my plate with the cattery and the donkey paddock.'

'Why can't you just sit in the sun with a book and forget all about the god-damned cats, and the donkeys come to that?'

'Because that would be lazy. Besides, it's far too boring to just sit in the sun.'

'Did you know that ducks are psychotic? My uncle was eaten by a duck.'

'I'm really sorry to hear that. Maybe the duck just went quackers?'

'You're a sicko, you know that?'

Ollie calls from the kitchen. 'Now what are you doing? Hurry up.'

'Time to go, old chap.'

He turns his head as if hiding a smirk. 'Have a nice cold dip. See you soon, wizened prune.'

Humph. I set off to the bedroom, change, and join Ollie for a freezing cold swim in the pool. Despite it being June, the water at this time of the year is still numbing and I can only just about manage a ten-minute foray into the cool depths before my body begins shivering all over.

'Very bracing,' I gasp as I jog over to fetch my towel. 'Can we go and have a bit of sun in the port now?'

Ollie dabs at himself with the towel. 'We could always have a dip in the sea?'

'Are you deranged?'

'Coming from you, I'd say that was a bit rich.'

In Port of Sóller, the first of the summer visitors can be seen walking slowly along the promenade in shorts and T-shirts and dawdling over double-decker ice creams in the cafes. In the sea, a few brave souls are screeching and splashing about while others huddle on the beach under towels. Though the sun is casting radiant light across the port, there is a cool breeze blowing in from the sea. I stand with Ollie on the promenade, looking at the yachts as they sway gently from side to side at their berths. From the sea an elegant schooner glides between the two rocky formations that form the craggy mouth of the bay. Its wooden flanks sparkle under the sun and the white sails billow in the breeze.

'It looks like a pirate ship,' observes Ollie. 'I wish it was.'

'Actually, given their historic record in Mallorca, I'd be quite happy if it wasn't.'

We head along to Santa Catalina at the farthest end of the bay, and take a seat at one of the cafes overlooking the boats. A waiter comes to take our order and, as he departs, I see Michel walking slowly along with a younger man in tow. I'm suddenly aware of his vulnerability as he laboriously marks out each paving stone with his stick before moving forward. I stand up and give a wave in his direction. He stops to study me and then, screwing up his eyes against the bright sun, returns the gesture with his stick. I watch as he leans towards his companion and, I assume, offers a few words of explanation.

'Who's that?' asks Ollie.

'It's the poet I told you about. Michel, or rather José.'

'Didn't you say he was a bit strange?' hisses Ollie.

'A little, but I think you'll like him.'

They now approach us, smiling. Michel reaches out his lean, mottled hand to Ollie. His companion shakes my hand, explaining that he is Ignacio, the nephew.

'I've heard much about you from my uncle,' he says.

'Likewise,' I reply. 'Will you join us?'

He hesitates for a moment. 'I hope you won't think me rude, but I have to pick up my wife from our olive grove. I was going to leave my uncle here for a little walk until we returned.'

I turn to Michel. 'Then you must stay with us.'

He smiles. '*Gracias*. That would be nice.'

We agree a designated point to meet in an hour and watch as Ignacio makes his way across the road to a parked car. Michel sits down at the table next to Ollie.

'You're a skinny young man. You remind me of myself at your age. Do you like football?'

Ollie smiles. 'Football and tennis.'

'That's good. What about picking almonds?'

'I can't say I've ever tried it but our new neighbour, Fernando, is inviting us to pick almonds with him in August.'

Michel laughs. 'When I was a boy, almond picking was a sort of family sport. We all went to help out. My brother and cousins and I would always end up firing them at each other.'

Ollie laughs. 'Sounds like fun.'

I turn to Michel. 'Can I get you a drink?'

He nudges Ollie. 'What are you having?'

'A double scoop of chocolate ice cream.'

'I'll join you.'

The waiter comes over and, smiling at Michel, takes his order. '*Donc, mi amic*, how are things? I haven't seen you here for a while.'

Michel nods. 'My nephew tries to get me to take the air on a Sunday but often I resist. What does air do for you?'

He pats my hand. 'I've known that lad since he was a baby. Ah, I love Santa Catalina. Did you know that it has been linked to the citrus trade since the fourteenth century?'

'No, I can't say I did.'

'It has an interesting history like the street names. They're *topónimos*. You know what that means, Ollie?'

He shrugs.

'Toponyms in English, descriptive place names,' I say.

Ollie frowns. 'Such as?'

Michel and Ollie excitedly accept their whopping ice creams from the waiter. They sit like fellow conspirators, licking their spoons and enjoying the first icy mouthfuls. I stir sugar into my iced coffee.

'You see, Ollie, certain streets bear the names of different prevailing winds and that's because the sailors and fishermen living in Santa Catalina harbour relied heavily on the winds.'

'Like the Tramuntana wind?' he asks.

'*Molt bé*! That's the northerly wind, and the most annoying for the fishermen here. There's also the Migjorn from the south, the Llevant from the east and Ponent from the west.'

Ollie regards Michel with interest. 'So there are streets named after those winds?'

'Oh yes, and there's also, let me think, Gregal, Mestral, Xaloc and Lleibeig.'

'Wow, you've got a good memory.'

'Like a fine wine, it matures with age.' Michel smiles and licks his fingers. 'This ice cream is delicious.'

'Was this port affected much during the Spanish Civil War?' I ask.

He wipes his lips with a napkin. 'Hugely. You know it became a secret submarine base for Franco? The Nationalists bought Italian-made submarines to make their attacks against the Republicans. Remember the Italians, like the Germans, were Franco's allies.'

I turn to face Michel. 'So there were a lot of military personnel based here at the time?'

He chuckles. '*Segur*! At one stage there were 300 Italian and at least 200 Spanish marines. Santa Catalina became a *zona militar*, where apart from hiding submarines they kept launchers and torpedoes secreted in hidden tunnels. It was all very secretive and the Sóllerics were kept well away.'

'But what if you were a fisherman?' says Ollie.

'Locals were allowed to carry on living here but they were surrounded by military and would have had to carry their authorisation papers at all times.'

It's inconceivable to imagine the merry Port of Sóller with its relaxed atmosphere today playing home to a huge mob of young Italian marines wearing black military garb and carrying weapons.

'But what if Sóllerics wanted to come to the sea for a swim or even take a stroll? Was that permitted?' I ask.

Michel gives a deep sigh. 'Look, I wasn't here then but what I've been told is that no one really visited here much. Sóller *plaça* was the centre of social activity and the concept of taking a stroll wasn't relevant at that time. Only fishermen took an interest in the sea.'

I call the waiter and order another coffee. Michel asks for mineral water.

'Many buildings and hotels here were requisitioned during the war to accommodate the military. There were few hotels in the port at the time – the Dennis, Marina, which of course still exists, Terramar, Costa Brava and the Marisol. All of them would have been forced to hand over rooms to Franco's supporters.'

'It must have been quite scary for them,' says Ollie.

'*Si*, no hotel owner likes to be forced to do such things,' agrees Michel.

'In my history lessons I learned that Mallorca was Nationalist and Menorca was Republican. Did the Republicans ever attack Mallorca?' asks Ollie.

'They tried with aerial raids. The Russian Air Force supported the Republicans and made several attacks on Palma but only once in Sóller and never the port.'

'Imagine if they had! They could have blown up all the Nationalists' submarines.'

Michel grins. 'You are a clever boy. Why didn't they attack the port? The most obvious place, no?'

Ollie hasn't an answer. 'Maybe they weren't very bright?'

Michel claps his hands together. 'Very funny! Or perhaps they didn't know what was hidden here.'

Ollie nods and pushes his bowl away from him. I laugh at his chocolate moustache, which he wipes off with the back of his hand.

'Do you live with your nephew?' he asks Michel.

'Yes, and his wife, Marina. His daughters are no longer living with us.'

'How old are they?'

'Sara is thirty and Pilar is thirty-four.'

Ollie raises his eyebrows. 'Oh, they're old.'

'Maybe to you, yes,' he laughs.

'What do they do?'

'Well, Ollie, one is a teacher in Barcelona and the other is a lawyer in Madrid.'

'Do you all get on well?'

I remonstrate but Michel gently raises his hand. I notice it quivers slightly with the effort.

'A good question. We do get on now but there are many sad things in our past that my nephew and I have had to resolve. We have built bridges to overcome them.'

'What sort of things?' asks Ollie.

I squirm a little in my chair but Michel is unbothered by his mini interrogation.

'Mostly about my brother, Joaquin. He died some years after the war ended. My family at the time held me partly responsible. It's a long story.'

'Were you responsible?' Ollie replies.

'In a way, yes. My brother spent many years in a concentration camp and prison on the Spanish mainland because the Fascists believed he was a Republican like me. He protested his innocence and insisted he was on their side, a Nationalist, like all my family, but they didn't listen. He was only able to return in the late forties and his health was apparently very poor.'

We sit in silence.

'Did you apologise to him?' says Ollie.

'I never had the chance. He died of pneumonia in 1955 before I returned to Mallorca but I have tried to make it up to his son and his family. I have to live with my conscience.'

He bows his head for a second. Ollie pats his arm solicitously.

'It could have been worse. I mean, he could have been shot or died in prison.'

I call the waiter and settle the bill. We set off slowly on our walk along the promenade.

Ollie looks out at the sea. 'If you weren't here at the time, your family shouldn't have blamed you for Joaquin's death. That's not fair.'

Michel places an arm around Ollie's shoulder.

'Si, *mi chico*, many things in life are just not fair.'

We arrive at the car park by the marina and Ignacio jogs across from his vehicle to greet us. An attractive, smiling woman waves at us from the passenger seat.

'I hope you've had a nice time,' Ignacio says. 'That's my wife, Marina. You must meet her properly over dinner one day.'

'That would be lovely,' I reply.

He kisses me on both cheeks and tousles Ollie's hair. 'I hope we'll meet again soon. Perhaps you too will join us for dinner?'

'Of course,' says Ollie.

Very gently he takes his uncle by the arm and gives him an encouraging smile.

'I'll visit again soon,' says Michel. 'Thank you for your words, Ollie.'

Together, uncle and nephew head back to the car while Ollie and I stand on the promenade, both deep in thought.

For the last few days, Geoff, the Scotsman's brother and his wife, Ali, a Yorkshire lass and proud of it, have been staying with us, following a holiday in the north of the island. Like me, Ali loves cooking and experimenting with recipes and as soon as I mentioned my wish to start making lemon curd, she was in to her stride. Producing a fail-safe recipe of her own, she then trotted off to Sóller town, returning with clear glass jars and greaseproof paper.

'Now,' she said, rolling up her sleeves, 'We can really make use of all those lovely lemons in your orchard. Such a pity to see them go to waste.'

I had to go for a meeting, so she shooed me out of the kitchen and set to work. By the time I'd returned, she'd already made about ten jars of lemon curd.

'Good God, Ali! You've been busy,' I exclaimed as I entered the kitchen, breathing in the citrus odour.

She gave me a huge wink. 'There's no time like the present. Now, I need you to taste three different versions. This one has more sugar.'

She held out a spoon. I had a taste.

'And this one is quite lemony.'

I took another.

'And the final one is quite creamy.'

Feeling like Goldilocks sampling the bears' three bowls of porridge, I declared that I liked the last one best.

'They're all good but the last is wonderfully rich.'

'Just what I thought,' she said, pleased as punch. 'Now then, I've bought you more jars and the nice lady in the kitchen shop said she'd discount on volume.'

I laughed. Ali obviously had visions of me starting my own lemon curd industry. Thinking about it, that wasn't such a bad idea. I mean, Teresa in the market and Xavier at Colmado sa Lluna would probably love to have a supply of home-made English lemon curd. I made a mental note to discuss this potential new enterprise with the Scotsman.

Today, Ali is once again in the kitchen, clearing up the dishes after breakfast and looking forward to a cycle ride with Geoff along the winding country road up to Fornalutx. Geoff has spent the last few days topping up his tan and swimming and is looking forward to some light exercise before they return to Scotland in the morning. We dust down our bikes on the front porch, inflate the tyres and wave them both off.

Alan sits down at the kitchen table. 'Ah, now I can have a quiet read of the newspaper.'

'Before you do, can I have your opinion about making lemon curd for the local shops and market?'

He takes off his reading glasses and surveys me for a second. 'Sorry, did I hear right? You want to supply the shops with lemon curd?'

'Yes, I know it sounds a bit barmy but since we have so many lemons it might be a good way of using them up.'

'Have you any idea how time-consuming that would be and for tiny profit?'

'I view it more as a public service. Besides, making in bulk isn't that hard. You could peel while I…'

He hoots with laughter. 'Aha! You mean to involve me in your little scheme? Well, you can forget that immediately. If you think I'm going to start peeling damned lemons all day, you're quite mistaken.'

I sigh. 'Oh well, I'll just have to manage on my own – or maybe I can bribe Minky and Orlando to help.'

I call to Minky. 'Fancy making some lemon curd in exchange for a chicken leg?'

Alan gives a dismissive shake of the head. 'You really are the limit. Mad as a hatter. Talking of which, haven't you got any real work to do?'

With an indignant sniff, I potter upstairs to get on with some 'real' work. Rachel has sent me a pile of releases to check and also her event plan for the drag hatter's tea party at The Dorchester. Barely an hour passes when the phone rings. A moment later, Alan bursts into the office with an ashen face.

'Whatever's wrong?' I ask, somewhat alarmed.

'You'll never believe it. My brother's fallen over the wall of a bridge.'

'What? Is he badly hurt?'

He sits down, obviously in some shock. 'That was Catalina calling. She says that Geoff was cycling round a bend and toppled over the little bridge into the *torrente* below. Luckily, it's dried up at the moment and he seems OK.'

I'm askance. 'But how on earth did he manage to do that? Anyway, the place I think you're talking about isn't a bridge.'

He stands up. 'I said we'd come up immediately so we'll learn more then. Thank heavens Catalina happened to be driving by just after the accident happened.'

I grab my handbag. 'Good old Catalina. She's always there when you need her.'

Some twenty minutes later we arrive at the bridge. Ali is standing by the offending wall with her bicycle and is obviously recovering from the shock of the incident, while Geoff sits nursing his injuries with Catalina by his side. A bevy of builders hang around their white van, offering sympathy and rural wisdom – old-fashioned advice about how to treat Geoff for shock and trauma. Their suggestion of a big tumbler of *herbes*, the local liqueur, doesn't seem to appeal to Geoff.

Catalina waves when she sees the car. 'I've called the ambulance. It's best to get Geoff checked out at the local medical clinic first.'

Ali comes over and gives us both a hug while the wounded soldier remains sitting on the wall. We are relieved to discover that he's compos mentis and able to talk.

'Whatever happened?' asks Alan, mystified.

'Ali will tell you,' he says feebly.

'It was quite bizarre,' she says, giggling with shock. 'One minute Geoff was pedalling away in front of me, and the next he'd disappeared.'

'The Fornalutx Triangle?' I suggest.

She laughs. 'Something like that. I came puffing round a corner and couldn't for the life of me think where he'd gone. I mean he's a bit faster than me, but not that fast.'

Alan grows impatient. 'So where had he gone?'

'Well,' she resumes, 'just as I came round the corner, I saw these workmen all leaning over the stone wall and shouting. I had no idea they'd just seen Geoff go tumbling over with the bike on top of him!'

Catalina continues. 'I arrived at that moment and one of the builders who I know asked if I could speak English to a foreigner who'd fallen over the wall, and there was Geoff!' She giggles at the memory. 'Poor Geoff. Luckily for him he fell on *cañas*, you know, dry canes, and that broke his fall. The builder said Geoff had pulled over against that old stone wall to let them pass, lost his balance and flipped over the side, three metres down.'

Luckily for Geoff the *torrente* was indeed dried up and so he wasn't carried off downstream in a clump of *cañas,* like a modern-day version of baby Moses. Instead, the burly builders ran down the bank and rescued both him and the bike.

An ambulance appears and two paramedics come over to inspect the invalid. They chat in Mallorquin with Catalina and, satisfied that Geoff is able to breathe and move, carefully transfer him to a stretcher in the back of the ambulance. We agree to follow them to the local clinic and, if necessary, on to one of the Palma hospitals. Catalina asks us to keep her abreast of news and off we go.

'I hope he'll be OK to get on the plane tomorrow,' says Ali anxiously. 'Trust Geoff to come a cropper the day before we leave!'

'It's one way of avoiding going back to work,' says Alan with a wink.

En route to the clinic, Alan drops me off at the house so that I'll be there when Ollie returns from a tennis game. I wonder what the doctor's diagnosis will be at the local clinic. Hopefully, there won't be any broken bones.

It's eight o'clock in the evening when Geoff, Ali and the Scotsman return. Having been told at the Sóller clinic that to err on the side of caution Geoff should have X-rays, they had all trooped off to one of the main Palma hospitals. Alan had followed the ambulance but lost track of it on the Cintura motorway, so that by the time he and Ali eventually arrived at the hospital Geoff was yet again nowhere to be found. After some time trying to discover his whereabouts in various departments, they were finally told he had been taken for tests and X-rays. Hours later, and to their immense relief, Geoff reappeared. It transpired that his ailments amounted to little more than some uncomfortable bruises and shock but the experience had left him in sombre mood, thinking about what could have happened had the river been swollen. Rather than stay at home, we all set off in good spirits to Agapanto restaurant in the port to celebrate his good fortune in living to tell the tale.

'Oh well, look on the bright side,' says the Scotsman, as we clink flutes of cava, 'you'll be able to dine out on this story for some time.'

'True,' says Ali, with a grin. 'Shame he won't have any war wounds to show for it, though.'

'You may all mock,' says Geoff with a sniff, 'but it wasn't funny at the time.'

'Of course not,' I reply, 'but you've definitely left your mark on Fornalutx. The locals will be recounting the story of the Flying Scotsman for years to come.'

'I'm afraid you'll have to pick up your bikes from Paco's orchard. Catalina told those builders to dump them at her father's house.'

'We'll have to walk up there and ride the bikes back,' says Alan.

'Fine,' giggles Ali, 'but whatever you do, don't stop to let any builders pass you on the way!'

We stand inside the sunny portals of Biniaraix's old church of Immaculada Concepció whose decrepit, weather-beaten front looks on to what might be described as one of the island's smallest *plaças* with its landmark village cafe but little else. Biniaraix is a tranquil and sleepy hamlet tucked away in the foothills of the Tramuntanas and situated halfway up the old country road between Sóller town and Fornalutx. With its distinctly Gallic charm it's not surprising that so many French expats settled here at one time, perhaps also drawn to the area by its past association with their country as a citrus trading route. These days most have returned to their native France, and the local inhabitants are mostly Mallorcan with a few foreigners thrown into the mix.

For most of the week the hamlet goes quietly about its business but on Sundays it is awash with parked cars as hikers and family picnickers congregate at the old public washstand to begin their trek along the cobbled paths leading up to the famous Barranc Gorge and the Cuba Reservoir beyond. The Cami d'es Barranc cobbled track once served as a route for pilgrims making their way to Lluc monastery over the mountains but it is now the playground for families and recreational walkers.

Finally, Jorge and Beatriz's big day has arrived and they, together with hordes of friends and family from Mallorca and Argentina, swoop on the church, tooting horns and yelling excitedly to one another. The church bells are chiming and locals come out onto the street to join in the fun. The Church of Immaculada Concepció, a simple limestone edifice, is nestled in a tiny cul-de-sac in the hamlet and is reached by about a dozen broad stone cobbled steps. Its large wooden, arched door is shielded from inclement weather by sturdy sheet metal, which has been hammered onto its surface. It may not be particularly aesthetic but it is at least practical. Today, the door has been thrown back to let in the sunlight and guests are clustered on the steps in readiness for the ceremony.

An unusual aspect of this wedding is that Jorge's lively and emotional family has arrived from Buenos Aires, and from the moment his mother walks in to the church she is in floods of tears. Jorge fixes me with a pained smile at the church door.

'My mother has just told Beatriz's mother that her daughter is lucky to have caught me. Can you imagine! I am so embarrassed.'

I giggle. 'Oh these things happen. Point me in her direction.'

He raises his eyebrows. 'Just follow the sobbing! My poor father is trying to keep a distance.'

Alan mutters under his breath.

'What did you say, old Scotsman?' I say.

'Nothing!' he says with a grin.

Ollie yawns. 'He said, "Typical woman!".'

'Oh shush! You little turncoat!' exclaims Alan.

We enter the church and are bombarded with kisses and hugs from our many shared friends. Pep and Juana have come with Angel and have bagged us seats in their pew at the rear of the church.

'It's so exciting,' says Juana. 'Beatriz is such a lovely girl. I've known her family for years so I sincerely hope Jorge will be good enough for her. He's lucky to have caught her.'

'Don't you start! Jorge's mother's been saying the same to Beatriz's mother, apparently.'

She stares at me aghast. '*Pues*, what a cheek! I shall go and have words with her.'

Pep rolls his eyes. 'You see the trouble you cause?'

'Me?' I say innocently.

He hits me on the head with the order of service. 'Listen, let's hope the priest is quick off the mark. Otherwise we can all nip out for a beer during the service.'

Alan laughs. 'Good thinking.'

Juana tuts loudly and bustles off in the direction of Jorge's mother seated near the altar. She is wearing an ornate gold suit with an enormous flowery hat and dabs dramatically at her eyes. Despite the sizzling temperatures outside, uncharacteristic for June, the church is dark and cool and the wooden pews cold to the touch. Several women are using their service sheets as fans, vigorously flipping them to and fro and causing a gentle breeze of incense and warm air to waft among the throng. Finally, with great fanfare the organ strikes up and everyone scrambles to their feet. As is typical at a Mallorcan wedding, many people are still not seated and are milling around at the back of the church as the bride arrives. Babies howl and toddlers crawl around on the stone floor, oblivious to what's going on. There are smiles and sighs of joy as beautiful Beatriz, in a stunning organza ivory gown, arrives at the foot of the aisle. She wears no veil and her rich ebony hair is drawn up on her head in an exotic floral arrangement. A slash of red in its midst turns out to be a deep-red rosebud. Jorge looks adoringly at her from the front of the church as she walks with poise along the aisle towards him, smiling and winking at friends on the way. A little girl runs out in front of them and, very gently, Beatriz bends down, her gown spread around her like a soft web, and kissing the child on the cheek returns her to her mother.

The feeling of informality and fun permeates even the service. The priest is relaxed and happy, smiling at the children and making little jokes with the family in the front rows. The music peters out and we kneel and bow our heads in prayer. Peering to my left, I catch the eye of a bleeding Jesus as he labours with a monstrous cross in one of the agonising stages of the Stations of the Cross. A statue of the Virgin Mary looks on beatifically from the side of the altar and various religious iconic images run the length of the white walls.

Ollie nudges me. 'What are you looking at?

'That poor Jesus. He looks exhausted.'

'Well, wouldn't you be?' he whispers impatiently.

The service rolls on. Pep is yawning and looking at the blue sky beyond the front door. I wonder if he's going to make a break for freedom.

'Don't even think about it!' I whisper.

Juana, who sits on the other side of Pep, shakes her head despairingly. We sing a Mallorcan hymn, the words of which I don't know, and then there are more prayers. Children are now congregating at the back of the church, others playing games with pebbles out by the bar and the babies continue to burble from the pews.

'It's extraordinary how different this is from an English service,' I remark quietly to Alan.

He offers me a wry grin. 'Unbelievable, but so much less stuffy isn't it?'

When the service is over, the organ blasts, the wooden doors are opened wide and the crowd pours out of the church down the steps, in hot pursuit of the happy bride and groom. Rose petals and rice grains are strewn all over the *plaça* and Beatriz screeches when a handful of rice is tipped unceremoniously down the front of her dress. Juana pulls me aside on the crowded street.

'By the way, I had a good talk with Jorge's mother. I told her that Beatriz's family was very wealthy and that she was considered the best chef in the valley.'

I gawp at her, surprised to learn this new information.

'I also told her that Beatriz was a brilliant seamstress and gardener. His mother was so impressed and thanked me profusely for this new insight on her daughter-in-law. The next thing she was all over Beatriz's mother, saying how wonderful it would be to have Beatriz in the family. The last I saw they were chatting away happily.'

'Well done for building bridges between them – I had no idea about all Beatriz's skills. She never mentioned her love of cooking when we met.'

Juana rolls her head back and laughs. 'You *idiota*! I was just making it up. Beatriz hates cooking and sewing and has never ridden a horse in her life but she's great fun and has a heart of gold.'

'So you were just trying to keep Jorge's mother happy?'

'Something like that. She'll only be here another two days and then we can all relax.'

In the melee, Pep and Alan beckon us over. I grab Ollie and Angel's arms and we manage to escape the throng.

'Let's make a dash for the reception venue now so that we get a good parking space,' says Pep as he attempts to light a cigar.

'I could do with a glass of *vino*,' enthuses Alan.

'Wasn't it a beautiful service?' I say to Pep.

He fumbles with his lighter. 'Beautiful? That poor young chap has just signed away his life. We should be wearing black armbands.'

Juana whacks him with her handbag as Angel and Ollie exchange whispers and giggles. Pep's cigar tumbles to the floor and is crushed as some children race by in a game of chase. Pep growls and gives Juana a dark look just as a smiling Jorge waves at us from amidst the crowd of well-wishers. 'We'll catch up at the reception.'

We nod and walk along the cobbled street in search of our cars. The sun is blisteringly hot and both cars are like mini saunas inside. We all clamber into our seats and roll down the windows.

'It's sweltering!' moans Juana.

Pep straps himself into his driving seat and calls to Alan from his window.

'Mark my words, that boy's life will never be his own.'

Alan walks over to Pep's car and, with a sympathetic pat on his shoulder, proffers a new cigar.

'Just what the doctor ordered,' smiles Pep, his mood suddenly lightening. 'What the hell! Let's go and celebrate and nab ourselves a big glass of *vino tinto*!'

THIRTEEN

PINE ISLANDS

A clutter of white buildings can be seen on the horizon, each crooked house piggybacking one on top of the other all the way up a small craggy hill to the tip of Dalt Vila, the old town of Eivissa. We are on a ferry heading towards the white island of Ibiza, better known as Eivissa to the people of the *Baleares*. Along with Formentera, its tiny neighbouring island, Eivissa is one of the two Pityuses, meaning 'Pine Islands', which form part of the Balearic archipelago. It was in 654 BC that the Phoenicians set their sights on Ibiza; they named the port Ibossim and dedicated it to their God Bes, later known as Ebusus by the Romans.

Ibiza, similarly to its sister islands, Mallorca and Menorca, has had its fair share of trials and tribulations over the years. Having being under the thumb of the Phoenicians, it was then invaded by the Carthaginians and later sacked by the Romans. As if that wasn't bad enough, when the Roman Empire finally collapsed, poor beleaguered Ibiza was invaded by the Vandals and then the Byzantines. At this point the Moors pitched up and the island fell under Islamic rule until King James I of Aragón reclaimed it in 1235.

Below the gaze of the sun, the town's old church of Santa Maria sparkles like a small diamond against the deep blue of the cloudless sky. Perched as it is on the very top of Dalt Vila along with a small outcrop of white houses, it seems at times like a mirage, lost in the haze of sea and sun, as our boat forges ahead across the plucky waves. The old fortified city is formed in layers, with the castle, church and museum at the summit giving way to a wild assortment of milky white houses and battered old ochre-hued buildings that spread out chaotically around the hill. More houses zigzag down to the port and reach out to the furthest rim of the coast. Beyond the city walls at the foot of the old ramparts of Sant Llúcia, and at the extreme end of the bay, is a slim finger of terrain known as Sa Penya, the old fishing quarter. It was this unaffected, tumbledown neighbourhood that inspired Isidor Macabich to write:

Mirant a tramuntana,
Linda d'una drassana,
Tomba dalt dos puntals,
Una antiga caseta,
Comuna nau, desteta,
Per jorns i temporals.
Pobre casulla trencat
De la boca del port!
No hi ha qui s'apiat
De sa dissort?

The Scotsman peers at the Catalan poetry book lying open on my lap. 'Who was Isidor Macabich?'

'A very well-known Ibicenco priest, poet and historian. He was born in 1883 and took quite a stand during the Spanish Civil War, organising labour unions under the auspices of the Catholic Church which wound him up in prison for a while.'

'Poor chap. So he was imprisoned by the Fascists in Ibiza?'

'Yes, but they let him out after several months.'

'So what's this poem about?'

I shrug. 'Well, I'm no Catalan scholar but I think a rough translation would be, "Looking towards the Tramuntanas, from the threshold of the shipyard, is a broken down old hut that seems defeated like a ship rocked by storms and the passing of time. Poor little hut, shattered by the mouth of the port. Won't anyone take pity on you in your plight?"'

'That's a rather sad sentiment.'

I slam the book shut and yawn. 'I think he just felt it sad to see a once lively enclave inhabited by fishermen going to the dogs. Of course, long after he'd died in the seventies the place was completely renovated. Historically Dalt Vila was the powerbase of the rich landlords, while the marina was where the fishermen, dockers and working class lived.'

'I wonder what they'd all make of it today,' he muses.

For the last ten years we have been popping over to Ibiza for the odd long weekend, and have noticed Eivissa town's gradual gentrification and the continuous developments and improvements being made to the towns and villages inland. Sa Penya is no exception, although there are scant fishermen there these days. Instead there are small lodging houses and hotels. Ollie sits up in his seat and observes the harbour as it comes into view.

'Look lively! It's ten o'clock,' he cajoles. 'We'd better get down to the car or we'll have to stay on until Denia.'

Alan laughs. 'The boat won't leave until all the cars bound for Ibiza have disembarked. Anyway, the captain will hang around in the port until all the passengers for Denia have boarded.'

'All the same,' I say, 'I think Ollie's right. We should join the queue before it gets too congested down in the lower deck.'

We walk through the lounge, the town of Eivissa now looming large through the wide panoramic windows. No matter how many times I visit the island by ferry, my heart always leaps with utter joy when I see the image of the port and the familiar houses and cafes by the harbour. Ibiza has an indefinable magic, a magnetic power that lifts the soul and is quite impossible to resist. We shall be staying just one night before sailing off to Menorca for the famous Sant Joan festival, before returning the following day for a few more nights. There's a thundering boom and a horn blasts loudly as we chunter into dock. We sit patiently in our faithful little Mini down in the inky bowels of the cavernous vessel, waiting for the boat to disgorge us and our fellow passengers on to the quay. Those without cars stand by the exit, clutching bags and cases, ready to dismount first. The large doors gradually creak open, rather like an enormous yawning mouth, and light pours onto the windowless deck, dazzling our eyes.

Alan starts the engine and before long we are clear of the ferry and driving slowly along the flat, open road leading from the port to the town. Crowds of locals have come to meet the boat, and *motos*, cars, bicycles, families on foot, dogs, officials and police mill around the place like a swarm of excitable wasps, yelling and laughing, yapping and blowing whistles. There are cries of '*Cariño!*', darling, '*Hijo mio!*', my son, '*Mi amic!*', my friend, as devoted mothers, lovers, fathers and friends embrace loved ones emerging from the shadows of the boat, weighed down with rucksacks and luggage. Alan progresses along the road carefully and stops when a policeman toots on his whistle and ceremoniously releases a barrier to let us through into the town district.

I lean out of the window, breathing in the balmy air. 'How I love Eivissa! It's so crazy. What time are we supposed to meet Pep and Juana?'

Alan chuckles. 'That all depends on what time the yacht arrived yesterday and how much *vino* they enjoyed at supper.'

Pep and Juana have been invited to spend two weeks touring the Balearic Islands with some wealthy friends aboard their luxury yacht. The husband is apparently some hotshot adviser within the Madrid government while the wife is a native of Ibiza. We have been invited to accompany them from Eivissa Port to Menorca for the famous San Joan horse festival that takes place each June.

We reach the small roundabout that joins the promenade. In its centre is a large, rather unremarkable obelisk, which I've never paid much attention to before.

'What is that monument?' Ollie asks.

'Believe it or not, the inscription says, *'Ibiza a sus corsarios'* which rather oddly seems to be commemorating the pirates that came to the island. Most of the time pirates were the scourge of island society, so I'm not quite sure why they erected it.'

'An ironic symbol, perhaps?' says Alan.

'Who knows but it is bizarre.'

Ollie tuts. 'You're both very dim. I read that in the past many Ibicencans were corsairs and they lived in the marina area. So if part of the population were pirates no wonder they set up the monument to them.'

'Thanks for putting us in our box,' I say. 'We'll get you to give us a history lesson later.'

We find a parking place and set off along some narrow cut-throughs into the town itself. Towering above us is Dalt Vila, below which runs a labyrinth of small streets full of boutiques, gift shops and cafes. The atmosphere in Eivissa town is unlike that of any other town or city in the Balearic Islands. For one thing it's as if time really didn't exist. People walk in an unhurried way, stopping to chat with friends as they amble along the cobbled and leafy streets in the bright sunshine. A wild-haired man is sitting cross-legged under a tree playing a flute, while a young barefooted woman in a white dress works at an easel.

Erstwhile home to the hippy set during the sixties, Eivissa still holds court to an eclectic group of itinerant young people seeking work in the tourist season who hang out in cafes on the popular

Vara de Rei, usually with a dog on a rope in tow. The dog appears to be the new accessory for happy wanderers who pitch up like would-be Robinson Crusoes on the island, wearing scruffy sea- and sand-wear and sporting the obligatory Balearic peasant straw basket slung over the arm. Even today in certain renowned cafes the unmistakable whiff of cannabis mingles with the breeze.

In the early seventies, in a book devoted to the Balearic Islands, Catalan writers Tony Catany and Maria Antònia Oliver wrote disapprovingly of the hippies that flocked to Ibiza ten years earlier, commenting on their disinterest in the islanders and their culture. They accused them of forming a sort of expat hippy clique that never bothered to interact with the locals. Furthermore, those who wafted around in flowing white dresses, old shorts and bare feet were often derided by locals when they left for the UK at the end of their sojourn wearing expensive city clothes and paying for the most expensive cabins on the boat back to Barcelona! Today, there appears to be a better merging of souls and greater integration as a strong contingent of foreigners have made the island their permanent home. Ibiza these days is as famous for its clubbing culture as for its rural beauty and yet the two live happily alongside each other. At the height of the summer season the island can become a little too club-centric and at night the streets in San Antonio, the main clubbing resort, are awash with young people en route to the all-hours music and dance dens from which they emerge bleary-eyed as day breaks. By September time the tourists have flown home and once again the island is able to regain its equilibrium and daily life is resumed.

Having set off from home at six in the morning to catch the early ferry from Palma, we decide to have breakfast and stretch out at a table in one of our favourite cafes in a shady square in the town. It is hard to imagine that this quiet town was once torn apart by historic wars and strife and in more recent times during the Spanish Civil War when it was bombed by Italian forces supporting Franco. Ollie kicks off his shoes and pours himself a Bitter Kas.

'Did you know that the Carthaginians who invaded Ibiza used Balearic stone-slingers in battle?'

I take a sip of coffee. 'As it happens I did, clever clogs! They were known as *foners*, and had the run of the islands from about 600 BC. They used a sling called a *fona,* a simple rope made of natural fibre with a leather pad, to fire stones at their enemies and prey they were hunting.'

Ollie interrupts. 'Our history teacher said the stones were as good as bullets because they went off like rockets, about twelve stones every minute. How cool is that?'

He wipes his mouth with his hand. 'Do you think they could kill people?'

'Stone dead,' says Alan with a grin.

'That's a terrible pun!' groans Ollie. 'Anyway, if that's the case, no wonder the Carthaginians employed them against the Romans.'

'Yes, you wouldn't want to get on the wrong side of a *foner*,' says Alan. 'Neus told me they were talented hunters and in Mallorca they used to fell animals in a matter of seconds.'

'Apparently, the Carthaginians used *foners* during the Punic Wars so they must have made fierce warriors. Even so, the Romans still conquered the Carthaginians and sacked Ibiza.'

'Where can I get hold of one of these slings?' asks Ollie hopefully.

Alan's mobile phone rings. He guffaws loudly and begins a merry banter.

'It has to be Pep,' I whisper to Ollie.

He shakes his head. 'I hope these friends of Pep's aren't boring if we're spending today and tomorrow with them.'

'I'm sure they'll be charming. Anyway, you can play with Angel and ignore all of us.'

He looks relieved. 'That's true.'

Alan pops his mobile back into his pocket. 'That was Pep. They're just surfacing and suggest we meet them at the boat in about an hour or so for a drink before lunch. In the meantime, we can dump our bags at the hotel.'

We finish our breakfast and spend a leisurely time exploring some of the narrow shopping streets before returning to the car. We have booked rooms at a small hotel up in Dalt Vila, which is tranquil and offers pretty views over a small square in the old town. We take the steep road leading up through the fortified walls to the hotel. The tiny shops and boutiques that are crammed in this historical part of the city offer unusual jewellery, hand-made leather bags and the famed Ibizan all-white cotton apparel – flowing dresses, hippy skirts, kaftans and Nehru shirts. There's no hard selling and the general tone of the area is relaxed and extremely laid back.

Half an hour later, having received a warm welcome at the hotel, we set off for the marina in search of Pep and Juana. The directions given to us by Pep are at best lazy and at worst utterly useless. Around the bay, facing the sea, is the newly built five-star Ibiza Gran Hotel and close by the luxurious El Hotel Pacha, both of which opened during our last visit to Ibiza. We search along the lines of smart boats until by luck we see both a Spanish and Ibizan flag flapping high up the mast of a handsome motor yacht. The white and blue livery and matching deck furniture gives it a distinctly naval feel. Pep is standing on the main deck, puffing a *puro* and looking somewhat anxiously up and down the promenade. With visible relief, he waves when he sees us.

'There you are. *Hombre*! Where have you been?'

'Your emailed directions could have been better,' says Alan, the master of understatement.

'*Mi amic*, I couldn't have been clearer. I told you its size and colour and where it would be berthed more or less. What more did you want?'

'The yacht's name might have been useful,' I say archly.

'The name?' He frowns and grabs the piece of paper in Alan's hand. '*Donc, si*, maybe I forgot to add her name. It's *La Marquesa*.'

'Yes, we know that now,' I reply.

He raises his arms. 'You've found us, so what does it matter? Now, come on board.'

He lends me a hand as I walk up the small ladder onto the stern. Ollie and Alan follow behind.

Pep grabs Ollie's hand. 'Give me a hug, *mi amic*. Angel is downstairs playing with his computer. Go and give him a surprise.' Ollie races down the steps to find his chum.

We step onto the gleaming deck and take in our surroundings.

'Hey, this is very plush,' I say to Pep, taking in the large U-shaped dining table and seating arrangement. Through sliding glass doors I can see a smart, fully furnished saloon.

'It's a Princess. They're beautiful boats,' says Alan admiring the craftsmanship.

'A Princess V52 to be exact. You don't think all my friends are poor like you? No, I know people of means,' sniffs Pep.

The glass doors slide open and a portly man with a large moustache and laughing eyes appears with a glass of cava.

'Pep, if you know someone with money, please introduce him to me too,' he says with a grin.

He comes forward and plants a kiss on both my cheeks.

'I am Enrique. How well do you know Pep?'

'Too well probably,' Alan replies.

'Ah, then you know he talks total rubbish! Please, let me get some drinks and introduce you to Isabella, my wife. She is chatting downstairs with Juana.'

He re-enters the saloon and is soon back again bearing a tray of assorted drinks and nuts. A glamorous brunette sporting a deep-red swimsuit and chiffon sarong appears behind him, followed by a relaxed and smiling Juana in shorts and T-shirt.

Juana makes the necessary introductions, and kisses are exchanged. We sit back in comfortable cream sofas and look out at the sea, its surface tinged gold by the burning sun.

'What a beautiful yacht you have,' says Alan.

Enrique gives a proud smile. 'Yes, our little Princess.'

'How many knots does she do?' he asks.

'Thirty-three to thirty-five,' he replies.

'That's impressive. It has two berths?'

'Two doubles, which seems a lot but we sail a great deal and entertain friends like Juana and Pep so it's been a worthwhile investment. Believe it or not, Pep and I met at Madrid University and we used to sail whenever we had the chance.'

'Really?' I say.

'Yes, you see, I'm not as stupid as you thought. I was quite a scholar and a talented sailor.'

Enrique laughs. 'He scraped an economics degree with a little bribery. As for the sailing, I taught him everything he knows.'

'Slander!' cries Pep, slapping his hand down on the wooden table in front of him.

Enrique pops a handful of salted almonds in his mouth and grins at him.

I turn to Isabella. 'So, I hear you are native to Ibiza.'

She takes a sip of her white wine. 'Yes, I spent my childhood here but my father was offered a great job in Madrid running a hotel group, so we left when I was in my late teens. These days we try to return every year to see my family.'

'Where do they live?'

'Mostly in Santa Eularia but it's changed so much since I was a child. It was just a small town with few tourists. Now it's one of the island's main resorts.'

I nod. 'But at least at this time of the year it's still relatively quiet.'

She unfurls her tanned legs and looks across the bay. 'I love the island out of season. It's always best to come before the summer kicks off to see it at its best. My favourite time is always now in June.'

'Do you go across to Formentera much?' I ask, looking for the little island in the near distance.

She gasps. 'Ah! It has some of the best beaches in the Med. Enrique and I sail over there whenever we come to Ibiza. This time it's a flying visit but we'll be back.'

'You'll meet Isabella's grandmother, Paja, tonight. We've invited her along with Isabella's parents for an early supper. She could tell you some fascinating tales about the island. She's eighty-seven and has a phenomenal memory,' says Enrique.

'That will be fun,' I reply.

'I should warn you that although she can understand Castilian well, she prefers speaking Eivissenc. You know it's a dialect of Catalan?' says Isabella.

I give a sigh. 'I'm just trying to cope with Catalan and Mallorquin, so I'm not sure I've got the stamina to tackle Ibiza's own dialect as well.'

She laughs. 'Well, when we reach Menorca tomorrow they'll all be speaking in Menorqui.'

I laugh. 'Oh, don't tell me!'

Pep looks at his watch. '*Vamos*. I've booked Ca n'Alfredo's on the Vara de Rei for one o'clock so we'd better get moving.'

Alan pats his stomach. 'Great. One of my favourites. They do superb oven-baked fish.'

'The best,' agrees Enrique, 'and also *arroz ciego*.'

'Doesn't that mean blind rice?' says Alan with a puzzled expression.

'Yes, it's supposed to mean that this seafood dish is so good that you don't even need to see it. The smell and taste is enough.'

We get ready to set off into town, suddenly remembering that the boys are on the lower deck. Juana bellows their names and a second later they appear in the saloon doorway.

'Hurry up or you'll miss the boat,' drawls Pep.

'You wouldn't really have left us there?' asks his son, Angel, incredulously.

'Time,' says Pep, grabbing each boy by the neck, 'waits for no one, especially when it involves the stomach.'

And with that we make our way along the quay in anticipation of authentic Ibicencan fishy delights.

High above the gently swaying boat, a small island of ice-white stars have formed in the brooding sky. Dalt Vila is suspended in the dark sky like a dazzling chandelier and music from restaurants in its cavernous belly occasionally drifts on the breeze, tantalising us with the odd vibrant chord or vocal flash of flamenco. We sit around the large horseshoe table on the yacht illuminated with small lamps, replete after a delicious dinner of assorted *tapas,* rosemary-baked lamb and strong Ibicencan wine. Isabella's parents, Vicente and Odila, now retired in Ibiza, have enjoyed the evening immensely and seem thrilled to see their daughter and son-in-law again. They have thirsted for news about Paula and Juan, the two teenage children of Enrique and Isabella, both of whom are studying at universities on the mainland. Paja pats my knee.

'Before I get sleepy and start speaking in Eivissenc, I must finish telling you about the civil war years here. As I mentioned earlier, the island was torn between the Fascists and the Republicans, just like Mallorca. Although in truth the civil war was often used for settling old scores with neighbours or even family.'

'Our family was *Frente Popular*, Republican,' says Isabella, stealing a quick glance in her husband's direction.

Enrique smiles. 'And mine in Madrid was staunchly Nationalist.'

Paja sighs. 'Anyway, we country people in Santa Eularia were mostly Republican. We held out against the Fascists on the island

and in the early months of the war, in the summer of 1936, my parents thought we'd be protected by the Republican government in Madrid, but it all went awry.'

'Who was in charge when war was declared?' I ask.

'The island was controlled by Commandant Juli Mestre Martí, a governor put in place by the Nationalist rebels who declared a state of war and began curfews and all sorts of ridiculous restrictions. I was only fourteen but I remember my parents being angry with him about the way he treated local people. All the same, they believed we'd be safe when the Republican Air Force Captain Alberto Bayo turned up with four thousand troops. He promised that Ibiza would remain in Republican hands, not the Fascist rebels. We all cheered and showed the left-fist salute and shouted, *"Viva La Republica!"* and sang and danced.'

'So naïve!' tuts Isabella.

The old lady pushes her white hair back from her face. 'It's easy to say that now. This Captain Bayo only stayed five weeks and decided to go on to Mallorca with his troops to attempt to take Palma from the Fascists. That was the end.'

'Why?' I ask.

'We were left unprotected here because the Republican government recalled Captain Bayo and his troops to the capital, Madrid. His expedition to Mallorca had ended in failure anyway. Things became chaotic here. Two boats full of civilian Anarchists, about five hundred or more, turned up one day in September, all on the side of *Frente Popular*, but they were unruly and their leader, Juan Yagúe, didn't have much control. We knew it wouldn't be long before the Nationalists seized control of the island again.'

'The final turning point came at noon on Sunday 13 September. In Eivissa town, mothers and young children had gathered along the waterfront as usual to enjoy the sun and sea air. Without warning, four enemy planes appeared on the skyline and dropped bombs directly on them. They didn't target buildings, no, just defenceless women and children. I know because I was one of them.'

Pep's cigar nearly drops from his mouth in surprise. We sit silently, shocked, embarrassed and uncertain of what to say. Paja dabs at her eyes.

'Forgive me, but to this day, I cannot forget the sounds, the smell of horror and palpable terror.'

Isabella clasps her grandmother's hand. 'Paja lost her best friend, Marga, that day. She was only twelve. Thank God Marga's mother and youngest daughter, Julia, survived. It was a fluke that any of them were in Eivissa town at all – a whim of Marga's mother to get away from the oppressive feel of Santa Eularia. Paja had gone with them and they'd been given a lift to Eivissa by a local doctor. It was just supposed to be a nice day out.'

Paja shakes her head. 'Fifty-five Ibicencans were killed that day, forty-two of them women and children under the age of ten. In retaliation, the Anarchists who were guarding Eivissa fortress killed 113 of their Fascist prisoners, a mixture of priests, right-wing supporters and one or two prominent men. Some claim it was 239, others more but, if my memory serves me right, there are only 113 names on the plaque in the fortress. Who knows the truth? All that bloodshed and butchery, and for what?'

Alan eyes me fretfully, wondering how to lift the sudden sad tone of the evening. The children are below deck playing cards and I am thankful that neither has been party to this sad piece of Ibicencan history.

'It must have been so terrifying for all the islanders,' I say feebly. 'So when did the Nationalists conquer Ibiza?'

'It was 20 September that Italian troops in support of Franco landed and set up a Fascist administration. After that, those Republicans who hadn't escaped by boat or hidden in the forests were rounded up and killed or, if they were lucky, imprisoned.'

'What was happening in Formentera, meanwhile?' I ask.

She gives a big sigh. 'The Formenterencs suffered the most in the war. They were farming people and very much supported the left. When the Fascists took over Ibiza and Formentera, they made life difficult for all of the Republican supporters. There were executions every night and terrible deprivation on Formentera. There was hardly any food, no fuel and a constant witch hunt that had whole villages turning against each other.'

She shakes her head. 'We are a devout Catholic family but most of the priests supported the Fascists and were rounded up and killed. That was something the Republicans did to their shame. Thankfully Ibiza's most famous priest, Isidor Macabich, survived that persecution.'

'And you survived,' I say.

Paja nods and smiles. 'Yes, many of us managed to survive. It was a terrible period but it was a long time ago and, thank God, old wounds have more or less healed. I even have a Fascist son-in-law!'

'Steady on!' cries Enrique. 'I wasn't even born then.'

We laugh a little stiffly, and Isabella's parents, who have sat quietly during the old lady's story, gently help her to her feet and say it is time to leave. There is a slight kiss of rain in the air and the boat begins rocking to and fro.

'We're in for a stormy night,' says Pep with a grin.

'Remember, whatever the weather, we're setting off at six in the morning,' says Enrique.

'Aye, aye, Captain,' says Alan. 'We'll be here.'

Angel and Ollie appear on the deck, yawning loudly.

'Come on *chicos*,' says Juana. 'We're all going to bed.'

We say our goodbyes and walk slowly along the marina with Paja and Isabella's parents back to their car.

'Will it take you long to get back to Santa Eularia?' asks Alan.

'No,' says Vicente. 'Only about thirty minutes. 'Well, it has been lovely to meet you all.'

Paja gives Ollie a hug and presses my hand to her cheek.

'I hope it didn't sadden you too much to relive those memories,' I say.

She sighs. 'Not at all because I relive them every day, not in bitterness but in sadness. It was a black period in Spanish history and everyone was a loser in the end. In civil war both sides share the blame and shame.'

Alan, Ollie and I huddle together in the fierce wind, watching as the car slips away into the velvety night. I study the deserted and gloomy marina, imagining the tinkling laughter and then the sudden screams of terror and confusion of those unsuspecting women and children as bombs rained down upon them. I try to push away the thought.

'Ready for a bracing walk up to Dalt Vila?' asks the Scotsman cheerfully.

Ollie groans. 'Can you give me a piggyback?'

Alan clasps us both around the waist.

'In your dreams, sonny Jim, in your dreams.'

FOURTEEN

WILD HORSES AND HAZELNUTS

We sprawl on the deck under the full strength of a fat and cheerful sun. A mild wind is blowing and the yacht forges ahead smoothly, nosing its way confidently across the buoyant waves in a north-easterly direction towards Ciutadella, in the west of Menorca. Some five hours ago, at six in the morning, Alan, Ollie and I had breezed along the marina with overnight cases to find our companions aboard *La Marquessa* in an exhausted and dishevelled state. While we had slept peacefully at our boutique hotel in Dalt Vila, they had experienced a wild and tempestuous night in the harbour and had slept little. Still, several strong coffees and a hearty breakfast en route had revived their spirits and soon everyone was wide awake and in good cheer. We had set off just after six o'clock, easing up the east coast of Ibiza from Eivissa town and following the west coast of Mallorca, past Sóller and the bays of Cala Tuent and Sa Calobra. Enrique and Pep had increased the boat's speed to twenty-nine knots as we headed out into open sea, hoping to cover the 163 nautical miles in less than five hours.

In sharp contrast to the stormy night, the sea is calm and the sky a radiant blue. Enrique emerges from the upper saloon and calls to the boys. They look up sleepily from the deck where they have been dozing happily in the sun. He has his laptop with him.

'*Venga chicos*, I thought you might like to know a little about the festival before we arrive. We'll be there in about an hour.'

They sit up and peer inquisitively at the computer screen. The Scotsman and I rise from our comatose position and join Enrique at the outside table.

'You know the fiesta of San Joan has been in existence since the early fourteenth century. It was held in June in honour of Saint John the Baptist and has become one of the most famous festivals in the world. Now, the whole thing kicks off on a Sunday with Dìa des Be, which we happen to have missed but I took some film of the event last year.'

'The actual day of Sant Joan is the twenty-fourth, isn't it?' asks Alan.

Enrique fiddles with the mouse. 'Yes, although on the 23 June at 2 p.m. on the dot the official festivities begin at the Palace of Caixer Senyor in the main square. The Sunday before the event there is the quaint ceremony in which a man depicts San Joan. Look here.'

He clicks the screen and there before us is a young man wandering barefoot down a cobbled street literally in sheep's clothing, with a huge and fluffy white sheep draped like a shawl around his shoulders. On his forehead is a red cross and, apart from sheepskin, he wears little else. The boys giggle.

'What on earth is he doing?' asks Ollie. 'And who are those men on horseback?'

'The *Home de Be*, man of the sheep, welcomes everyone to the festival to the sound of flutes and drums. Accompanying him are the *caixers*, riders, who represent the social order of the town as it was in medieval times; churchmen, nobility, craftsmen and country folk.'

Angel points at the sheep. 'That must weigh a ton.'

'*Seguro*! The man chosen for the task must be very strong to carry a live sheep. It is a great honour. You see he has the cross of San Juan on his brow.'

I study the screen. 'Does he have to carry the sheep for a long time?'

He laughs. 'Long enough. Anyway, today the event begins at 2 p.m. at the palace of the Caixer Senyor, meaning nobleman. There is music and *primer toc*, which means the first notes played on the *flabiol*, a small flute made from cane. It makes an eerie, high-pitched sound.'

Alan claps his hands together. 'I hear the local brew, *pomeda*, is flowing throughout the festival.'

Enrique nods. 'Yes, that's right – Mahon gin and lemon. Everyone drinks a little bit too much of the stuff. Be careful, it's fairly strong.'

Juana and Isabella join us. They have been relaxing and chatting at the bow of the boat.

'I have been to the San Joan fiesta more than ten times and I never get bored with it,' proclaims Isabella. 'My family used to go every year.'

'Where did you stay?' I ask.

'We were lucky. My father had good friends living there so we always stayed at their home right in the centre of the town. We had the best view.'

Enrique turns off his laptop. 'We won't do so badly this time. We have an invitation to view the event from one of the buildings in the Pla de Born today.'

'How's that?' Alan asks.

'I have some contacts through my work in foreign affairs,' he mutters modestly. 'Right, I'd better relieve Pep in the cockpit. Look, there's Menorca now.'

We all leap up and turn to face the bow. Sure enough, land is coming into view.

Ollie and Angel begin packing up their cards and books.

'Steady on, boys, we're not quite there yet,' smiles Enrique. 'Let's organise a little Mahon gin and lemon juice before we arrive.'

Isabella swishes through to the saloon in a beautiful embroidered dress.

'Can I help?' I call after her.

'No, you just enjoy the sea air.'

'By the way, Alan, the hotel I've booked you three into for tonight and tomorrow is just off the Pla de Born. You'll love it. I only wish you would have stayed on the boat with us,' says Isabella.

Alan shakes his head. 'Listen, it's very good of you but there just wouldn't be enough space for us all. Besides, it will be nice for us to explore Ciutadella on foot.'

'Well, we shall enjoy the fiesta together at least,' she smiles.

Thirty minutes later we are all sitting on deck enjoying delicious *pomeda* with ice. The boys, however, stick to Coca-Cola.

'I could get used to this,' says the Scotsman, flicking an almond into his mouth.

'That's reminded me,' says Isabella. 'There's a fun event tomorrow night which involves throwing hazelnuts. It's a bit crazy but in the past young swains apparently used to bring their girlfriends bags of whole hazelnuts as a sign of affection. Today it's just a bit of silliness, but young people enjoy it.'

Ollie perks up. 'That sounds cool. Can Angel and I go?'

'So it's a big hazelnut fight?' says Angel with a grin.

She tuts. 'It isn't supposed to be violent. Everyone just throws the nuts in a spirit of fun. No one is supposed to be aggressive about it.'

'I'm not sure if it's such a good idea,' I say. 'Besides, you might be in bed by then. Let's see.'

The boys groan.

Pep arrives and lights a *puro*. He jiggles his hips and pushes his cap firmly over his wild grey hair. 'Tonight's the night for partying. This is one of my favourite events!'

Juana rolls her eyes. 'The minute you start embarrassing us, I shall be off.'

He claps his hands together. 'Great! I shall be free to get up to mischief.'

The stunning town of Ciutadella rises before us as it sits slightly above the busy harbour.

'Right,' says Enrique, 'We are going to dock a little way out with the other boats and take the dinghy in. Can you gather your belongings?'

All around us yachts large and small bob on the glistening waves. The sun is hot on my back and when I lick my lips they taste of sea brine. Cheers rise from the large gathering of souls milling in the harbour. It seems the celebrations are about to begin.

The air is thick with the smell of cordite, sweat, manure, heat and horse. A giant swell of people is crushing us on both sides and whistles, pipes, drums and cheers rent the air. Sweat drips from my forehead as a hot red sun spreads needles of heat across the vast and magnificent Pla de Born. Thundering along the cobbled streets, which have been strewn with sawdust, comes another powerfully built, sleek and black Menorcan steed. On its back is a tall rider clad in traditional black frock coat, white breeches, black tricorn and polished black boots. He raises a musical pipe and then thrusts the horse into the crowd to the cries of, '*Jaleo! Jaleo!*' Immediately the horse rises up on to its hind legs and whinnies loudly. Ollie squeezes closer as the gigantic hooves pound the air. Dust flies and young men run forward trying to touch its flanks or, so it seems, tip the horse backwards. The rider laughs and, with a quick crack of the whip, gallops ahead to join his companions.

Ollie raises his eyebrows. 'That was a bit close. I thought it was going to tumble down on top of us! Why are they all shouting *jaleo*?'

'It means "merry-making" or "uproar" in Spanish. I suppose it's a way of goading the riders into rearing their horses in the air. Wait for it, here comes another.'

We move back and watch as a horse speeds past, rearing up and then pressing on towards the front of the Bishop Marroig's seventeenth-century palace. I stand on my tiptoes to survey the crowd and decide that at least 10,000 people must have crammed into the square. I feel a tap on my shoulder and Enrique is indicating with his eyes to follow. We beat a retreat, grappling with the swaying crowds, and finally find ourselves on the perimeter of the square.

'I have some friends – officials – who would like us to join them in one of the historic buildings. Come! I have sent the others on ahead.'

Ollie and I scramble after him and finally find ourselves on an expansive balcony in full view of the square. Angel rushes over to Ollie and pats his back.

'Where did you go?' he yells.

Ollie shrugs. 'My mother and I got separated in the crowd.'

A waiter appears with Pep at his side and offers me a glass of *pomeda*.

'Just what the doctor ordered,' I gasp.

Ollie accepts a Coca-Cola with some relief. A group of stylishly dressed men and women are watching the event from the other side of the terrace. I surmise that they must be some of Menorca's top brass. Pep talks to the waiter and he returns with some chairs.

'Sit, sit,' instructs Pep. 'We all found each other but gave up looking for you and Ollie. Then Alan spotted you in the crowds. Wasn't it crazy down there?'

'Mad but exhilarating. Why do the crowds shout *jaleo*?'

'Ah, that's an instruction for the rider to rear up on his horse. Sometimes the young guys bait the horse-rider to rise higher. It's just for fun.'

Alan comes over with a huge smile on his face. 'The wanderer returns! One minute you were next to me and then you'd vanished.'

I turn to him. 'I know. Ollie wanted to get closer to the horses and the crowd closed in around us.'

Enrique and Isabella, carrying glasses of gin, come over to join us.

'Isn't it heavenly up here?' Isabella sighs. 'You know this is the heart of Ciutadella. Of course before you awful British came in the eighteenth century and conquered the island, this city was the capital.'

'I apologise for our ancestors,' says Alan.

'So you should,' cries Pep. 'What a po-faced lot they were. Even now Mahon, the present capital, smart as it is, has that straight-backed, upper-class British feel. It's hard to eradicate.'

Enrique frowns. 'That's not fair. I think the British did a good job with the architecture in Mahon, although I prefer the ochre and terracotta walls of this old city. It has such panache and a richness of history.'

'Were the locals angry when the capital was moved to Mahon?' asks Ollie.

Enrique shrugs. 'Not really. The Menorcan aristocracy, the bishop and the church refused to leave Ciutadella and lived a way of life distinct from their British rulers. Part of the reason why the city still retains its Moorish feel and grand palaces is precisely because it was left to its own devices by the British.'

Pep takes a sip of his gin. 'The town has a violent history. It was vanquished by the Romans, then the Moors and in 1558 Turkish corsairs attacked and enslaved three thousand inhabitants, carting them off to sell at the Istanbul markets.'

'What happened?' says Angel.

'A brave Menorcan doctor named Marcos Martí negotiated with the Turks using money acquired by the Pope, and all were returned to Ciutadella.'

'A happy ending,' says Isabella.

'Happy endings don't exist,' snorts Pep. 'They rebuilt their city in splendour, were minding their own business and then the acquisitive Brits turned up.'

'That's enough Brit bashing for one day,' laughs Alan. 'Go and get us another drink.'

Pep wanders off, his arm slung chummily around the shoulder of the very polite waiter. I worry that the officials might think we're abusing their hospitality but Enrique seems laid-back about it all and says that today is open house. Enrique lights a cigarette and wanders over to shake the hands of some of the other guests at the far end of the terrace. A distinguished older man hands him two bags. Smiles and nods are exchanged.

'Lucky *chicos*!' says Enrique, returning to us and approaching Angel and Ollie. 'That kind gentleman works for the Ciutadella council and has given you both a bag of goodies. There's a T-shirt for you both with the red and white flag of San Joan.'

The boys fall on the bags in great excitement and strip off their T-shirts, replacing them with the festival ones. They have been given leaflets, pens and even a replica Menorcan steed.

We drain our glasses.

'I think we should re-enter the fray,' says Enrique. 'It's the *caragol*, the snail, when the riders form loops around the crowds. The horses look so beautiful.'

'Why is there such an emphasis on horses at this festival?' I ask.

Enrique shrugs. 'It harks back to medieval days when the aristocracy would have jousting matches and show off their horses. The Menorcan horses are famous worldwide so these days it's an opportunity to demonstrate their skills and beauty. Anyway, let's get going. There'll be time to rest on the boat later before the evening celebrations.'

We look down at the heaving crowd and then follow Enrique back down the stone staircase into the deafening scrum. This time, though, we stick close together.

The sea is thick and viscous like rich black oil. A sky heavy with amber stars smiles down at the dancing and singing crowds as they make their way from the waterfront to the open strip of land where the *juegos peligrosos* will take place.

'Dangerous games?' Alan asks with alarm. 'How dangerous?'

Pep giggles. 'Oh, it's nothing. Just a bit of jousting and racing.'

The boys are intoxicated by the dark balmy night, the crowds of happy, laughing people and the promise of danger. Everyone gathers for the horse events, jostling for the best view and whistling and calling out to the riders. A man begins playing a guitar while his companion bangs loudly on a *tambor*, a taut hide drum, and sings a Menorcan *glose*.

'What is he saying?' I ask Pep.

'The song is about how annoying women are and how they need to be controlled.'

'I don't believe you,' I say.

'That's wise,' he says, 'because I completely made that up.'

'I think you've had far too much *pomeda*,' chastises Juana.

'Good, then I can go to bed happy and laughing and wake up with a bad hangover. That's how it ought to be,' he chortles.

Angel and Ollie giggle wildly and cover their faces with their hands when an old man topples sideways, knocking over his companion as he tries to down some *pomeda* from an upturned *flacon*. The two men roll about on the ground in fits of laughter until some fellow spectators help them to their feet, amid much cajoling and harmless taunts.

As we jostle with the crowd a pipe sounds and before we know it there's the pounding of sharp hooves and a horseman rushes headlong through the darkness, lance at the ready. Strung up high between two poles is a rope from which a round peg is suspended. The aim is to spear the peg through the middle. The first horseman misses. The crowd roars and there's the sound of stamping feet. Another horseman pounds through the dust, raising his lance high and this time spearing the peg. The crowds are ecstatic, jumping and clapping in glee. The contest continues, the smell of gin, sweat and hot dust assailing our nostrils. A young man waggles a *flacon* of alcohol in my direction before crashing to the ground. Laughing, one of his companions lifts him to his feet and carries him off to a nearby tree to sober up.

The event livens up as greater numbers of riders manage to accurately spear the pegs. They thunder along the parched earth with grim determination, spurred on by the hysterical baying of the crowd. When their energy is spent they trot away from the track to rest for a while, knowing that the rest of the races will soon commence.

It is an hour later that the hazelnut-throwing battle takes place, by which time we have all had far too much *pomeda* and are desperately in need of our beds. Ollie and Angel beg to take part and, on the insistence of Enrique, the boys get their way. My memory is of the sound of cracking nuts, screams of laughter and thousands of ducking bodies, many with their eyes clad in big protective glasses. Ollie and Angel have the time of their lives, ending up on their backs and giggling at the end of the fight when they discover a small arsenal of hazelnuts has worked its way inside their T-shirts and down to their trousers and socks. The rest of us have shielded our faces with our arms as best we can during the debacle, although are surprised to find no aggressive behaviour. Quite to the contrary, most combatants aim in the air with their caches of nuts to avoid causing injury to fellow revellers. At two in the morning we finally wander back to the hotel and flop exhausted into our beds while the others return to the harbour. How they negotiate the walk back to the yacht we don't know – or care for that matter – because at this hour our only concern is sleep and the illuminated hotel lobby is a miraculous and welcome sight.

It is early afternoon the next day when we arrive at Ibiza's small airport outside Eivissa town. Having left Ciutadella in the morning by ferry for Mallorca, we then caught the island hopper from Palma airport, a twenty-minute flight back to Ibiza. We said our farewells to the sleepy and hung-over occupants of *La Marquessa* before we left Menorca. The brief flight has been bumpy so I am relieved to touch down at Eivissa Airport. Ollie leans against my shoulder.

'I loved Menorca but I'm always glad to return to Ibiza.'

'What about Mallorca then?'

'That's different because it's home.'

Alan grapples with his wallet, pulling out folded bits of paper and crumpled receipts. 'I hope I've got the parking ticket safe.'

I give him a sharp look. 'Woe betide you if you haven't.'

He spends an anxious few moments examining every receipt until in relief he waves the ticket in the air. 'Bingo! We're in business. Isn't it a blissful thought? Four more days of holiday. I could get used to this life.'

'Me too,' echoes Ollie.

He stands up, rucksack over his shoulder. 'The plane's stopped. Shall we get moving?'

The journey has been effortless, although with all the exhaustion from the celebrations we've slept most of the way and now leap to our feet. Ollie leads the way and soon we're descending the small flight of steps into the warm air. A crush of people wait ahead of us, bearing suitcases and rucksacks.

'Shall we hang out in Eivissa town tonight?' yawns Alan.

'Where else? The hotel's expecting us. We can set off on our island tour tomorrow.'

Ollie frowns. 'We are going to stay at Hotel Victoria, aren't we?'

This Swedish hotel on a secluded hill near San Antonio has always proved a favourite haunt for us all.

'Of course. We'll stay there from tomorrow night,' I reply.

We make our way into the airport arrival lounge.

'No more festivals for a while,' says Alan sleepily as we walk with the others to the exit.

'Absolutely,' I reply. 'I think the San Joan fiesta might be enough to keep us going for another year. Now for some quiet nights in Ibiza.'

The sun bathes us in white light as we emerge from the arrivals lounge and hail a taxi into Eivissa town. The taxi driver follows the main road to the car park in the town where we have left the Mini. We bid him farewell and head for our hotel in the car, stopping at a local newspaper shop on the way. Alan buys a local paper and scans the front page.

'Thankfully, there doesn't seem to be much happening on the island.'

Ollie takes it from him and begins browsing the pages.

'That's just how I like Eivissa town,' I say. 'Peaceful and tourist-free.'

Ollie looks at us both with a sadistic smile. 'Actually there's a report here about an amazing fiesta which kicks off at ten tonight in the village of Sant Josep.'

Alan grabs the newspaper and hits him on the head with it. 'Well, don't expect us to join you.'

'Did you say Sant Josep? It's one of my favourite villages,' I exclaim in mock delight.

'Yes, me too!' says Ollie, giving me a nudge.

'You can't be serious,' puffs the weary Scotsman.

'Well, it's only half an hour away from Eivissa town. If it starts at ten, we could be back at the hotel by about four in the morning,' I say.

'Exactly,' grins Ollie.

Alan stops and looks at us both as if we've completely lost our minds.

'You really want to go to an all-night fiesta?' he asks incredulously.

'Only kidding,' I reply with a wink.

Ollie laughs and gives him a punch on the arm. 'You never learn!'

FIFTEEN

MAD HATTERS

Wednesday 2 p.m., the office, Mayfair

Rachel stretches her long legs across her desk and reads a passage out loud from *Private Eye*. She tosses the magazine on the desk and shrieks with laughter.

'I love it when Greedy George gets a pasting in *Private Eye*. They've really gone to town on his Chinese donkey gambit.'

I pull the magazine towards me. 'We're not supposed to be laughing at our clients when they get caught out in the press, Rachel. It's our job to keep them in the clear.'

She throws a ball of scrunched paper at me. 'Oh, says she, who stitched him up in the first place!'

'I can't think what you mean.'

'You can't fool me. I know that you got in touch with that donkey charity and spilled the beans on George. And do you know how I know?'

I give her an exasperated expression. 'Go on then.'

'When you were last in the office, you left a doodle on a Post-it note with the name Alicia and the words Donkey Defence Trust. I looked them up on Google and found Alicia was a trustee.'

'Aren't you a regular sleuth? OK, well I did talk to Alicia but I hadn't bargained on her organising heckling demonstrators outside the Havana store.'

She laughs. 'Your secret's safe, although Sarah knows. She noticed the Post-it too but of course wouldn't tell George. Given how many scrapes you get yourself into, you're lucky that we employ very discreet people.'

'Well, pretty soon I won't have to worry about all this PR nonsense.'

'You wish! So where are you up to with Dynamite Communications?'

'Amazingly, I've had some excellent conversations with Gillian, the managing director, and I'm impressed with their offer document. I'm seeing her later today and if that goes well I'll get you to meet her before I go back to Mallorca this week.'

'Blimey! You seem really keen.'

'Actually, I think this is it. Simon Rendall has done us proud as a broker. It really seems to be just what we're looking for and there's no question of Gillian's not wanting to take on our staff.'

'That's fantastic. Fingers crossed for your meeting, then. By the way, harking back to the donkey theme, how are your donkey plans coming on in Mallorca?'

'You'll be pleased to learn that the new cattery is just about finished and Stefan and his men are sorting out the donkey paddock as we speak.'

She giggles. 'How I pity poor Alan.'

'By the way, did I tell you about my idea to sell lemon curd locally?'

She narrows her eyes. 'Please tell me you're joking.'

'Of course I'm not. I've just given samples to several stores in Sóller.'

'Martha Stewart comes to the mountains!' she crows. 'May I ask why?'

'It seemed like a good way of using up our excess lemons. Mind you, it is quite time-consuming.'

She gets up and tosses her keys and Filofax in her handbag. 'It's an insane idea and probably completely unprofitable.'

'But fun.'

'No, I don't think it's fun. The sooner you knock it on the head the better. You've got more than enough on your plate. Why go looking for more headaches?'

I get up and pull my papers together. 'You have a point. So it's countdown for the big event. Do you think we'll keep our mad hatters under control?'

She shrugs. 'We've got an impressive guest- and press-list confirmed. I just hope Marcus and Pippa Darley behave themselves tomorrow. Actually, Bruno's the biggest worry.'

I frown. 'Why? I think he'll do us proud as the drag hatter compère. He was calm as a cucumber at the rehearsal this morning and the models were fantastic.'

'They're drag queens, not models, remember,' she corrects.

'Whatever they are, it was an outstanding performance and the new hat range is fantastic.'

She stands by the door, handbag over her shoulder and clutching a pile of files. 'You've really thrown yourself into this mad event. I never thought it would come off but somehow it has. Let's just hope it's a success.'

'The Dorchester seems to think so. I spoke to Concetto, the guest relations manager who's a complete perfectionist, and he loved the rehearsal.'

'That's a good sign I suppose.' She looks at her watch. 'Gosh, must be off for my meeting with Alicia and Charlie Romstead. I'll see you at The Dorchester tomorrow.'

She scurries out of the office, issues some instructions to Sarah and is gone. I walk over to the window and look down at the scrawny branches of a tree far below the window. Here we are in July and the poor trees in this city are sad, drooping and practically devoid of leaves. The street is teeming with the usual cheerless foot soldiers going about their day-to-day business and also a few bewildered backpackers holding maps up to their noses. Sarah pops her head around the door.

'How are you doing? Want another coffee?'

'Thanks but I'd better get going to this meeting.'

She nods slowly. 'Is this the new agency you're talking to?'

'Yes, it could be the right one this time.'

'It'll be sad to disband the company. We've had a fun time together.'

She's right. In the rush to find a company to merge with I've barely given myself a minute to think about how it will feel when we all go our separate ways. I regard the girls in my office as family.

'Life has to move on and you're a go-getter so in some ways this could present new opportunities for you.'

'Maybe,' she says thoughtfully. 'I suppose I'll have to decide whether I want to find something completely different or stay with the new company.'

'It's an important decision but why not wait until I suss out Dynamite first?'

She smiles. 'Of course. Anyway, I've got enough to think about with this mad hatter's tea party tomorrow, and next week I'm off to help the Claverton-Michaels' with a summer fun day.'

I gather up my files and handbag and head for the door. 'Let's hope you don't meet any ghosts.'

She laughs. 'That wouldn't worry me at all. We've had ghosts at home since I was little.'

'Are you kidding?'

She nods her head. 'My parents have an old coaching inn in Kent. We're always hearing spirits clattering about in the kitchen, even ghostly horses neighing in the courtyard. It's quite comforting if you're at home alone.'

I walk down the stairs to the reception in some confusion. It would never have crossed my mind before that a ghost could make good company.

5 p.m., Dynamite Communications, Mayfair

Gillian Simpson sits across from me at the large wooden table. Dynamite's offices occupy the top floor of a modest building just off Bond Street and enjoy a spectacular view from their wide rear windows of the black slate rooftops of Mayfair. In fact, all I can think about is the sequence from *Mary Poppins* with the chimneysweeps dancing across the roofs. Gillian pushes back a stray lock of black hair, a bemused look on her face.

'You seem very taken with the rooftop view.'

I force my eyes to focus on the woman in the crisp suit before me.

'Yes, I must admit to having a fascination with rooftops.'

'Not a morbid preoccupation with leaping from them?'

'An interesting thought, but no. In truth it has more to do with *Mary Poppins*.'

'Chimneysweeps?' she suggests brightly.

'Exactly.'

She offers me a butternut biscuit and takes one herself. We sit chewing thoughtfully.

'We could sing the song if you like. You know, *"Chim chimney, chim chim cher-ee"*.'

I shake my head. 'No, that won't be necessary. Therein madness lies.'

She giggles. 'It's good to know I'm not the only nut around here. So, what do you think, shall we merge so that you can go off and live in la la land?'

'That sounds good. I mean, if you're happy for me to duck out after a year then I think we've got a deal.'

She smiles. 'Good. I think, as you say, we'll keep George Myers and Dannie Popescu-Miller out of the contract. They've made it pretty clear that they'd like you personally to carry on handling their PR work, which is fine by us. We're after your travel and UK business mostly.'

I gather up my belongings. 'I'll get our lawyers to check through the contract this week and then get Rachel in to meet you.'

'You're comfortable if we aim for the merger in September? We'll have August, which is a dead month, to wind things up and to move your staff over here.'

I nod. 'Yes, I think it's do-able.'

She bends forward and kisses me on both cheeks. Spanish customs are catching on fast in London.

'Here's to new beginnings! Call me with a time for us to get together with Rachel.'

I leave the office, a lightness to my step. Finally, it seems that I've found the right company. It will be a low-key, simple merger with no fanfare and fuss and for the first year I will become a monthly commuter, supporting the new company and the clients until everyone has learned the ropes. I shall then be footloose and fancy-free in Mallorca. After several years of constantly hopping on and off planes, it will be a joy to have the time to concentrate on new projects in the hills, such as my cattery. Moving to Mallorca was a gamble that now seems to be paying off. I always knew that I would have to work hard in order to fulfil the dream and now I feel huge satisfaction knowing that I've earned my small slice of paradise in the mountains. My excitement is almost palpable. I hail a cab to Havana's showroom, feeling brave enough to cope with any new madness that Greedy George may throw at me.

7 p.m., Havana Leather, St James's

Richard, Greedy George's beleaguered shop manager, is sitting on a stool behind the counter with his long legs folded coquettishly in front of him. The air conditioning is on full blast, so I instinctively reach for my cotton cardigan as I stride through the showroom.

'Too chilly for you?' trills Richard.

'I know it's July but it's like a mini Siberia in here. Can you turn it down a shade?'

He rolls his eyes and gives me an impish grin. 'You're just acclimatised to the sun, sweetie. We poor Londoners can't cope with this heatwave.'

'Why are you still working at this hour anyway?'

He leaps down from his stool and slinks over to me. 'It's stocktaking tonight. Always a bore.

I've got a hot date later so don't keep him here too long.'

I laugh. 'Trust me, we're just having a quick catch-up and I'm off.'

There's the sound of heavy footsteps from above and then a voice bellows from the landing. 'What are you rattling on about, Ricardo? Go and get some drinks and stop moaning, you old queen.'

Richard nudges me. 'Isn't George a joy to work for?'

I give him a conspiratorial wink and plod up the stairs. I've barely reached the landing when George impatiently accosts me at his office doorway. He's had his grey hair cropped ultra-short so that it resembles a newly trimmed Mediterranean lawn.

'Come on, guv, we haven't got all day. I thought you were supposed to be a marathon girl?'

'What's the rush? I've had a long day.'

He ushers me into the room. 'Long day? Tell me about it. Anyway, come and have a look at this fab clobber. It's for one of my new winter ranges.'

'Winter?' There's always something bizarre about discussing cold seasonal wear in the middle of a sweltering summer.

He claps his pulpy hands together. 'It's the Biggles flying range. What d'you think of this?'

He grabs a brown leather flying hat from the glass table and jams it down on his large head. The leather chin-straps hang loose and the sheepskin border around his furrowed brow gives the appearance of beige curly hair. I erupt into giggles.

'I can't decide whether you look like Churchill, a distraught lamb or a bulldog.'

'You're fired.'

'If I'd known that's all it took, I would have called you Churchill before!'

'It's the distraught lamb I object to, not bleeding Churchill. What's wrong with it?'

'Nothing. It's just that it's not quite you. Anyway, what are you trying to do, appeal to would-be pilots?'

'You don't need to be a pilot to wear a Biggles hat, guv. They're all doing them now – Armani, MG, all the cool brands.'

'So, how much are they going to retail for?'

'About two hundred quid at a guess.'

I shake my head. What kind of person would spend that sort of dosh in order to look like a, well, distressed lamb?

Richard barges through the doors with a tray. 'Some chilled champagne and salted almonds.'

'You're a treasure,' I say.

'Oh, listen to Mother Teresa of the Mountains. Careful Ricardo, or she might adopt you and tether you up with her goats and donkeys.'

'Things could be worse, George. I could carry on working here,' sniggers Richard.

'Oh, aren't we the wit? Anyway, guv, what's happening with your donkey project? I'm off them after that bloody donkey trust put the kybosh on my new range. Liu Chan was well peed off.'

'I'm sure it was all for the best. Anyway, there's nothing more to report just yet. Suffice to say it's progressing.'

George begins humming 'Old Macdonald' and gives Richard a shove.

'Put the damn tray down. I'm gagging for a drink.'

I move a pile of Biggles hats to one side of the table to make room for the tray.

'Hey Richard, try on one of these hats,' I say, holding a sample out to him.

He puts the tray down and gingerly picks it up. 'It's a bit kitsch but it could have its uses.'

He slips it on his head and, as I expected, he looks rather handsome. 'That really suits you, Richard.'

He waltzes over to George's large mirror in front of the mantelpiece and examines himself. 'You're right. I do look rather groovy but then I have naturally fine features.'

George slaps the table. 'Get out of here, you idiot.'

Richard drops the hat back on the table with a chuckle. 'I'll leave you in peace.'

'Help yourself to a glass of fizz downstairs,' mumbles George.

'I will, thank you.'

Maybe I should invite Richard to my mad hatter's tea party event tomorrow. He'd love all the drag queens.'

'Nah, don't spoil him. By the way, do you know where the term 'mad hatter' comes from?'

'Tell me.'

'Apparently hatters in the nineteenth century used to use mercury for making felt hats. The poor sods would get mercury poisoning and go barmy.'

'Trust you to know about that,' I sigh.

'So,' says George. 'What's new? Any fresh ghostly sightings of late?'

'Nothing like an old gag, eh? Actually, I do have some big news…'

'You're selling up?' he sits up and takes a large gulp from his glass.

'I really think I've found the right company to merge with. It's called Dynamite Communications.'

'Naff name but you can't have everything,' he chortles.

'That aside, I think it's just the right size and the clients are synergistic. You'd like the MD, Gillian Simpson.'

'Well, let's drink to the merger but listen up, as agreed you'll continue to work with me on a freelance basis. I'm not going to start getting to know this new bird, Gillian.'

'But I thought you just fired me?'

'Today,' he grins, sipping his champagne. 'But tomorrow's a different kettle of fish.'

Thursday 8 a.m., the club, Mayfair
Standing outside the club I am relieved to see a vibrant blue sky above and a small gathering of sparrows happily pecking on a discarded bread roll by a rubbish bin – a few small signs of the natural world to keep my spirits up before returning to Mallorca. I see the amber light of an empty black cab heading towards me along the busy street and put out my hand. It pulls over just as a hysterical Irish voice yells my name from the front door of my club. Now what? Bernadette, clad in a red working overall and gripping a yellow duster in one hand, is scurrying down the front steps. Behind oversized glasses she sports a violent shade of glittering, sea-green eyeshadow, her red hair blazes in the emerging sunlight and on her feet are – oh don't tell me – pink, furry pompom slippers. She waves frantically at me and it is at that moment that I notice the briefcase in her free hand. It looks suspiciously like mine – the one that I no longer have in my grip.

'You left your briefcase at reception, you daft brush!' she yells as I walk towards her.

'Mother of God, making me come out in me slippers in a public street. Whatever next?'

She pokes her head through the cabbie's open passenger window. 'She's a hopeless case. Make sure she hasn't forgotten her wallet too! There's nothing between her two ears.'

Amid peals of manic laughter, I watch as she shuffles back to the club's front door.

'Sorry about that,' I say in some embarrassment as I settle myself in the back of the cab.

The cabbie grins. 'Mothers, eh? What would we do without 'em?'

5 p.m., Drag Hatter's Tea Party, The Dorchester, Park Lane
The Dorchester ballroom is in crimson and cream livery, and wild, blood-red roses are strewn dramatically and liberally across the guests' tables and on the floor of a raised T-shaped stage running through the centre of the large room. What looks like snow, but is in reality dendritic salt, has been scattered all about to give a feeling of Christmas despite the fact that London is experiencing a heatwave. Each table of eight well-heeled guests sports at its centre a large card replica figure of the Mad Hatter from *Alice in Wonderland* with the words, 'Drag Hatter's Tea Party'. Discreet waiters waltz around the tables, offering tea and cucumber sandwiches, scones with cream and glasses of champagne. A pair of drag queens have been kitted out in surreal fur costumes to resemble two of Lewis Carroll's characters, one a dormouse carrying a teapot and the other a March hare. They teeter about the room in spindly heels, flamboyant fur and felt winter hats. Bruno, The Drag Hatter compère extraordinaire, has spent the last forty minutes conducting the most bizarre hat show I have even seen. The models, all towering drag queens who, like Bruno,

perform at Drag Haven in Soho, have thrilled guests with a son et lumière show in which they danced, gyrated and sang in glorious, exotic hats. Beside themselves with delight, Pippa and Marcus Darley stood by the side of the stage clapping frantically. At the end of the show, Marcus took his bow on the stage with Bruno and the team and rushed over to my table.

'It's been a sensation. The press love the new range! I can't believe how brilliant Bruno was and weren't the drag queens a riot?' he exclaims excitedly.

I agree that the show has been an unquestionable success. He sits down, beckoning to his wife to join us. Pippa saunters over in high heels and a long white, crushed silk gown. On her head she wears a crimson hat that resembles a giant cherry with a single white plume emerging from its centre.

'We've made *The Sunday Times*, and *Grazia* is going to do an interview and feature on the new range. I'm ecstatic,' she cries.

Rachel, who has been sitting in some bemusement throughout the proceedings, raises her teacup.

'Hats off to you! The collection really is superb and Bruno was a star.'

As if on cue, Bruno waves from the side of the stage where he is besieged by adoring guests and fashion press. He wears a foppish, wavy wig, top hat and giant spotted bow tie. His faithfulness to the original Tenniel book illustration of the Mad Hatter wanders at that point because from the waist down he is clad in Lycra hot pants, fish nets and glittery red platform boots.

'I always loved the original drawing of the Mad Hatter with his winged collar and spotted bow tie,' observes Rachel.

'Bruno's interpretation is certainly novel,' I mutter. 'Unforgettable in fact.'

'Absolutely,' shrieks Marcus Darley. 'Oh, it must be at times like this that you miss London life and question your rural existence.'

He stares at me intently.

I ponder his words for a few seconds. 'You're right, Marcus. Nothing could quite match this event in my valley but who knows, perhaps we could bring the drag hatter concept to Sóller?'

He raises both hands in the air. 'Oh really? Well count us in. Do Mallorcans wear many hats, then?'

Rachel nearly spills her tea mid sip.

'Not really, Marcus,' I laugh. 'I was being ironic.'

He smiles. 'You may laugh but stranger things have happened.'

'The day you stage a drag hatter's tea party in the Sóller valley, I'll eat my hat.'

He chinks my glass and beams. 'Then let's drink to that.'

SIXTEEN

DANCING IN THE STREET

A plump golden sun squats aloft the Tramuntanas, surveying the lush green orchards and pine forests below. In the sizzling heat of July the frogs and lizards vie for shelter in the dark crevices of the rock wall by the pond and the portly goldfish hide in the entangled weeds deep below the water's surface. Whistling cheerily as he saunters along the track is Jorge, his long tresses fastened back into a neat ponytail. His yellow sack is flung over his right shoulder and in his hand he clasps a small package. He's about to buzz at the gate when he suddenly notices me observing him from the doorway. I open the gate and wait until he's reached the shadow of the steps. He throws his bag on to the porch and sits down heavily on the top step.

'This heat is a killer. I've drunk about four litres of water today.'

I offer to get him a glass but he shakes his head.

'No thanks, I don't want to overdose on the stuff. I'm knocking off for lunch soon anyway. I'll have a cool beer then.'

He hands me the package which I see is a book from an American antiquarian bookshop. Inside is a 1937 edition of a book by Elliot Paul, an American journalist and author who lived in Ibiza during the Spanish Civil War.

'I've been waiting some time for this book.'

I hold it up to Jorge. He takes it from my hands and reads the jacket's cover. 'It's a bit gloomy, isn't it? All about Franco's invasion of Ibiza.'

I shrug. 'I find it a fascinating subject. It's a tragic episode in Spanish history but I can't imagine living here without knowing something of its past.'

He sighs. 'I don't know much about it and I don't see the point of poring over books. What's the point of digging up the past? The Spanish government wants to exhume all these bodies from the Spanish Civil War. What for? All it does is give rise to old enmities.'

He has a good point. Sometimes it's best to let sleeping dogs lie.

'So, how's married life?'

He pats his stomach. 'I've put on four kilos.'

'I can see. Isn't it women who are supposed to pile on the weight when they get hitched, not men?'

'The trouble is that I love cooking and now that I come home to Beatriz, I've an excuse to spend time in the kitchen.'

I laugh. 'Life's for living. A few kilos won't kill you.'

A wasp flits in front of me and I take a swipe at it.

'Be careful doing that. It just makes them angry.'

'We're being plagued by them at the moment. They've got nests everywhere.'

He frowns and follows my gaze to one of the window ledges.

'*Hombre*! That's a huge nest. Get Alan to knock it down. Best to burn them and do it at dusk when they're not buzzing about.'

'We've got nests hanging outside every window. It seems to have happened overnight.'

He looks perplexed. 'That's very odd. Maybe it's something about the house or its position.'

'Who knows?' I reply.

'Why not go to the *ferreteria* and get a solution to ward them off?' he suggests.

'Good idea. Thanks.'

He pulls the bag over his shoulder and stretches. 'I'd better be off. See you soon.'

I watch as he sets off down the path. Today I am expecting a call from Gillian Simpson about the company merger. There have been a few points on the final contract that our lawyer has queried but, other than that, we're about to agree final terms. Rachel has met with Gillian and the team at Dynamite and thinks the company suits us perfectly. Can this really be it? The big break?

There's a hooting at the gate and Catalina arrives. The car skids across the gravel and stops abruptly a few feet from me.

'Hey, I've just been into Sóller. Sa Mostra begins today and the *plaça* is already decked out with the stage and lights. Have you seen it?'

'Not yet, but I've got the programme. It looks exciting. They've got Indian and Russian dancers this year. Hopefully we can pop along tomorrow night.'

She bustles up the steps. 'This heat is going to kill me.'

'You and Jorge both. He's just been complaining.'

She nods. 'I just spoke to him on the track. He says you've got a wasp problem.'

As usual news travels faster than sound in this town.

'We seem to be attracting them in droves.'

She tuts and barges into the *entrada,* dumping her wicker basket on a chair. 'I'll give you the name of a solution to drive them away but maybe we can knock the nests off the windowsills now.'

'I'm not sure. Jorge advised against it during the day.'

She waves her hands in the air. '*Hombres*!' Men.

Alan potters into the kitchen at the sound of Catalina's voice.

'Would this solution you're talking about work on stray cats? I'm sick of them peeing all over my saplings. Enough is enough!'

'Just hose them with water,' she says as she marches across to the sink. 'Some people put chilli pepper on the soil. They don't like that.'

'Poor little things. That would be a dreadful thing to do,' I cry.

The Scotsman mumbles something under his breath. 'Anyway, let's forget the damned ferals for a moment. Come and have a look at what Stefan's done in our field.'

'Of course, you haven't seen it!' I say.

'Si, si the paddock and cattery. I am dying to inspect my brother's work. Stefan told me you've agreed a price on the donkeys and they'll be arriving soon.'

'Mother and daughter are packing their bags as we speak. They'll be here next month. We have some early cat-boarders arriving around the same time so it will be all hands to the pump,' I reply.

'I need a coffee. What about you?' Catalina asks.

'An iced one would be great but come on, let's go and do a tour of the land first.'

We set off down to the field. Salvador and the hens have been moved to a newly installed stone house with a wider and grassier run that backs onto a shady wall. For once the old boy looks positively chirpy as he struts about with his bossy entourage in tow. Cordelia sits serenely in the hen house observing the rest of the gang, enjoying the sunshine. Beyond the hen enclosure is the paddock in the middle of which is a sturdy wooden shelter for the donkeys. The whole zone has been protected by strong fencing and a small gate includes Pep and Juana's plaque with the names Minny and Della.

Catalina smiles. 'It's nice that you are calling the donkeys after your eccentric elderly aunts. They would have loved that.'

She examines the wooden fencing. 'It's very strong. That's good. There's quite a lot of shade too, which is ideal for donkeys.'

We walk over to the wooden cattery building, which sits in its own small, fenced-off garden. 'What do you think?'

'Very nice,' she enthuses. 'Now all you need is some guests.'

'Do you want to look inside?' asks the Scotsman.

She nods enthusiastically. We open the gate and walk around the small garden. Alan proudly shows her his newly planted bushes of rosemary and climbing jasmine. We enter the small building and she walks into each cat run, examining the mesh surrounds and testing the bolts.

'It's secure and also there's lots of light, which is good,' she observes.

'And shade outside,' I add. 'We've had this special overhang created to protect the cats from the sun.'

'Good,' she mumbles.

'And now for the vegetable patch,' says the Scotsman with gusto.

A row of curly lettuces and cucumbers greet us. Beyond them is a huge area of aubergines.

Catalina's eyes bulge. 'When are you going to eat all that lot?'

'We're giving some away and bottling the rest.'

Back in the kitchen over iced coffee, Catalina begins to notice the wasps.

'They're flying in all the time. It wasn't like this last week when I came.'

Alan marches over to the kitchen door. 'This was the first nest and now loads more have suddenly appeared. They seem to form the nests overnight.'

'That's it!' says Catalina.

She disappears into the outside bathroom beyond the *entrada* and re-emerges with a bucket and two large sweeping brushes. '*Venga!*'

Alan sucks in his cheeks. 'I'm not sure about this. Maybe we should do it later.'

Catalina sweeps past him, shoves a brush in my hand and off we go. We start off downstairs knocking the nests off each window lintel and then crushing and setting them alight. Few wasps actually fly out so I imagine they're all dozy or out on wasp business in the valley.

'You know this is very dangerous. In the UK they have special companies to do this. They're sort of wasp-busters in special protective suits.'

She thinks this is very funny. 'How ridiculous. We've got our sunglasses and rubber gloves. What more do we need?'

At the end of two hours we've cleared every wasp nest. We sit in the kitchen guzzling cold water from the fridge while the Scotsman looks on in satisfaction. 'Good work. Let's hope the blighters don't come back.'

Catalina raises her eyebrows. 'You must buy this solution or they may return. Once they like a place they tend to stay.'

Ollie bangs open the front door having returned from a game of tennis with Angel. With flushed face, he flings down his sports bag and takes a seat at the kitchen table.

'You'll never believe it, but there's a big swarm of wasps in the courtyard,' he says.

We troop over to the front door to witness a volatile cloud of wasps hovering over the front lawn. It appears that we haven't solved the entire problem. Drastic action is needed. Let's hope the *ferreteria* can indeed dispel the fiends once and for all.

Finishing the call with Gillian, I jubilantly replace the mobile in my pocket. I'm alone, so grabbing the nearest cat, Minky as it happens, I do a little dance of joy around the courtyard. He protests after a few minutes and leaps out of my arms, obviously deciding that I've completely lost my head. It's a done deal. The quest to find a company with which to merge is over. Gillian Simpson of Dynamite Communications and I have now formally agreed to join forces. I'm sure the staff on both sides will be thrilled. How can it have all been so easy in the end? We have agreed that in two months' time, my staff will relocate to her offices along with all our files and computers to herald a new beginning. As I prance about in the sun I am suddenly aware of a face watching me through the gate. Oh no, how embarrassing is this? Michel has a strange smile on his face.

'Is this where the expression "mad dogs and Englishmen" comes from?' he says looking up at the blazing sun.

Despite the heat he is wearing a smart straw hat, shirt and tie and cotton jacket. I rush over to give him a hug.

'I'm so happy you're here. I've just had some wonderful news.'

His face crinkles with delight. 'Please, tell me.'

'I've just agreed to merge my company which means that I'm not going to have to commute back and forth to London all the time. I'll return once every month for a year and then that will be it.'

He shakes his head, absorbing the news. 'I am very happy for you. Now you'll be able to spend more time with your friends, of which I count myself one.'

I take his arm and lead him up the steps to the *entrada*. 'I'll still have a few private clients to look after. Some wanted me to continue to represent them myself.'

He laughs. 'Don't tell me, one of them is that funny man who makes pilots hats?'

We enter the kitchen. 'You've got such a good memory, Michel. Yes, I've promised to carry on working for George Myers and also Dannie Popescu-Miller, a client in America.'

He slides his walking stick under his chair. 'I think you're wise to keep a few clients of your own for now. Who knows what the future may hold.'

Michel looks beyond the kitchen door. The terracotta pots on the patio are full of aromatic herbs and flowers and the intoxicating fragrance drifts into the kitchen.

'I wish I could carry that fragrance home with me,' he says quietly.

'Would you like to sit outside in the shade?'

He shakes his head. 'I like it here in the cool, if that's OK. It also means we avoid the wasps.'

I laugh. 'You must be psychic. We've just had a plague of wasps but fortunately the good old *ferretería* gave us a solution in spray form which has sent them packing.'

He smiles. 'For now, at least.'

I pour us both some freshly squeezed orange juice and sit down opposite him at the kitchen table.

'Maybe we should celebrate with a glass of cava?'

Michel lets out a little gasp. 'I don't think I could manage it at this hour. It's not even six o'clock. When is Ollie home? I have something for him.'

I survey my watch. 'In about an hour. Can you stay until then?'

'Maybe,' he says. 'Let's see.'

He is still for a few seconds. I watch as he fingers the fabric of his jacket, removing a tiny thread of cotton before he resumes. 'I feel it's time to finish my story for you. Then when we next meet there will only be the present and future to discuss.' He pauses. 'Although, my own future is somewhat limited.'

'There's plenty of life in you yet,' I chide. 'Don't forget Mallorca has scores of centenarians.'

'That's true. But it doesn't bother me anyway. I am at peace with myself these days.'

'So, tell me more. We never talked beyond your time in Valencia.'

He sighs. 'When I defected from POUM and became a Communist I had even less control over my destiny and I travelled further away from Madrid and my beloved Sofia. We corresponded, as you know. After all, you found her letters in your garden.'

'It's incredible that you kept them for all these years.'

He smiles. 'Without them my life would have had no purpose. I have read and re-read them ever since the war. Beyond my family, they are the only thing I treasure.'

He pauses. 'To cut a long story short, after Valencia I travelled with the Communist troops to Teruel and towards the end of December 1938 I was based back in Barcelona. That is when Barcelona was finally taken by the Nationalists. There was a bloody battle and the Republican government retreated to Gerona but the Fascists and Franco were victorious.'

'How so?'

'Once they won Barcelona, the stuffing was kicked out of the Republican side. The Fascists became pretty invincible. I trembled to think that Madrid would be next and that Sofia might be caught up in the mayhem.'

'Were you able to warn her?'

He spreads out his hands on the table. 'Oh, she knew what was happening. After her sister, Elena, died she became quite a die-hard for the Republican cause. She held out in abysmal and freezing conditions in the university quarter with her comrades, all of them half-starved and lacking artillery. Her father and even her mother abandoned her. All she had left in the world was me, and I was miles away.'

I take a sip of orange juice, totally gripped by his account.

'Barcelona fell to Franco's troops on 26 January 1939 and that is when I made my escape. I left for Madrid unbeknown to my Communist colleagues. I assume they thought I'd been killed in battle.'

'How did you get to Madrid?'

He gives a hollow laugh. 'I walked and thumbed lifts, careful not to own up to my status as a soldier unless I knew I was with supporters of the left. Finally, exhausted and half-starved myself I arrived in Madrid. It was a bitterly cold winter and for the first few days I made little headway at entering the town because there was heavy shooting and confusion.'

'But did you find Sofia?' I ask impatiently.

He pats the air with a shaky hand. 'On the last day of February I made my way to the university quarter and after enquiries discovered that Sofia was alive and at the makeshift hospital. I rushed there and found her delirious and full of fever. She had consumption and malnutrition and was dying.'

My throat feels paralysed and I feel tears well in my eyes.

Michel stares blankly at the table, his fingers feeling the grain of the oak. He finally meets my eyes. 'She lasted until the fifth of March. I was with her when she breathed her last. Even in her delirium she knew who I was and called out my name, not Michel but José.'

He covers his eyes with his hands and then weeps silently, his shoulders quivering with the effort. I rise and bring him some tissues and for the next five minutes we share a feeling of untold grief. He wipes his eyes and takes my hand in his. 'After we buried her I fought like a madman against the Fascists, determined to die in the final battle for Madrid. On 28 March the city fell to Franco and, although I was badly wounded, somehow I survived and was cared for by Republican sympathisers and eventually – with false papers – dispatched to Paris to a Republican safe house. Franco announced the end of the war on 1 April 1939, a fitting date for your English humour,' he says with a little chuckle. 'I wanted to die and was in a deep depression for months, but in the end the instinct to survive took over. I started a new life in Paris, one without light or purpose.'

I blow my nose. 'I don't know how you coped.'

He gives a little snort. 'Trust me, my story is that of a blessed soul compared to some of the wretches I met after the war. You know, many believe that when the civil war ended so did the violence and persecution but in some ways it was just the beginning.'

'What do you mean?'

'I will never forget that in August of 1939, a group of fifty-six teenagers from the Socialist Party, Juventud Socialista, who had been imprisoned for some time, merely for being young Socialist supporters, were taken to the Cementerio de la Almudena in Madrid by Franco's army and shot by firing squad. Thirteen were just young innocent girls of sixteen or seventeen years old and after their deaths they became known as *La Trece Rosas*, the thirteen roses. There was a letter written by Julia Conesa, one of the girls, to her mother before her death. It was so noble.'

We sit quietly.

'And so you were in Paris when World War Two came?'

He nods. 'Yes, and what a hellish event that was. Luckily, I was too broken to really notice the deprivation and horror. I'd seen so much already and without Sofia I lost all notion of fear of death.'

I sigh deeply. 'Can I pour a glass of cava now?'

'What for?'

'To celebrate life and the lives of Sofia and Elena and all the other brave souls who lost their lives so pointlessly, whether Republican or Nationalist.'

He considers this for a moment. 'That concludes my tale and so yes, let us celebrate life. One day I hope you'll come to my home and look at photos of Sofia and my family. I can also show you all my poetry books. Most are now out of print, of course.'

I open a bottle of cold cava from the fridge and laugh when Michel catches his breath as the cork pops.

'This feels very decadent.'

'Hardly,' I smile.

We chink glasses and Michel coughs at the first taste of bubbles.

'It's a long time since I've had cava. Now, may I also raise my glass to your future enterprises? Congratulations on divesting the company. Here's to the future – for all of us.'

We sit savouring the cold cava until the front door slaps open and Alan and Ollie stand smiling at us from the *entrada*.

'Michel, I presume?' beams the Scotsman. 'At last we meet and just at the right time. It looks as though we're celebrating something?'

Michel shakes Alan's hand and ushers him to the seat next to him.

He turns to Ollie and gives him a hug. 'I have a bag of fossils for you. They were embedded in the sand and soil near Can Repic beach in the port.'

Ollie thanks him and begins examining them with delight.

'So why the cava so early?'

'I was concluding my sorry tale,' says Michel, 'but there is a real reason we are celebrating.'

I pour Alan a glass of cava and a smaller one for Ollie. They stare at me in some anticipation.

With a smile I turn to them. 'I have some very good news.'

It's ten o'clock and Sóller *plaça* is bursting with locals and tourists who've come to watch the dance troupes taking part in Sa Mostra, the annual dance festival held in Sóller during July. Each year, different groups visit from overseas and there is great excitement about which countries will be performing. The shows are completely free of charge and the programme of events continues for a week. The last performance has ended to great applause and now hordes of people are doing ad-lib folk dancing in the street. Mateo the waiter approaches our table outside Café Paris.

'Can I get you anything else?'

Pep yawns. 'No thanks. I think we've had more than enough rosé. Anyway we should go and join the dancing.'

Ollie and Angel groan. 'No way are we going to dance.'

'Why ever not?' taunts Pep. 'You might both find yourselves some nice girlfriends.'

They face each other with screwed up noses.

'Urgh,' says Ollie.

'*Si*, we only like supermodels,' adds Angel.

'Then you'll both end up being monks,' shrugs Pep with a giggle.

Alan finishes his wine. 'Come on then, Juana. Show me some Mallorcan folk dancing.'

I look at him in horror. 'You're not really going to get up and dance?'

He turns to face the street. 'Everyone else is, so why not? Come on!'

Juana grabs my arm. 'Don't be so stuck up and English, *venga*!'

Protesting loudly, I follow the others into the bustling street and find myself being whisked around to the music by Pep. Even when he dances he manages to keep his *puro* wedged firmly between his teeth. Alan and Juana appear to be doing a hybrid waltz while Angel and Ollie mock from the sidelines.

'What a way to end a perfect day,' I say to Pep.

He pulls the cigar from his mouth and smiles broadly. 'Yes, freeing yourself from the business in London is reason enough to dance in the street tonight. It's fantastic news.'

'And also,' I say, 'because we're all so lucky to be alive and safe, living on the most beautiful island, away from war zones. My new friend Michel has taught me that.'

He shrugs. 'Yes, sometimes we forget how lucky we are – every day we should celebrate life and forget the little irritating things that get in the way.'

Alan reaches across and tugs my hand. 'Here's to new horizons – and that includes learning Mallorcan folk dancing.'

And with that he stumbles and both he and Pep tumble to the ground like a pair of skittles.

Ed is in serious mode. I can tell by the way he is articulating every word very clearly. I pull my legs up under me on the warm stone wall and push the mobile against my ear. My concentration is waning as I watch the new generation of baby frogs diving off into the pond.

'So Irina is no more?' I say absentmindedly.

He gives a titter down the line. 'Heavens, you make it sound as if she's snuffed it. Yes, it's all over but I have something important to tell you.'

'Oh?'

'I've met someone unbelievably special.'

I groan. 'Oh, please, spare me.'

'You can cut the cynicism. This time it's for real. She's a brilliant psychoanalyst and Japanese.'

For once I'm interested. A psychoanalyst could prove even better than a nurse.

'So why on earth is she interested in you, other than as a patient?'

'Very funny. She and I have a lot in common as it happens. We met via a cultural site. Did you get the image of her I sent?'

'Hang on.' I fumble with the phone and find a downloaded image of a serene and smiling woman with an intelligent and beautiful face. I call Ed back, having managed to cut him off.

'She looks amazing.'

'Told you. She's called Rela. Can we all get together when you're back in town?'

'You bet. I'm crossing my fingers and toes this time. Has Jane met her yet?'

Jane is a close mutual university friend and Ollie's godmother. What she says is of crucial significance to me.

'She loves her. They got on famously.'

I'm stunned. For once the signs are good. Perhaps after all this time Ed's finally met the one. I finish the call and feel Johnny's eyes boring into me from his favourite hidey-hole. He's chewing on an insect.

'It seems as though Ed's met a fantastic girl.'

'She must need her head seeing to,' he rasps. 'Any friend of yours can't be too sane.'

I give a sniff. 'It's brilliant news. I feel like dancing in the street.'

'Spare us that spectacle! And playing Cupid doesn't suit you. I gave up on romance long ago.'

'That's why you're such an irascible old toad.'

'True, but you wouldn't have me any other way.'

I finish our script. 'You're right. I wouldn't have you any other way.'

And with a 'bah humbug', he plops into the pond.

SEVENTEEN

HAPPY ENDINGS

A mesmeric sea the colour of wild bluebells glistens in the bay, watched over from aloft a craggy rock by the weary old lighthouse of Port of Sóller. Yachts sway gently from side to side as they sit tantalisingly close to the shore, tethered and waiting for a maritime adventure. Running along the deserted esplanade, I breathe in the sharp odour of ozone mingled with seaweed and a faint suspicion of sage. Jordi is just opening up his car hire kiosk for the day and gives me a sleepy '*Hola*' and brief wave. Despite it being the height of the tourist season, few people venture out of bed at this early hour. I find the tranquillity magical. As I sprint past Can Repic beach, all I can hear is the regular pounding of the waves against the rocks, the cry of an eagle and the excited quack of a lone white duck. At the far end of the port, three fishermen are mending their nets which are sprawled out on the ground before them. They give me a cursory nod when I pass by. In the last year, all vestiges of military presence have been erased from this part of the port, in deference to islanders keen to erase such reminders of the Spanish Civil War. The forbidding building inscribed with the Latin words, *'Todo Por La Patria'*, literally meaning 'all for the country', has been demolished. Nothing, as yet, replaces it and so I am free to run wildly in a large open space overlooked on three sides by open sea.

As I do a U-turn and head back along the esplanade, the impeccably dressed elderly mother of Pep Erias, yet another Pep I know, who owns a culinary shop in Calle sa Lluna, calls out to me from the patio of her flat.

'Still running, *reina*?'

We exchange greetings and I plod on until I hear a familiar tooting behind me. A large red face is now parallel with mine as the *moto* hiccups slowly along.

'You're up early!'

'I like to beat the sun, Gaspar. It's the only time to run in August.'

'Segur!' he laughs. 'When can I come running with you again? I need to lose weight and get fit.'

I have been expecting this. 'I thought your doctor didn't recommend it?'

I stop to catch my breath as Gaspar pulls into the side. *'Pues,* he says I can start going for gentle runs. When Jorge was delivering the mail he told me you're never going back to England again.'

'That's a slight exaggeration. I'm merging my company which means I'll be in Sóller most of the time but will need to return to London for a while.'

He beams. 'Great. That means you'll have plenty of time to take me running.'

'D'acord. We'll discuss a programme for September.'

He nods cheerfully and drives off, the exhaust of his old bike popping and spluttering out grey smoke as he goes.

Back at the track I bump into Neus, who appears to be in deep discussion with Rafael.

'We were just discussing you. I hear from Jorge that you're not going to be returning to England so much?'

I laugh. 'Is anything sacred in this town? Yes it's true, Neus. I'm changing my way of life.'

'That's good,' she smiles. 'It can't be healthy doing all that travelling and it's not fair on Alan having to cook while you're away. Men find it so hard.'

I narrow my eyes and am about to protest but see Rafael giggling. '*Si*, it's so tough being a helpless man. I hardly eat at all and there's no one to help with my washing. My girlfriend is always working in Palma.'

He gives me a stealthy wink.

Neus shakes her head. 'Terrible. This is what female emancipation has come to! I couldn't imagine leaving poor Bernat to cook for himself.'

I watch her closely. 'So how are things between you and Bernat? Are you doing his cooking now?'

Rafael slaps his knee. 'Isn't that nice. What a lucky *tio* he is!'

A lucky chap indeed. She is a little coy. 'It's better to take things slowly but he has asked whether I'd consider getting engaged.'

Rafael and I look at each other in astonishment.

'Oh that's fantastic, Neus! Congratulations.' I give her a hug.

She pushes me gently away. '*Pues*, don't make a big fuss. We're old people after all. We'll take our time.'

Rafael whoops and claps his hands together. 'Wait till I tell the neighbours.'

'They probably all knew even before Neus,' I say.

'Well, I have to get to the market so can't stand around chatting. When are your donkeys arriving anyway?' she asks.

'In just a few days now. I'm so excited. Wolfgang and Helge are arriving tonight so they'll be here just in time for the big event.'

'They haven't been back here for months,' says Rafael. 'Have they been in Berlin all this time?'

I shrug. 'They've a busy life over there.'

'I'm going to visit Berlin for a clown seminar next month so I might look them up.'

'All you people flying around. Why can't you stand still and enjoy life?' exclaims Neus.

'That's exactly what I intend to do, Neus.'

I jog along the track to find the Scotsman busy mowing the front lawn. He stops when he sees me in the courtyard.

'It's getting so hot. Just as well you ran early. We seem to have an ant infestation.'

'Really?'

'It's terrible. I've been spraying the whole house. Your office is seething with the little devils.'

I do some stretching and climb the stairs to my office. Sure enough a huge army of ants is marching across my desk and down the wall by the window. I wonder if Ollie's left a discarded chocolate packet around but there's no evidence of it. Last month we had a hellish job getting rid of the wasps, now we have a new plague.

The Scotsman pops his head around the door. 'I think I'll go off to the *ferreteria* to get something to kill them off. That wasp solution I bought from the shop was brilliant so they must have something to combat ants.'

'Let's hope so.'

I use some paper to wipe the ants from my desk, and then open my emails. There's a pile of new product information I've got to rewrite for Greedy George and several press releases for checking from Rachel. Gillian Simpson of Dynamite Communications has sent through some notes on logistics for the new office arrangement, together with a visual plan of the desks that will be designated to my staff. It seems hard to believe that in a month's time our offices will be vacated and I will no longer be involved in the day-to-day operations of the company. Everything has gone surprisingly smoothly. The lease on our offices had nearly expired so it wasn't difficult to terminate the agreement and a removals company has been booked to transfer our equipment and files over to Dynamite's offices. Everything seems to be under control. The clients have been expecting the merger for some time and are happy with the new arrangements. Only George, Dannie and Manuel of H Hotels have asked me to personally continue helping them directly with their PR needs and all are happy for me to be based in Mallorca.

The phone rings. Rachel is very chirpy.

'How are things?'

'Good. What about you?'

'We're all ploughing on. We've just begun clearing cupboards and files for the move. It's bizarre what odd things you find tucked away.'

'Such as?'

'Well, Sarah's just come across a fragrant Santa lizard. Do you remember Greedy George's great Christmas invention?'

I give a yelp. 'Oh no! Not the Santa lizard with the moving head? I thought we'd got rid of all those press samples.'

'Most, but these were hidden behind some press cutting files. Who knows, they could become a collector's item.'

We laugh.

'I'll get on with the work you need checking. First I've got to fumigate the office. We seem to have a plague of ants.'

'The ten plagues of Egypt?'

'Something like that.'

'By the way, Gillian's going to get me working on some fantastic new travel brands. It's a shame I'll be off to Yorkshire soon.'

'What's your timeframe?'

'I'm not sure. Ben can take up his programming job any time but I need to find something. We may wait until the New Year to get cracking or even longer. I quite like the idea of working at Dynamite for a while.'

The concept of Rachel relocating to Yorkshire still seems strange to me given her love of London life but then many people believed I'd never survive in rural Mallorca. How wrong they were.

I finish the call and potter off to my bedroom to inspect signs of ant invasion and to my horror see a phalanx of ants progressing steadily across the quilt. The bathroom is also under siege as they smother the tap in search of moisture. Let's hope the *ferreteria* can come up with a solution quickly. Ollie calls up to me from his bedroom.

'You should see all the ants on my desk. It's weird.'

I scramble down the stairs, dismayed to see a swarm of the horrors all over his table, desk, and walls.

'It looks quite cool,' he says cheerfully.

'Cool isn't the word that immediately comes to mind, Ollie.'

He yawns and stretches across to a book by his bed. 'I've just finished this book on horse whispering. Joe Pentman's father was a genius. He could make horses do almost anything.'

'Who's Joe Pentman?' I ask absentmindedly.

'You know, my coin dealer friend in the States.'

'Of course. How could I forget? Any good deals going on?'

He nods modestly. 'I've just bought a Roman coin from him. It's in reasonable condition. He's taking one of my Sri Lankan 1950s coins in exchange.'

'That doesn't sound like an even deal.'

He sighs heavily. 'Of course it is. The coin I'm giving him is in practically mint condition and is quite rare actually.'

I quickly demure, realising, not for the first time, that I am way out of my depth when it comes to numismatics.

'Anyway, I'm fairly sure I can use some of the book's horse whispering techniques on the donkeys when they arrive.'

'That would be helpful. Can you instruct me?'

He raises his eyebrows. 'I'm not sure how quickly you'd catch on. Maybe I'll try first and if it works I'll lend you the book.'

'It can't be that difficult.'

He eyes me dismissively. 'Look, mother, donkeys can be dangerous. They're not fluffy toys. Leave it to me for now.'

Scanning his bookshelves he pulls out his coin collections and we examine them together. He gives me a running commentary on their value and history. Some time later we hear the door slam and the Scotsman appears gripping his wicker basket.

'Any luck?' I ask.

'I've got a toxic potion that has to be diluted and sprayed around the exterior of the house to prevent the ants getting in. Apparently they're desperately after water in this heat. I'm going to get started now.'

He potters off.

'That sounds hopeful,' I say.

Ollie leans on his elbow. 'I'm not so sure he'd be good with dangerous substances. I'd better go and help.'

He gets up and joins his father in the kitchen. It's wonderful that a twelve-year-old boy feels so much more capable to deal with risky tasks than his ageing parents. And if I'm totally honest, these days, he probably is.

It's 7 a.m. and Fernando, our newest neighbour now living on our track, is singing a *glose* at the top of his voice as he drives his battered old jeep up the winding hill to the Sóller tunnel. Ollie and I squat in the open back, getting thrown around as he takes the corners sharply. Alan sits up front, enjoying the view and pleasant aromatic air.

'What's that song about?' I yell at Fernando above the sound of the engine.

'It's based on a poem by Maria Antonia Salvà i Ripoll. You must have heard of her?'

Ollie gives me a blank look.

'Vaguely,' I say. 'My friend Neus once mentioned her.'

He nods enthusiastically. 'Well, she was one of the first major female bards to write in the Catalan language. She was born in Palma and wrote at least six poetry books. We studied her at school.'

'Remind me of her era? I ask.

'She was born in the late eighteen hundreds but was still around in the nineteen fifties. Amazing woman. You know she travelled the world at the turn of the century with another of our famous poets, Miguel Costa i Llobera. Now he did a poem called…'

'"Pi de Formentor"!' yells Ollie.

'*Molt bé*, Ollie. It's all about a pine tree.'

'*Si, si*,' replies Ollie with some impatience.

'Ah, your favourite!' I tease.

'The most boring poem on the planet,' he mutters under his breath.

'Now to change the subject,' yells Fernando. 'Today I'll have three men helping us collect the almonds. We're meeting them directly in S'Egletia. It's going to be tough work but we'll down tools at ten for a *merienda* break and then work on until two. *Vale?*'

I like the sound of the *merienda* break when normally crusty big rolls are handed around full of ripe tomato slices, chorizo sausage and Serrano ham. The idea of bashing down almonds in the heat has less appeal but we did ask Fernando some months ago whether we could join him and he has never forgotten.

Some fifteen minutes beyond the Sóller tunnel, we take a right towards S'Egletia village. As we progress along the narrow, windy road, Fernando points out the almond fields on either side.

'Two of those are mine. We'll pick the guys up at the church and set to work.'

At the junction, Fernando parks up outside the small church. He rests against his door.

'It's not much of a village, is it? More of a road junction with a church and bar.'

Alan sighs. 'Well, it must have been a useful stopping-off place back in 1838 when Chopin and his lover George Sand made their laborious way by horse and carriage to La Cartuja, the monastery in Valldemossa.'

Fernando furrows his brow. 'She was the awful French woman who came to live here for a year and wrote scandalous things about us Mallorcans.'

Ollie giggles. 'Why, what did she say?'

'I've never read her book, *A Winter in Mallorca*, because I heard it insulted the locals. She was a very odd woman, Ollie. She dressed as a man.'

'Weird,' says Ollie.

I nod. 'The book is quite an interesting take on the epoch but she is rather mean and biased about the locals, you're right, Fernando.'

Three well-built young men saunter over to us with smiles on their faces. They represent the rest of the almond-picking workforce for the day. They jump in the back of the jeep with Ollie and me and we set off back up the road and turn right at an old wrought iron gate. Fernando opens it and climbs back in the car. A moment later we are in the middle of a large field bursting with almond trees.

'This is spectacular,' says Alan, stepping down onto the grass. 'They look very healthy.'

Fernando watches as the three guys walk off to a small shelter where piles of canvases are stored. He turns back to Alan. 'These trees are in good shape but my almond field in Lloseta is in a bad way. We've had a termite problem and half the trees have died. The government agriculture department doesn't seem to have an answer.'

'What sort of termite is it?' I ask.

He shrugs. 'It's called *xilófago*, a bug that attacks the bark of trees. It's a menace.'

The men stride over, their sleeves rolled up. 'Shall we get going?'

We're each given a two-litre bottle of water and a long bamboo stick.

'Now, the guys will lay down the canvasses beneath the trees and you can begin beating the branches to knock the *ametles* down.'

'The what?' says Alan.

'*Ametles*, almonds in Catalan,' I hiss.

He pulls a face. 'Do they just fall down?'

'Hopefully,' laughs one of the guys. 'Most of the soft outer shells have come away. They should just fall.'

We troop after them to one of the first trees. The cicadas are already hissing in the long grass and a grinning sun leaps up from behind the distant Tramuntanas. It's going to be a scorching day. I soak an old cotton scarf in cold water and tie it around my neck. Ollie does the same. We're all wearing straw hats. Once the canvasses are spread, the men show us how to beat the branches. Sure enough, almonds scatter all over the sheet. This impresses Ollie and, with his shorter bamboo stick, he begins thrashing at the tree. We tackle one tree between us until the men inspect it and decide it's time to move on to the next. After the initial ease with which we knock down the almonds, we find the task is getting tougher as the temperature rises. I wipe sweat from my eyes with my shirt sleeve but within a few minutes my face is running. Ollie and I sit in the shade and gulp back some warm water.

'Wow, this is tough work,' I say.

'It's only nine o'clock,' he groans. 'We've got another hour to go.'

We struggle on, the sizzling sun on our backs and the hot grass tickling our shins. Alan is working on a far off tree with one of the men and making good progress. A veritable mound of cork-coloured almonds lie at his feet. Fernando suddenly breaks from his work and ambles over to us. 'Come on, let's get into the shade and have a snack.'

Gratefully we follow him to a small shack where he has stored foil-protected *bocadillos*, rolls, and a cooler box full of beer and Coke. We fall on the food like ravenous creatures, savouring the rich tomato chorizo rolls and bowls of home-cured olives. The three men seem unaffected by their morning's work and smile cheerfully as we pour cool water over our heads.

'You're doing well. Let's keep at it a few more hours and that will be enough for the day,' says Fernando.

Ollie picks at one of the almond shells. 'Do you ever eat these when they're green?'

'*Segur*. Lots of Mallorcans eat young, unripe *ametles verdes*. We pick them around April and eat them with salads and ice cream. They're delicious.'

Ollie lies back against a stone wall. 'Aren't there machines that can remove the almonds off the trees? It seems like a lot of work.'

'For big production some farmers use machines with pincers that shake the tree and make the almonds fall but I've only got two fields so it's not worth it. I use the local cooperative to shell the nuts mechanically. That's the hardest job.'

'Do you sell the almonds?'

'No. I don't produce enough really. I give them to the family mostly, and friends. I'm not in it for the money, that's for sure.'

The three guys chew on their rolls and laugh. 'We get paid in almonds, Ollie.'

'Exactly, and that's how I'll pay you three.'

Alan tuts. 'Oh, we don't expect anything. You always give us a sack anyway. That's more than enough.'

Fernando shakes his head. 'I'll give you a few sacks to keep you going.'

We finish our short *merienda*, our break, and get back to work. By midday everything is beginning to itch – my arms, head and legs. A mixture of sunburn, ant bites and scratches are the culprits.

Fernando claps loudly. 'Time to gather up the canvasses.'

We pull in the laden sheets and gather the nuts into the same shelter where we scoffed our earlier snack, finally setting off at one o'clock for the local bar. The owner greets Fernando like a brother and soon we are seated at a long wooden table and treated to *flacons* of Rosado wine and ice-cold water. Dishes of salad, chips and pork chops are passed down the table, along with green olives, bread and *aioli*, the Mallorcan garlic mayonnaise.

'Hard work?' laughs the bar owner, obviously amused at our bright red faces.

'Really tough. It looks easy from a distance.'

He nods. 'When I was a kid, my parents got us special dispensation from school for several weeks to join the almond harvesting at the farm. Every night we had to remove the almond husks. It was much harder than being at school.'

'I bet!' says Alan, taking a long sip of wine.

'It's really been fun though, hasn't it?'

Ollie and Alan regard me cautiously, wondering whether the sun has finally gone to my head.

'If it's been such entertainment,' says Fernando mischievously, 'you're welcome to join us for the rest of the week.'

Alan coughs heartily. 'A lovely idea, Fernando, but perhaps one day is enough for us feeble Brits.'

He slaps Alan's back. 'You've done very well. I'd never have got my sons to spend that much time harvesting in the heat.'

'Now you tell us!' I say. 'Why didn't we stop earlier?'

'*Hombre*! Why would I have done that,' he winks, 'when you were all having such a great time?'

It's a sweltering evening and all the windows are thrown open in the cosy kitchen. Beyond the house in the velvety darkness comes the penetrating and urgent rasping sound of the cicadas and the distant hoot of an owl. I turn my head distractedly, breathing in the sweet aromatic smells of summer as they waft through the open windows. Michel rests his head on one hand, observing me while Marina, the wife of his nephew, Ignacio, clears away our dinner plates.

'So another chapter ends,' says Michel simply.

I turn to him and smile. 'In England we say one door closes and another opens.'

He nods. 'Yes, I know that expression. I feel that we have been on an odyssey together, you and me. An incredible journey of the memory. To think that two strangers can be brought together by random sheets of paper.'

Ignacio flicks some breadcrumbs from the tablecloth and touches his uncle's hand. 'As long as you feel more able to deal with the past now. That is what matters.'

Michel puffs out his bottom lip and touches his chin with a quivering hand. I study the raised veins, turquoise by candlelight, and the translucent skin. 'I'm not sure, my dear nephew, whether we are ever capable of dealing with our past but we can at least learn to forgive ourselves and to open a new chapter in the book of life.'

Alan catches my eye and raises an eyebrow, uncertain whether to speak. He remains silent.

'Looking at these old photos of my beautiful Sofia is like a stab to the heart and yet it makes me feel alive once more. In facing the past maybe we have a future. I don't know. Maybe these are just the ramblings of a very old man.'

Reaching in front of me, I hold one of the black and white photos to the candlelight. Sofia stares back at me, a playful smile gracing her rosebud lips, her long dark hair entwined on one shoulder.

'She really was beautiful, Michel,' I sigh. 'Like an angel.'

He pushes another dog-eared image towards me. 'This is her sister, Elena. Have I already shown you that one?'

I have pored over this image and hundreds more for the best part of three hours, only putting them aside to have the dinner prepared for us all by Marina. She remains like a shadow, courteous and smiling but wary of imposing during what she seems to regard as a rather personal conversation in which she has no role.

Alan yawns and rubs his eyes. 'It's been a wonderful evening but I feel we have overstayed our welcome and should make for home.'

'Not at all!' exclaims Ignacio. 'But Ollie is nearly asleep so I think we should continue our friendship over another meal on another day.'

'Next time at our house,' I say.

'Thank you, that would be nice,' he replies.

We rise from our seats and head in a small group to the front door. I hold back and wait for Michel as the others spill out into the quiet, dark street.

'I want you to have this photo of Sofia,' he says, thrusting the small smiling image of her into my hands. I feel my eyes prick with tears. 'This way you will always remember her and me and our story will live on.'

I kiss his cheek and together we head for the door.

We drive into the courtyard, car windows open to allow the balmy night air to rush inside. It has been a magical evening, one which I shall never forget. Michel's nephew and his wife invited us for supper at their home in Sóller town, and finally I was able to see the house and the many photographs of Sofia, her sister, Elena, and Michel's family. It was poignant to revisit the letters and poems which I had originally discovered caught in the trees of our orchard, but now the jigsaw was complete.

Michel showed us his many poetry books and his single novel, written in French, which he gave me to read at my leisure. Maybe in sharing his life story Michel's load had become lighter, well so it seemed to me. He had a new animation, a look of hope and genuine happiness to be sitting with his family at supper. It warmed my heart and made me realise how fortunate I had been to have crossed his path.

Ollie wearily steps out of the car and yawns. 'There are loads of scops owls about. Listen.'

We stand on the gravel listening to the strange cry that sounds so like the intermittent bleep of a submarine sonar. Our house is in darkness and the silhouetted forms of fast-winged bats swoop low around the front garden, before disappearing over the field. Brilliant white stars litter the skies, and a half moon leans over the mountain tops. Footsteps break us from our silent reverie and there at the front gate is Helge.

'*Hola* neighbours! Can I disturb you for some garlic?'

We rush over to greet her and her husband, Wolfgang, who is hanging behind in the shadows.

'So you've abandoned Berlin for Sóller?'

'For six weeks this time,' says Wolfgang.

It still amuses me that we all converse in Spanish, given that neither party can speak the other's language.

'Let's have drinks later this week,' says Helge.

Ollie is delighted to see his German heroine again and extracts a promise from her to play football the following day.

'I haven't had a chance to go shopping yet and have run out of garlic for my pasta dish. Have you a clove?' she asks.

'Eating at eleven-thirty? That's late even by Mallorcan standards,' I reply.

I give her a bulb of fresh garlic from the market and a handful of parsley and chives.

'Thank you so much. We'll see you tomorrow.'

We watch as they saunter off across the courtyard and along the track to their *finca*.

'Makes a change from borrowing milk and sugar,' laughs Alan.

'True,' I say.

We enter the house and are greeted by three ever-hungry cats.

'Have you noticed?' asks Ollie, emerging from his room. 'There aren't any ants.'

We turn on lights and inspect all the rooms. They've vanished.

'A miracle,' I cry.

'No, just my brilliance combined with the power of a secret potion,' he says with a smile.

A bright sun burns in the morning sky and the Tramuntanas are suffused with light. Johnny and the frogs are quacking and splashing wildly about in the pond while the cats lie soporifically on the warm walls of the porch. The strays are stretched out in their own private encampment by the stone hut in the front garden and the cicadas trill unceasingly in the palpitating heat. We stand in the courtyard waiting in excited anticipation for Jacinto, the man who talks with donkeys. Pep called to say he would be arriving at ten o'clock and we have been keeping a vigil for the last twenty minutes. Suddenly there's the sound of a car and Pep pulls into the courtyard.

With a wicked smile he throws open the driver's door. 'Ah! The welcoming committee. You shouldn't have.'

'We're waiting for Jacinto, not you!' I say, tilting my old straw hat back on my head to peruse his face.

He gives a cackle. 'Yes, but if it wasn't for me you'd never have met the donkey whisperer.'

'True,' says Alan.

Pep taps Ollie's arm. 'Is the paddock all prepared?'

'I think so,' he replies nervously. 'We've got their food and water ready and the shelter's full of hay.'

He places a hand on his shoulder. '*Excelente*! Jacinto will be proud of you. What about the champagne?'

'Do donkeys drink alcohol?' asks Ollie in stunned surprise.

'No, you foolish *chico*, for officially declaring the paddock open. We smash the bottle on the gate.'

'And waste a good bottle of cava?' cries the Scotsman. 'Not on your Nelly. We'll cut a ribbon instead.'

He darts inside the house and emerges with a long piece of red Christmas tape and scissors. 'I'll go and run a tape across the paddock gate. Be back in a moment.'

Ten minutes later, when we are beginning to worry that the donkeys will never come, there's the gentle, methodical sound of hooves and there, walking slowly down the track, is Jacinto with Rosa and her small, very furry, brown daughter.

'They're coming!' cries Ollie. 'Oh, isn't the baby beautiful!'

Pep offers the Scotsman a cigar and together they puff contentedly on their *puros*.

Jacinto walks into the courtyard, the two donkeys plodding behind him. He pats their hides and says a few calming words. Shaking their ears, they step forward and aim straight for Ollie. His eyes open wide and in delight he reaches out to touch their noses as they both nuzzle up to him. I hear him speaking to them in a low voice and Jacinto laughs.

'I have competition! A young donkey whisperer.'

We all stroll over to welcome the new members of the menagerie. The two females lift their heads and, with snuffles and snorts, survey their surroundings. Their tawny brown fur is warm and incredibly soft.

Jacinto pulls a cloth from his pocket and wipes his brow under his old cloth hat. 'I have told Rosa that she will now be known as Minny and her daughter as Della. They are content with this. Shall we take them to the paddock now?'

We form a little entourage, walking down the steep slope into the field and across to the orchard. Jacinto and Ollie talk together and seem to be sharing a little old-fashioned donkey wisdom. Reaching the paddock gate, Alan gives Ollie the scissors while I hover with a camera. The donkeys and Jacinto stand by his side.

With as much gravitas as he can muster, Ollie faces us all.

'I now declare this paddock officially open! Welcome Minny and Della to your new home!'

He cuts the red strip of Christmas tape stretching across the gate. We all clap and whoop. Jacinto stares at us in bemusement and laughs. No sooner is the gate tugged open than both animals gallop into their new abode, flicking their manes and winnowing happily.

'They are happy,' says Jacinto simply. 'You have my instructions and now you must spend your time getting to know them. Ollie will be the guide.'

Ollie nods his head gravely.

'But Jacinto,' he asks, 'what if something goes wrong or we don't understand what they want?'

He tousles his hair. 'Oh, you'll know all right but if you have any worries just call me and I'll come and talk to them. *Chico*, go in there and chat with them.'

I watch as Ollie ambles across the grass of the paddock and joins mother and daughter at the wooden shelter where they are drinking water. Kissing my hand and then pushing his hat down firmly on his head, Jacinto slips off wordlessly across the field. Pep gives us a wink and strolls over to the paddock. He opens the gate and joins Ollie at the shelter. I watch as they both fondle the donkeys.

The heavens are now a radiant blue and in the distance a flock of birds streak across the sky in perfect formation like the Red Arrows.

'Well, this is it,' Alan says. 'The donkeys are here and tomorrow the cattery will be receiving its first guests. We're going to have our hands full.'

I smile. 'And in just over a week, I kiss goodbye to the PR company.'

He whistles and gives me a hug. 'A new life beckons. Are you ready for it?'

I throw my old straw hat high into the air. 'I don't know about you, but I've never been so sure.'

A Lizard in
my Luggage

MAYFAIR TO MALLORCA IN ONE EASY MOVE

ANNA NICHOLAS

A LIZARD IN MY LUGGAGE

Mayfair to Mallorca in One Easy Move

Anna Nicholas

ISBN: 978-1-84024-565-3   Paperback   £8.99

Anna, a PR consultant to Mayfair's ritziest and most glamorous, had always thought Mallorca was for the disco and beer-swilling fraternity. That was until her sister hired an au pair from a rural part of the island who said it was the most beautiful place on earth. On a visit, Anna impulsively decided to buy a ruined farmhouse.

Despite her fear of flying, she kept a foot in both camps and commuted to central London to manage her PR company. But she found herself drawn away from the bustle and stress of life in the fast lane towards a more tranquil existence.

Told with piquant humour, *A Lizard in my Luggage* explores Mallorca's fiestas and traditions, as well as the ups and downs of living in a rural retreat. It is about learning to appreciate the simple things and take risks in pursuit of real happiness. Most importantly, it shows that life can be lived between two places.

'*A beautifully written and highly entertaining account of the upside of downshifting*'   DAILY MIRROR

'*A witty and devilishly intelligent foray into the highs and lows of a new life in Spain*'   XPAT magazine

GOATS FROM A SMALL ISLAND

GRABBING MALLORCAN LIFE BY THE HORNS

ANNA NICHOLAS

GOATS FROM A SMALL ISLAND

Grabbing Mallorcan Life by the Horns

Anna Nicholas

ISBN: 978-1-84024-760-2   Paperback   £7.99

Life on the small island of Mallorca is entertaining and fascinating for Anna Nicholas, who moved her family to a rural mountain setting for a more *mañana* existence. But it's never simple.

She pursues her dream of opening a cattery, is devastated by the abduction of her beloved toad, and becomes fixated with Myotragus, the extinct goat that roamed Mallorca in ancient times. Meanwhile, trying to cut loose from her PR agency and its clients in London and New York, she finds herself among nutty Russian models and amorous rock climbers.

Hilarious, informative and brimming with memorable characters, *Goats From A Small Island* is a delightful tribute to Mallorca's rich way of life.

Have you enjoyed this book? If so, why not write a review on your favourite website?

Thanks very much for buying this Summersdale book.

www.summersdale.com